기본은 **꾹꾹**, 실력은 **쑥쑥**

숨마 주니어®

SUMMA CUM LAUDE 「최우등 졸업」을 의미하는 라틴어

WORD MANUAL

숨마 주니어®

중학 영어교과서

WORD MANUAL 3

중학 3학년 주요 800어휘 25일 완성

예문 + 독해지문을 통한 어휘력 및 독해력 향상

중학 영어교과서

WORD MANUAL 3

이 책을 지은 선생님

고미라 _ 상경중학교
정지윤 _ 언남중학교
이지애 _ 목암중학교
박여울 _ 충주여자고등학교
조금희 _ 세종과학고등학교
박선하 _ 서울보성고등학교

1판 1쇄 발행일 : 2014년 10월 30일

펴낸이 : 이동준, 정재현
기획 및 편집 : 김기진, 최원준, 김다래
디자인 : 굿윌디자인

펴낸곳 : (주)이룸이앤비
출판신고번호 : 제2009-000168호
주소 : 서울시 강남구 논현로 16길 4-3 이룸빌딩 (우 135-963)
대표전화 : 02-424-2410
팩스 : 02-424-5006
홈페이지 : www.erumenb.com
ISBN : 978-89-5990-267-5

이 책을 펴내면서

“영어를 잘하는 방법이 있나요?”

영어 선생님들께 질문을 했습니다.
공통적인 의견은 ‘먼저 단어를 많이 외우라.’ 입니다.

하지만 영어 단어를 외우는 것은 정말 힘든 일이지요.
외우고 외워도 자꾸 잊어버리게 되는 영어 단어…

“어디 쉽고 효율적으로 학습하는 방법은 없는 걸까요?”

해답은 문장 속에서 단어의 의미를 파악하며 학습하는 데 있답니다.
그렇게 해야만 살아있는 생생한 뉘앙스와 정확한 쓰임까지 체득하게 되는 법이지요.

“맞습니다!”

이 책은 여러분이 문장에서 단어의 의미를 익히고, 더 나아가 독해지문 속에서
어휘의 쓰임을 확실하게 마스터하게끔 설계되어 있답니다.

“So, don’t worry and just follow me!”

– 이룸이앤비 영어연구실 –

이 책의 구성과 특징

Part A : 학습할 표제어 및 예문

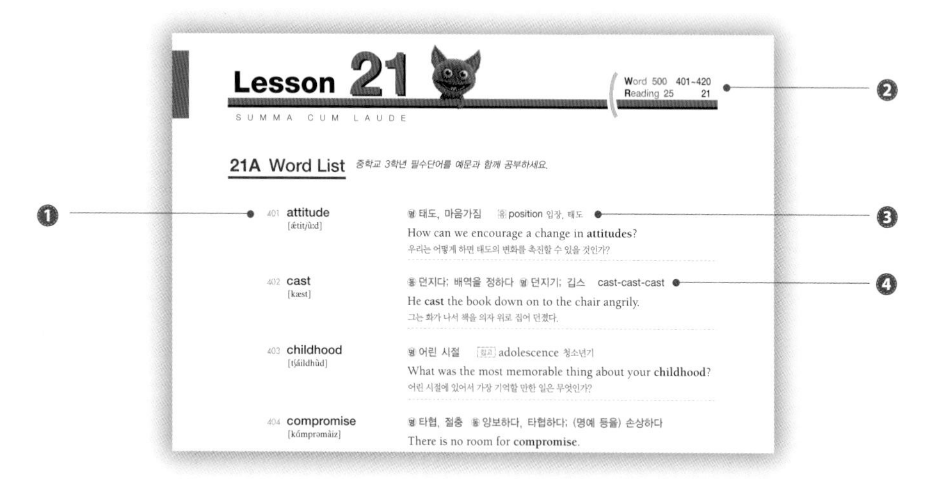

Lesson 21

SUMMA CUM LAUDE

Word 500 401~420
Reading 25 21

21A Word List 중학교 3학년 필수단어를 예문과 함께 공부하세요.

401 attitude [ǽtitjùːd]
명 태도, 마음가짐 유 position 입장, 태도
How can we encourage a change in **attitudes**?
우리는 어떻게 하면 태도의 변화를 촉진할 수 있을 것인가?

402 cast [kæst]
동 던지다; 배역을 정하다 명 던지기; 깁스 cast-cast-cast
He **cast** the book down on to the chair angrily.
그는 화가 나서 책을 의자 위로 집어 던졌다.

403 childhood [tʃáildhùd]
명 어린 시절 참고 adolescence 청소년기
What was the most memorable thing about your **childhood**?
어린 시절에 있어서 가장 기억할 만한 일은 무엇인가?

404 compromise [kɑ́mprəmàiz]
명 타협, 절충 동 양보하다, 타협하다; (명예 등을) 손상하다
There is no room for **compromise**.

❶ 빈출어휘 500개를 엄선하여 최적화된 예문과 함께 수록
❷ 학습할 전체 분량에서 해당 단원의 위치를 의미
❸ 표제어의 주요 파생어, 유의어, 반의어 수록
❹ 불규칙 동사의 변화형 제시

Part B · C · D · E : 각 학년 수준에 맞는 다양한 유형의 연습문제

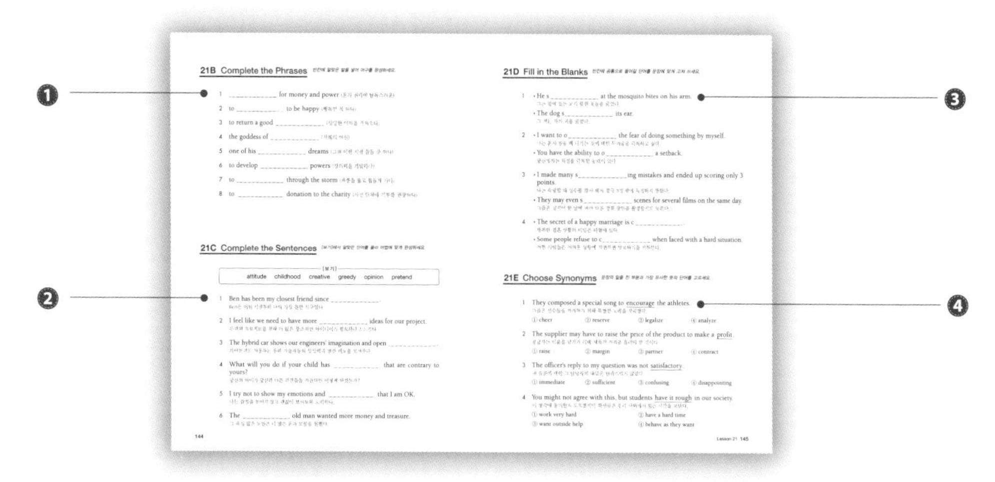

21B Complete the Phrases

1 ____________ for money and power
2 to ____________ to be happy
3 to return a good ____________
4 the goddess of ____________
5 one of his ____________ dreams
6 to develop ____________ powers
7 to ____________ through the storm
8 to ____________ donation to the charity

21C Complete the Sentences

[보기] attitude childhood creative greedy opinion pretend

1 Ben has been my closest friend since ____________.
2 I feel like we need to have more ____________ ideas for our project.
3 The hybrid car shows our engineers' imagination and open ____________.
4 What will you do if your child has ____________ that are contrary to yours?
5 I try not to show my emotions and ____________ that I am OK.
6 The ____________ old man wanted more money and treasure.

144

21D Fill in the Blanks

1 • He s____________ at the mosquito bites on his arm.
• The dog s____________ its ear.
2 • I want to o____________ the fear of doing something by myself.
• You have the ability to o____________ a setback.
3 • I made many s____________ing mistakes and ended up scoring only 3 points.
• They may even s____________ scenes for several films on the same day.
4 • The secret of a happy marriage is c____________.
• Some people refuse to c____________ when faced with a hard situation.

21E Choose Synonyms

1 They composed a special song to encourage the athletes.
① cheer ② reserve ③ legalize ④ analyze
2 The supplier may have to raise the price of the product to make a profit.
① raise ② margin ③ partner ④ contract
3 The officer's reply to my question was not satisfactory.
① immediate ② sufficient ③ confusing ④ disappointing
4 You might not agree with this, but students have it rough in our society.
① work very hard ② have a hard time
③ want outside help ④ behave as they want

Lesson 21 145

❶ 어구 완성하기
❷ 어법에 맞게 문장 완성하기
❸ 공통으로 들어갈 단어 쓰기
❹ 문장에서 유의어 찾기

Part F : 독해지문과 내신 대비 연습문제

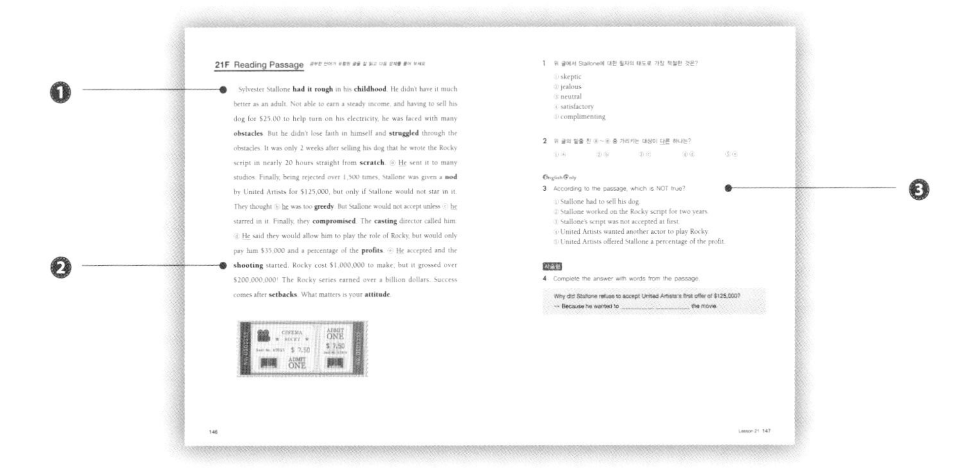

❶ 교과서 주요 어휘를 포함하는 흥미로운 지문 수록
❷ 독해지문 내에서 어휘의 쓰임을 정확히 익힘
❸ 서술형을 포함한 다양한 유형의 문제로 내신 시험 완벽 대비

Workbook : 마무리 단어 테스트 및 Dictation

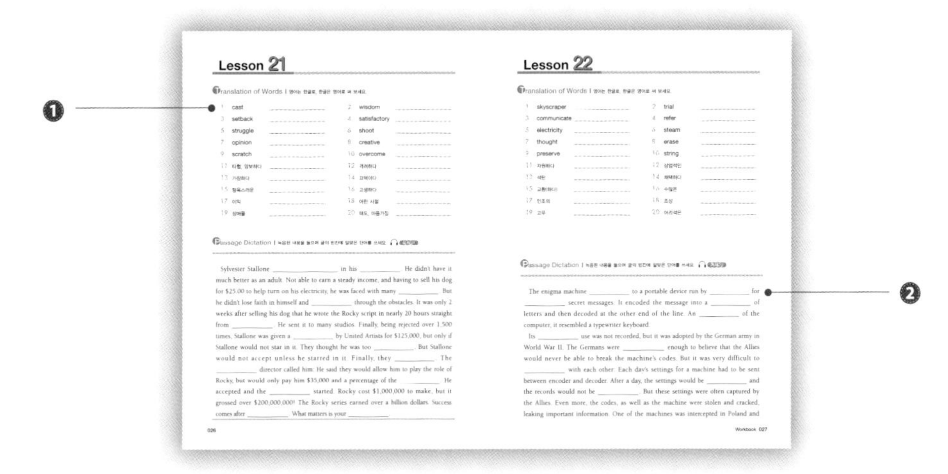

❶ 단원별로 학습한 어휘를 다시 한 번 확인해 볼 수 있는 단어 테스트 수록
❷ 원어민의 발음을 들으며 지문의 빈칸을 채워 완성하는 Dictation 수록

이 책의 학습 Plan 1 · 2

학습자의 계획에 따라 2가지 방법으로 학습이 가능합니다!

Plan **1** **어휘 집중 학습형** : 각 Lesson별 단어를 충분히 익히고, 독해지문은 나중에 따로 공부하는 방법

Plan **2** **어휘 + 독해 학습형** : 단어 학습과 그 단어가 포함된 독해지문 학습을 한번에 하는 방법

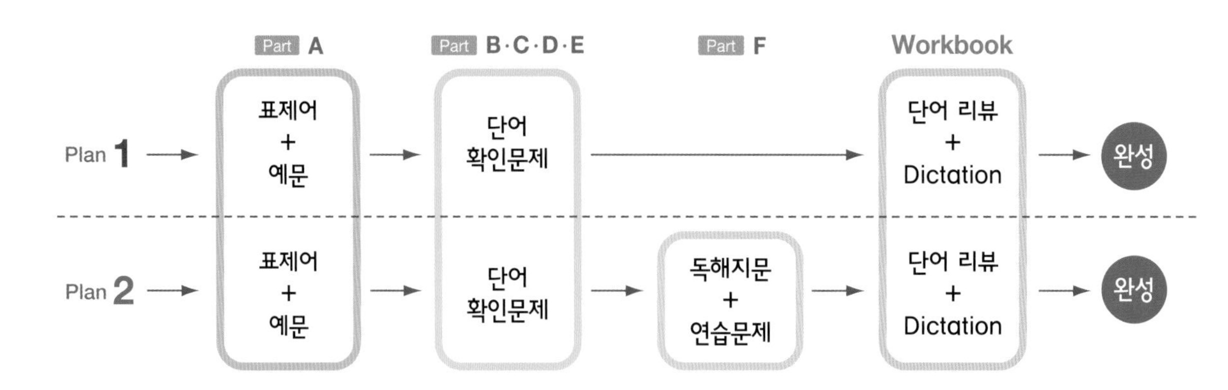

선생님들의 추천 학습 Tip

① 하루에 하나의 **Lesson**을 학습하세요.

② 하나의 **Chapter**가 끝나면 **Speedy Check-up**을 통해 외우지 못한 어휘를 정리하여 틈틈이 학습하세요.

③ 학습용 **mp3** 파일을 활용하세요. 등·하교시간, 쉬는 시간에 학습용·복습용으로 알차게 활용하세요.

④ **〈학습 스케줄러〉**에 학습한 날짜를 기입하면 전체적인 어휘 학습 진도를 한눈에 파악할 수 있습니다.

⑤ 독해지문 문제풀이가 부담스럽거나 단기간에 전체 어휘를 먼저 학습하고 싶다면 독해지문 코너를 건너뛰고 Plan **1**의 방법으로 학습하는 것을 제안합니다.

Plan 1 어휘 집중 학습 스케줄러

먼저 전체 어휘를 집중해서 공부하고 어휘학습이 충분하다고 판단되면 독해는 추후에, 학습한 단어를 확인해 가면서 따로 공부할 수 있습니다.
자신의 계획에 따라, 공부한 날짜를 써 가면서 학습하세요.

어휘 집중 학습

	Lesson 1	Lesson 2	Lesson 3	Lesson 4	Lesson 5
단어 및 확인문제 학습 Part A·B·C·D·E	월 일	월 일	월 일	월 일	월 일
워크북 학습	월 일	월 일	월 일	월 일	월 일

	Lesson 6	Lesson 7	Lesson 8	Lesson 9	Lesson 10
단어 및 확인문제 학습 Part A·B·C·D·E	월 일	월 일	월 일	월 일	월 일
워크북 학습	월 일	월 일	월 일	월 일	월 일

	Lesson 11	Lesson 12	Lesson 13	Lesson 14	Lesson 15
단어 및 확인문제 학습 Part A·B·C·D·E	월 일	월 일	월 일	월 일	월 일
워크북 학습	월 일	월 일	월 일	월 일	월 일

	Lesson 16	Lesson 17	Lesson 18	Lesson 19	Lesson 20
단어 및 확인문제 학습 Part A·B·C·D·E	월 일	월 일	월 일	월 일	월 일
워크북 학습	월 일	월 일	월 일	월 일	월 일

	Lesson 21	Lesson 22	Lesson 23	Lesson 24	Lesson 25
단어 및 확인문제 학습 Part A·B·C·D·E	월 일	월 일	월 일	월 일	월 일
워크북 학습	월 일	월 일	월 일	월 일	월 일

독해를 통한 어휘 확인 학습

	Lesson 1	Lesson 2	Lesson 3	Lesson 4	Lesson 5
독해 학습 Part F	월 일	월 일	월 일	월 일	월 일

	Lesson 6	Lesson 7	Lesson 8	Lesson 9	Lesson 10
독해 학습 Part F	월 일	월 일	월 일	월 일	월 일

	Lesson 11	Lesson 12	Lesson 13	Lesson 14	Lesson 15
독해 학습 Part F	월 일	월 일	월 일	월 일	월 일

	Lesson 16	Lesson 17	Lesson 18	Lesson 19	Lesson 20
독해 학습 Part F	월 일	월 일	월 일	월 일	월 일

	Lesson 21	Lesson 22	Lesson 23	Lesson 24	Lesson 25
독해 학습 Part F	월 일	월 일	월 일	월 일	월 일

Plan 2 어휘 + 독해 학습 스케줄러

어휘 학습을 한 후, 독해지문까지 마무리하며 단원 내에서 완벽하고 효율적으로 학습할 수 있습니다.
자신의 계획에 따라, 공부한 날짜를 써 가면서 학습하세요.

	Lesson 1	Lesson 2	Lesson 3	Lesson 4	Lesson 5
단어 및 확인문제 학습 Part A·B·C·D·E	월 일	월 일	월 일	월 일	월 일
독해 학습 Part F	월 일	월 일	월 일	월 일	월 일
워크북 학습	월 일	월 일	월 일	월 일	월 일

	Lesson 6	Lesson 7	Lesson 8	Lesson 9	Lesson 10
단어 및 확인문제 학습 Part A·B·C·D·E	월 일	월 일	월 일	월 일	월 일
독해 학습 Part F	월 일	월 일	월 일	월 일	월 일
워크북 학습	월 일	월 일	월 일	월 일	월 일

	Lesson 11	Lesson 12	Lesson 13	Lesson 14	Lesson 15
단어 및 확인문제 학습 Part A·B·C·D·E	월 일	월 일	월 일	월 일	월 일
독해 학습 Part F	월 일	월 일	월 일	월 일	월 일
워크북 학습	월 일	월 일	월 일	월 일	월 일

	Lesson 16	Lesson 17	Lesson 18	Lesson 19	Lesson 20
단어 및 확인문제 학습 Part A·B·C·D·E	월 일	월 일	월 일	월 일	월 일
독해 학습 Part F	월 일	월 일	월 일	월 일	월 일
워크북 학습	월 일	월 일	월 일	월 일	월 일

	Lesson 21	Lesson 22	Lesson 23	Lesson 24	Lesson 25
단어 및 확인문제 학습 Part A·B·C·D·E	월 일	월 일	월 일	월 일	월 일
독해 학습 Part F	월 일	월 일	월 일	월 일	월 일
워크북 학습	월 일	월 일	월 일	월 일	월 일

이 책의 **오감 만족 학습법**

다음 순서에 따라 학습해 보세요. 어휘 학습과 더불어 〈듣기〉, 〈쓰기〉, 〈말하기〉 영역 학습에도 도움이 됩니다.

1 해당 Lesson의 **표제어**를 눈으로 훑어보며 알고 있는 단어는 옆에 **표시**합니다.

2 「**단어 mp3**」 파일을 들으며 발음을 확인하고 **따라 읽어** 봅니다.

3 Part **A** **표제어**와 **예문**을 여러 번 읽으며 학습합니다.

4 책을 덮고 「**단어+예문 mp3**」 파일을 들으며 각 단어의 **의미**를 떠올려 봅니다.

5 Part **B·C·D·E** 연습문제를 풀어보고, **틀린 단어**는 예문과 함께 다시 읽어 봅니다.

6 ④단계를 반복 학습하고 Part **F**의 독해 지문을 **해석**하고 **문제**를 풉니다.

7 ②단계를 반복하고, Workbook **단어 테스트**를 풀어 봅니다.

8 「**독해 mp3**」 파일을 들으며 Dictation을 완성합니다.

9 하나의 Chapter가 끝나면 Speedy Check-up을 확인하고 **오답노트**로 활용합니다.

<<< 학습용 mp3 파일 구성 >>>

하나! 단어 mp3 | 둘! 단어+예문 mp3 | 셋! 독해 mp3

- **mp3 파일**은 이룸이앤비 홈페이지(www.erumenb.com) **학습자료실** ⇨ **듣기자료실**에서 무료로 다운 받을 수 있습니다.

이 책의 차례

표제어 500 / 확장어휘 300 / 독해 25

5 Chapter

Workbook
(책 속의 책)

Chapter 1

Lesson 1

SUMMA CUM LAUDE

Word 500 001~020
Reading 25 01

1A Word List

중학교 3학년 필수단어를 예문과 함께 공부하세요.

001 **awkward** [ɔ́:kwərd]

형 어색한, 서투른; 곤란한

She finally broke the **awkward** silence.

그녀가 마침내 어색한 침묵을 깨뜨렸다.

002 **calculate** [kǽlkjulèit]

동 계산하다, 산출하다 명 calculation 계산, 산출

This service makes it easy to **calculate** tax rates.

이 서비스는 세율 계산을 쉽게 한다.

003 **conflict** [kɑ́nflikt]

명 갈등, 충돌 동 대립하다

The basic reason for the war was a **conflict** between two cultures.

그 전쟁의 근본적인 이유는 두 문화 사이의 갈등이었다.

004 **creature** [krí:tʃər]

명 생물, 생명체, 사람 동 create 창조하다

We should teach our children to respect all living **creatures**.

우리는 아이들에게 살아있는 모든 생명체를 존중하는 것을 가르쳐야 한다.

005 **deserve** [dizə́:rv]

동 ~을 받을 만하다 (자격이 있다)

Practice makes perfect and effort **deserves** praise.

연습하면 완벽해지고 그 노력은 칭찬받을 가치가 있다.

006 **effective** [iféktiv]

형 효과적인; 시행되는 명 effectiveness 유효, 효과

It is not **effective** to study all day.

하루 종일 공부만 하는 것은 효과적이지 않다.

007 **fable** [féibl]

명 우화, 꾸며낸 이야기

I have loved Aesop's **Fables** since I was a child.

나는 어렸을 때부터 이솝 우화를 정말로 좋아했다.

008 **fever** [fí:vər]

명 열, 열병; 흥분

Eating chocolate can help reduce a high **fever**.

초콜릿을 먹으면 고열을 내리는 데 도움이 될 수 있다.

009 **forbid** [fərbíd]

동 금지하다 forbid-forbade-forbidden 유 prohibit

Scott **forbade** her to see his child.

Scott은 그녀가 자신의 아이를 보는 것을 금지했다.

010 **frustrate**
[frʌ́streit]

동 좌절시키다, 방해하다 형 frustrated 좌절한 명 frustration 좌절

The attempt to attack the building was **frustrated** by the police.
그 건물을 공격하려는 시도가 경찰에 의해 저지되었다.

011 **method**
[méθəd]

명 방법 참고 approach 접근법, 처리 방법

My boss came up with a new **method** of solving the problem.
내 상사는 그 문제를 해결할 새로운 방법을 생각해냈다.

012 **overweight**
[óuvərwèit]

형 과체중의, 비만의 참고 chubby 통통한

Females are very sensitive about being **overweight**.
여성들은 과체중이 되는 것에 대해 매우 민감하다.

013 **prevent**
[privént]

동 막다, 방해하다 명 prevention 방지

The heavy rain **prevented** me from going out.
나는 폭우가 내려서 외출하지 못했다.

014 **protest**
[prətést]

동 항의하다, 반대하다 명 항의, 반대

Many people continued to **protest** against the policy.
많은 사람들이 그 정책에 대해 계속 항의했다.

015 **sight**
[sait]

명 시력, 시야, 광경

Joseph lost his **sight** as a baby.
Joseph은 어렸을 때 시력을 잃었다.

016 **strike**
[straik]

동 세게 치다, 공격하다 명 파업 strike-struck-struck(stricken)

He suddenly **struck** the table with his fist.
그는 갑자기 주먹으로 탁자를 세게 쳤다.

017 **timid**
[tímid]

형 소심한, 용기(자신감)가 없는

Her boyfriend was too **timid** to propose to her.
그녀의 남자친구는 너무 소심해서 그녀에게 청혼하지 못했다.

018 **yell**
[jel]

동 소리치다, 고함치다 참고 scream 비명을 지르다 shout 외치다

I heard someone **yelling** my name.
나는 누군가가 내 이름을 소리쳐 부르는 것을 들었다.

019 **as though**

마치 ~인 것처럼 유 as if

Always behave **as though** nothing had happened, no matter what has happened.
어떤 일이 일어나더라도, 항상 아무 일도 일어나지 않았던 것처럼 행동하라.

020 **depend on**

신뢰하다, 의존하다; ~에 달려 있다

You are the sort of person I can **depend on**.
당신은 내가 의지할 수 있는 그런 부류의 사람이다.

1B Complete the Phrases
빈칸에 알맞은 말을 넣어 어구를 완성하세요.

1 a ________________ writer (우화 작가)

2 a scientific ________________ of data analysis (자료 분석의 과학적인 방법)

3 a highly ________________ treatment (매우 효과적인 치료법)

4 at first ________________ (첫눈에)

5 ________________ attention (주목을 받을 만하다)

6 an ________________ silence (어색한 침묵)

7 an ________________ man (비만인 남성)

8 a social ________________ (사회적 생물)

1C Complete the Sentences
[보기]에서 알맞은 단어를 골라 어법에 맞게 완성하세요.

[보기]
depend on　yell　as though　conflict　timid　protest　fever

1 He acted ________________ he were a little child.
그는 마치 어린아이인 것처럼 행동했다.

2 The teacher ________________ at her for being late again.
선생님은 또 늦은 것에 대해 그녀에게 소리를 쳤다.

3 A high ________________ in children can be scary for the parents.
아이들의 고열은 부모들에게 무서운 것일 수 있다.

4 A lot of things ________________ when he will come.
많은 것들은 그가 언제 오느냐에 달려 있다.

5 They made signs to ________________ the government's decision.
그들은 정부의 결정에 반대하는 취지의 서명을 했다.

6 I was too ________________ to go out with girls.
나는 여자들과 데이트하기에는 너무 소심했다.

7 I have some ________________ with my parents.
나는 우리 부모님과 몇 가지 갈등을 가지고 있다.

1D Fill in the Blanks 빈칸에 공통으로 들어갈 단어를 문장에 맞게 고쳐 쓰세요.

1 • He continued to p______________ his father's innocence.
그는 아버지의 무죄를 계속 항변했다.
• It originally started out as a peaceful p______________.
그것은 원래 평화로운 시위로 시작되었다.

2 • He d______________ the credit for an economic boom like this.
그는 이러한 재정적 호황을 누릴만한 자격이 있다.
• The report d______________ a closer look.
그 보고서는 좀 더 면밀히 검토할 가치가 있다.

3 • He found the drugs that are e______________ against cancer.
그는 암에 효과가 있는 약을 발견했다.
• The law became e______________ on January 15, 2014.
그 법안은 2014년 1월 15일에 발효되었다.

4 • This study's results c______________ with those of other papers.
이 연구 결과는 다른 논문들의 결과와 상충된다.
• Science sometimes comes into c______________ with religion.
과학은 때때로 종교와 갈등한다.

1E Choose Synonyms 문장의 밑줄 친 부분과 가장 유사한 뜻의 단어를 고르세요.

1 Students are forbidden to have cell phones in school.
학생들이 교내에서 휴대전화를 소지하는 것이 금지된다.
① invited ② delivered ③ prohibited ④ allowed

2 Don't be frustrated by the obstacles you encounter in life.
여러분의 삶에서 부딪히게 되는 장애물에 좌절하지 마세요.
① devoted ② discouraged ③ promoted ④ concerned

3 Nothing is going to prevent me from going there.
어떤 것도 내가 그곳에 가는 것을 막지 않을 것이다.
① enable ② chase ③ stop ④ reject

4 He hit the horn and yelled at the other driver.
그는 경적을 울리며 다른 운전자에게 소리쳤다.
① angered ② shouted ③ approached ④ rushed

1F Reading Passage 공부한 단어가 포함된 글을 잘 읽고 다음 문제를 풀어 보세요.

Here's one of Aesop's **fables**. Having dreamed that a **timid, overweight** old man saw his only son killed by a lion, he was afraid that the dream was a vision of what was actually going to happen.

(A) One day he stood in front of the lion and **yelled**: "Curse you! It is because of you and my father's dream that I must stay here like a woman. How can I pay you out?" And as he spoke he **struck** his hand against the wall **as though** he would knock out the lion's eye.

(B) To **prevent** it from coming true, ______________, he built a very terrific hall raised high above the ground and kept his son there under guard. The hall was decorated with pictures of all sorts of **creatures**, including a lion; but the **sight** of them only made him more **frustrated**.

(C) A thin, sharp piece of stone went in under his nail. He felt severe pain and had a high **fever**. Before long he died. So although it was but a painted picture, the lion had caused the boy's death, and <u>the **method** his father used</u>, finally, was not **effective**.

1 위 글의 주어진 문장 다음에 이어질 글의 순서로 가장 적절한 것은?

① (A) — (C) — (B)
② (B) — (A) — (C)
③ (B) — (C) — (A)
④ (C) — (A) — (B)
⑤ (C) — (B) — (A)

2 위 글의 빈칸에 들어갈 말로 가장 적절한 것은?

① however
② although
③ for example
④ therefore
⑤ similarly

English Only

3 According to the story, which is true?

① The old man saw his only son killing a lion.
② The old man's son blamed the lion for his situation.
③ The old man's son attacked the lion's legs.
④ The old man ordered his only son to hide himself underground.
⑤ The old man's son painted a picture of a lion on the wall.

서술형

4 Fill in the blanks to complete the answer. Use words from the passage.

What does the underlined phrase mean?
→ The old man had his son stay in a hall __________ __________ __________ the ground.

Lesson 2

SUMMA CUM LAUDE

2A Word List

중학교 3학년 필수단어를 예문과 함께 공부하세요.

021 **abstract** [æbstrǽkt]
형 추상적인, 관념적인 반 concrete 구체적인
The painter is very famous for his **abstract** paintings.
그 화가는 추상화로 매우 유명하다.

022 **accuse** [əkjúːz]
동 고발〔기소〕하다, 비난하다 명 accusation 고발, 기소
The man was **accused** of theft from a shop.
그 남자는 상점에서 절도죄로 기소되었다.

023 **blossom** [blάsəm]
동 꽃이 피다, 꽃을 피우다 명 (유실수나 관목의) 꽃
Apple trees **blossom** in April.
사과나무는 4월에 꽃을 피운다.

024 **breathe** [briːð]
동 숨을 쉬다, 호흡하다 명 breath 숨, 호흡
When I woke up, I could hardly **breathe**.
잠에서 깨어났을 때 나는 숨을 쉬기가 무척 어려웠다.

025 **cheerful** [tʃíərfəl]
형 발랄한, 쾌활한 참고 cheer 환호; 환호하다
She's a very **cheerful** and confident employee.
그녀는 매우 쾌활하고 자신감 있는 직원이다.

026 **cling** [kliŋ]
동 달라붙다, 매달리다, 고수하다 cling-clung-clung
My sister is always **clinging** to me.
내 여동생은 항상 나에게 달라붙어 안 떨어진다.

027 **desperate** [déspərit]
형 절망적인, 필사적인 부 desperately 절망적으로
Hundreds of people grew increasingly **desperate**.
수백 명의 사람들이 점점 더 절망적으로 변해갔다.

028 **emergency** [imə́ːrdʒənsi]
명 비상(사태), 응급 상황
Always call 119 in case of **emergency**.
비상시에는 항상 119로 전화하라.

029 **erupt** [irʌ́pt]
동 (화산이) 분출하다, 분출되다 명 eruption (화산) 분출
Mount Toba could **erupt** again at any time.
Toba 화산은 언제든 다시 분출할 수 있다.

030 **expert** [ékspəːrt]

명 전문가 반 amateur 아마추어, 비전문가

I want to become a computer **expert** in the future.
나는 미래에 컴퓨터 전문가가 되고 싶다.

031 **indeed** [indíːd]

부 정말, 확실히, 참으로

Did you **indeed** finish the work?
당신은 정말로 그 일을 끝냈나요?

032 **injury** [índʒəri]

명 부상, 상처 동 injure 부상을 입다[입히다]

My father couldn't work because of an **injury**.
우리 아버지는 부상을 당해서 일을 할 수 없었다.

033 **miracle** [mírəkl]

명 기적, 불가사의한 일 형 miraculous 기적의, 기적적인

They don't believe in **miracles** any more.
사람들은 더 이상 기적을 믿지 않는다.

034 **produce** [prədjúːs]

동 생산하다, 만들다 명 production 생산(량)

This tree is very old, but always **produces** big fruit.
그 나무는 매우 늙었지만 항상 큰 열매를 생산해 낸다.

035 **purchase** [pə́ːrtʃəs]

동 구매하다 명 구매, 구입

I recently **purchased** some books online.
나는 최근 온라인으로 책을 몇 권 샀다.

036 **recall** [rikɔ́ːl]

동 기억해 내다, 상기하다, 회상하다 유 recollect

I couldn't **recall** his name when I met him on the street.
나는 길에서 그를 만났을 때 그의 이름을 기억해 낼 수 없었다.

037 **recover** [rikʌ́vər]

동 회복하다, 되찾다 명 recovery 회복, 되찾음

He **recovered** from knee surgery.
그는 무릎 수술에서 회복했다.

038 **replace** [ripléis]

동 대신하다, 교체하다 명 replacement 교체, 대체(물)

The black ink cartridge needs **replacing**.
검정색 잉크 카트리지는 교체할 필요가 있다.

039 **strength** [stréŋkθ]

명 힘, 기운, 강점 형 strong 강한 동 strengthen 강화하다

A new device gives patients the **strength** to walk again.
새로운 장치는 환자들에게 다시 걸을 수 있는 힘을 준다.

040 **worth** [wəːrθ]

형 ~의 가치가 있는, ~해볼 만한 명 가치, 값어치

His plan was risky, but it was **worth** a try.
그의 계획은 위험했지만, 시도해볼 가치가 있었다.

2B Complete the Phrases

빈칸에 알맞은 말을 넣어 어구를 완성하세요.

1 an ______________ on education (교육 분야의 전문가)

2 an ______________ painter (추상화가)

3 in a ______________ situation (절망적인 상황에 처해 있는)

4 a ______________ drug (특효약, 기적의 약)

5 ______________ him of theft (그를 절도 혐의로 기소하다)

6 ______________ the effort (노력할 가치가 있는)

7 with all one's ______________ (온 힘을 다해)

8 be in ______________ (꽃이 활짝 피어 있는)

2C Complete the Sentences

[보기]에서 알맞은 단어를 골라 어법에 맞게 완성하세요.

[보기]

breathe emergency indeed replace recall erupt abstract

1 Sometimes it's nice to ______________ memories of childhood days.
가끔씩 어린 시절의 기억을 떠올리는 것은 좋다.

2 Breakfast is ______________ the most important meal of the day.
아침은 정말로 하루 중에 가장 중요한 식사이다.

3 This compass could be useful in an ______________.
이 나침반은 비상 상황에서 유용하게 쓰일 수 있다.

4 Paper bags have been ______________ by plastic bags.
종이봉투는 비닐봉투로 대체되었다.

5 An ______________ idea can be interpreted in many different ways.
추상적인 생각은 여러 다른 방식으로 해석될 수 있다.

6 My three-year-old has been having trouble ______________ for a month.
나의 3살짜리 아이가 한 달 동안 호흡하는 데 어려움을 겪어 왔다.

7 A volcano in Indonesia ______________ causing 10,000 deaths.
인도네시아의 한 화산이 분출해서 만 명의 사망자를 냈다.

2D Fill in the Blanks
빈칸에 공통으로 들어갈 단어를 문장에 맞게 고쳐 쓰세요.

1 • He made a d_______________ attempt to save his friend from drowning.
그는 물에 빠진 친구를 구하기 위해 필사적인 노력을 했다.
• It is true that religion attracts d_______________ people.
종교가 절망에 빠진 사람들의 마음을 끌어당긴다는 것은 사실이다.

2 • The region p_______________ wheat and corn and has many herds of cattle.
그 지역에서는 밀과 옥수수를 생산하고 많은 무리의 소 떼들을 사육한다.
• The drug, if taken daily, p_______________ bursts of energy.
그 약을 매일 복용하게 된다면 그것은 엄청난 양의 에너지를 만들어 낸다.

3 • Stretching is a great exercise to r_______________ from fatigue.
스트레칭은 피로로부터 회복할 수 있는 훌륭한 운동이다.
• Doctors say he is likely to r_______________ his sight and work again.
의사들은 그가 시력을 되찾아 다시 일을 할 것 같다고 말한다.

4 • This novel is w_______________ reading twice.
이 소설은 두 번 읽을 가치가 있다.
• The sharing of experiences was of great w_______________.
경험을 공유한다는 것은 훌륭한 가치가 있는 것이었다.

2E Choose Synonyms
문장의 밑줄 친 부분과 가장 유사한 뜻의 단어를 고르세요.

1 The ability to adapt to change is one of his many <u>strengths</u>.
변화에 적응하는 능력은 그의 많은 강점들 중의 하나이다.
① strategies ② advantages ③ shortcomings ④ diversities

2 He couldn't play the game due to a serious <u>injury</u>.
그는 심한 부상으로 인해 그 경기에서 뛸 수 없었다.
① error ② attack ③ worry ④ wound

3 The old is always <u>replaced</u> by the new.
오래된 것은 항상 새로운 것으로 대체된다.
① isolated ② substituted ③ decreased ④ guaranteed

4 I felt so embarrassed when I couldn't <u>recall</u> her name.
나는 그녀의 이름을 기억해 낼 수 없었을 때 무척 난처했다.
① recollect ② recover ③ compete ④ frustrate

2F Reading Passage

공부한 단어가 포함된 글을 잘 읽고 다음 문제를 풀어 보세요.

On June 23, Jim Smith heard the **desperate** screams of a woman whose son was **clinging** onto the veranda. "It wasn't a normal scream, so I knew it was an **emergency**," said Jim. "It was a scream **produced** in the most urgent moment in one's life" (ⓐ) He couldn't ignore the situation. He ran 30 meters and spread his arms wide, much like a goalkeeper ready to block a shot. (ⓑ) "It all happened so fast. It's a **miracle**. I couldn't really think, not even for a second," Jim **recalled**. (ⓒ) True to his words, catching a 17kg child falling from 15 meters high is **indeed** a miracle. (ⓓ) "It would be the same as being hit by an object travelling at 70km per hour," an **expert** said. (ⓔ) Although he was unable to move comfortably due to **injuries** and had a bit of difficulty **breathing** for a moment, Jim is **recovering** in the hospital. The boy luckily suffered from just a nosebleed. The boy's parents came to the hospital and asked Jim what he wanted. But he didn't want any reward. He said saving a life was **worth** the risk.

1 위 글의 제목으로 가장 적절한 것은?

① Turn Your Crisis Into Your Opportunity
② A Mother's Unconditional Love for Her Son
③ A Miracle Happens to Those Who Believe It
④ Your Children Cannot Be Safe, Even at Home
⑤ A Falling Boy Miraculously Rescued by a Man

2 글의 흐름으로 보아, 주어진 문장이 들어가기에 가장 적절한 곳은?

> At that moment, the boy's fingers slipped, and he fell right into Jim's ready arms, which lasted only 15 to 20 seconds.

① ⓐ ② ⓑ ③ ⓒ ④ ⓓ ⑤ ⓔ

English Only

3 According to the passage, which is NOT true?

① A boy was clinging onto the veranda.
② Jim heard a desperate scream of a woman.
③ Jim caught a boy falling from 15 meters high.
④ Jim had no injuries from the accident.
⑤ The boy's parents came to the hospital to see Jim.

서술형

4 What does the underlined the situation mean in the passage? Write your answer in Korean.

____

____

Lesson 3

Word 500 041~060
Reading 25 03

3A Word List

중학교 3학년 필수단어를 예문과 함께 공부하세요.

041 **aim** [éim]

명 목표, 목적 동 목표하다, 겨누다

Our main **aim** is to play well, not to win.
우리의 목표는 이기는 것이 아니라 경기를 잘하는 것이다.

042 **authority** [əθɔ́:rəti]

명 권위(자), 권한; 인가 참고 authorities 당국

She wanted to learn how to speak with **authority**.
그녀는 권위 있게 말하는 법을 배우고 싶어 했다.

043 **contrast** [kɑ́ntræst]

명 차이, 대조 동 대조하다 참고 in contrast to ~와는 대조적으로

There is a big **contrast** between the two cities.
두 도시 사이에는 큰 차이점이 있다.

044 **corridor** [kɔ́:ridər]

명 복도, 통로

I saw one boy running along the **corridor**.
나는 한 소년이 복도를 따라 뛰어가는 것을 보았다.

045 **guarantee** [gæ̀rəntí:]

동 보장(약속)하다 명 보장; 품질 보증서

We cannot **guarantee** their safety if they leave here.
그들이 이 곳을 떠난다면 우리는 그들의 안전을 보장할 수 없다.

046 **launch** [lɔ:ntʃ]

동 시작(개시)하다, (상품을) 출시하다

No country has the right to **launch** an attack on another country.
다른 국가에 대한 공격을 개시할 권리는 어떤 나라에도 없다.

047 **opportunity** [ɑ̀pərtjú:nəti]

명 기회 유 chance 참고 occasion 경우, 기회

You shouldn't miss the **opportunity** to make a fortune.
부자가 될 기회를 놓쳐서는 안 된다.

048 **permanent** [pə́:rmənənt]

형 영구(영속)적인 유 everlasting 영원한 반 temporary 일시적인

Exposure to loud music can cause **permanent** hearing damage.
시끄러운 음악에 노출되는 것은 영구적인 청각 손상을 초래할 수 있다.

049 **possibility** [pɑ̀səbíləti]

명 가능성, 가능한 일 형 possible 가능한

There is not much **possibility** of his coming on time.
그가 시간에 딱 맞춰 올 가능성은 그리 크지 않다.

050 **principle** [prínsəpl]

명 원칙, 원리, 신조 참고 in principle 원칙적으로

You need to stick to your own **principles** and beliefs.
당신은 자신의 원칙과 믿음을 고수해야 한다.

051 **pursuit** [pərsú:t]

명 추격, 추적, 추구 동 pursue 추구하다, 추적하다

The **pursuit** of happiness may make you less happy.
행복을 (지나치게) 추구하는 것은 당신의 행복감을 떨어뜨릴 수도 있다.

052 **quality** [kwɑ́ləti]

명 질(質), 품질, (사람의) 자질, 특성 참고 quantity 양, 수량

The test results show a decline in the water **quality** of the lake.
검사 결과는 그 호수의 수질 저하를 보여준다.

053 **relate** [riléit]

동 관련시키다 참고 related to ~와 관련되어 있는

Causes of hunger are **related** to poverty.
굶주림의 원인은 가난과 관련되어 있다.

054 **religion** [rilídʒən]

명 종교 형 religious 종교의, 종교적인

The conflict between science and **religion** is a hard problem.
과학과 종교 사이의 갈등은 어려운 문제이다.

055 **shelter** [ʃéltər]

명 주거지; 피신처 동 보호하다

It is impossible for human beings to survive without **shelter**.
인간이 주거지 없이 생존하는 것은 불가능하다.

056 **succeed** [səksí:d]

동 성공하다, 뒤를 잇다 명 success 성공 형 successful 성공적인

My daughter **succeeded** in getting a job abroad.
나의 딸은 해외에서 취직하는 데 성공했다.

057 **surface** [sə́:rfis]

명 표면, 지면, 수면, 외관

It takes twice as long to stop when the road **surface** is wet.
도로면이 젖어있을 때는 정지거리가 2배 길어진다.

058 **therefore** [ðɛ́ərfɔ̀:r]

부 그러므로, 따라서

She couldn't stay in one place long and **therefore** has few friends.
그녀는 한 장소에 오래 머무를 수 없어서 친구가 별로 없다.

059 **whisper** [wíspər]

동 속삭이다, 귀엣말하다, 험담하다 명 속삭임

I think it's rude to **whisper** in front of other people.
나는 다른 사람들 앞에서 귀엣말하는 것은 무례하다고 생각한다.

060 **be willing to**

기꺼이〔흔쾌히〕 ~ 하다

They **are willing to** sacrifice for the environment.
그들은 환경을 위해 기꺼이 희생하려 한다.

3B Complete the Phrases
빈칸에 알맞은 말을 넣어 어구를 완성하세요.

1 freedom of ________________ (종교의 자유)

2 a ________________ ownership (영구적인 소유권)

3 in ________________ of happiness (행복을 추구하는)

4 a great investment ________________ (좋은 투자 기회)

5 in ________________ with (~와 대조를 이루어)

6 in terms of ________________ (품질의 관점에서)

7 be ________________ to run a risk (기꺼이 위험을 무릅쓰다)

8 ________________ to business (사업과 관련된)

3C Complete the Sentences
[보기]에서 알맞은 단어를 골라 어법에 맞게 완성하세요.

[보기]

whisper quality corridor aim possibility principle surface

1 There is a low ________________ of an allergic reaction.
알레르기 반응이 일어날 가능성은 낮다.

2 He leaned over and ________________ something in my ear.
그는 몸을 기울여 내 귀에 무엇인가를 속삭였다.

3 I walked along the ________________ pretending to be talking on my phone.
나는 전화 통화를 하는 척 하면서 복도를 따라 걸어갔다.

4 Be careful of icy ________________ on the roads.
길 위에 얼어있는 면을 조심하시오.

5 The ________________ of this research is to provide evidence.
이 연구의 목적은 증거를 제공하는 것이다.

6 China took measures to enhance product ________________.
중국은 제품의 질을 향상시킬 조치를 취했다.

7 She acted on the ________________ of self-sacrifice.
그녀는 자기희생의 원칙에 따라 행동했다.

3D Fill in the Blanks *빈칸에 공통으로 들어갈 단어를 문장에 맞게 고쳐 쓰세요.*

1 • If you want to s_______________, you have to set a specific goal.
성공하기를 원한다면 구체적인 목표를 세워야 한다.
• Economic planning cannot s_______________ in present conditions.
현재와 같은 조건에서는 경제 계획이 성공할 수 없다.

2 • The basic components are food, clothing, and s_______________.
기본적인 요소에는 식량, 의복, 집이 있다.
• Many dogs abandoned by their owners are in the animal s_______________.
주인이 버린 많은 개들은 동물 보호소에 있다.

3 • I have no a_______________ to increase the number of students in the course.
나는 그 코스의 총 학생 수를 늘릴 권한이 전혀 없다.
• This investment was made without the president's a_______________.
이 투자는 회장의 인가 없이 행해졌다.

4 • It is interesting to c_______________ this approach with that of the company.
이 접근 방식과 그 회사의 방식을 비교하는 것은 흥미롭다.
• The situation of urban residents showed a sharp c_______________ with that of farmers.
도시주민의 환경은 농민의 환경과 확연한 대조를 보여 주었다.

3E Choose Synonyms *문장의 밑줄 친 부분과 가장 유사한 뜻의 단어를 고르세요.*

1 Food poisoning may cause <u>permanent</u> damage to the body.
식중독은 신체에 영구적인 손상을 줄지도 모른다.
① desirable ② temporary ③ fixed ④ everlasting

2 This project is <u>related</u> to my special interests.
이 프로젝트는 나의 특별한 관심사와 연관되어 있다.
① expected ② indifferent ③ occurred ④ connected

3 We <u>guarantee</u> to deliver your goods within two days.
우리는 2일내로 여러분의 상품을 배달할 것을 보장합니다.
① happen ② promise ③ deserve ④ mistake

4 The <u>aim</u> of this lecture is to help patients to be independent.
이 강의의 목적은 환자들로 하여금 독립적이 되도록 돕는 데에 있다.
① goal ② process ③ amount ④ selection

3F Reading Passage

공부한 단어가 포함된 글을 잘 읽고 다음 문제를 풀어 보세요.

In a 12-year study at Babson College, Dr. Robert Miller, an **authority** on businessmen education, searched for the reasons for success or failure among the students who graduated from the business school. Some went on to build successful businesses, but most did not. He discovered that those who built successful businesses had a special **quality**. It was that they had the ______________ to **launch** their businesses with no **guarantees** of success. They **were willing to** risk failure in the pursuit of their dreams.

Professor Miller called this the "**corridor principle**." He said that when you launch toward your goal, however distant, you begin to move down a corridor of time. As you move down this corridor, other doors of **opportunity** will open up on either side of you. But you would not have been able to see these other doors of opportunity if you were not already in motion down this psychological corridor toward your goal.

Most people who **succeed** in life achieve their success in an area completely different from the field in which they started off. But because they were in motion, they saw opportunities and **possibilities** that they would not have been aware of if they had waited until everything was just right. And the reality is that everything will never be just right.

1 위 글의 제목으로 가장 적절한 것은?

① Let Go of the Past to Succeed
② Opportunity Favors Those Ready
③ Risk Failure If You're to Succeed
④ Set a Specific Goal for Achievement
⑤ Build More Relationships to Do Business

2 위 글의 빈칸에 들어갈 말로 가장 적절한 것은?

① accident
② honesty
③ leisure
④ evidence
⑤ courage

English Only

3 According to Dr. Robert Miller's study, what is the reason students failed in business?

① Because they didn't graduate from business school.
② Because they didn't set a high goal to continue to achieve.
③ Because they didn't start their businesses with risk of failure.
④ Because they didn't have enough funds to launch their businesses.
⑤ Because they didn't know about the field in which they started off.

서술형

4 Complete the answer. Arrange the words given in order.

If you want to see doors of opportunity open up for you, what should you do?
→ We have to (down, toward, goal, our, move) ________________________.

Lesson 4

SUMMA CUM LAUDE

Word 500 061~080
Reading 25 04

4A Word List

중학교 3학년 필수단어를 예문과 함께 공부하세요.

061 **adapt** [ədǽpt]
동 맞추다, 조정하다; 적응하다 명 adaptation 적응
Intelligence is the ability to **adapt** to change.
지성이란 변화에 적응할 수 있는 능력이다.

062 **aggressive** [əgrésiv]
형 공격적인, 대단히 적극적인
My dog gets **aggressive** when I leave the house.
우리집 개는 내가 집을 나서려고 하면 공격적으로 변한다.

063 **boast** [boust]
동 뽐내다, 자랑하다 유 brag (심하게) 자랑하다
Mom always **boasts** about me to her friends.
우리 엄마는 항상 나를 엄마 친구들에게 자랑한다.

064 **casually** [kǽʒuəli]
부 우연히, 아무 생각 없이, 무심코
She glanced **casually** over her right shoulder.
그녀는 무심코 자신의 오른쪽 어깨 너머를 흘낏 보았다.

065 **characteristic** [kæ̀riktərístik]
명 특징, 특질 형 특유의 유 feature 특색, 특징
Diversity is a basic **characteristic** of human society.
다양성은 인간 사회의 기본적인 특징이다.

066 **clap** [klæp]
동 박수를 치다 명 박수 (소리)
She **clapped** her hands in delight.
그녀는 기뻐서 박수를 쳤다.

067 **conduct** [kəndʌ́ct]
동 수행하다; 지휘하다 명 행동; 수행
The team **conducted** a survey about consumer psychology.
그 팀은 소비자 심리에 관한 설문조사를 수행했다.

068 **declare** [dikléər]
동 선언(선포)하다; 신고하다 명 declaration 선언, 선포
Americans **declared** their independence from Britain.
미국인들은 영국으로부터의 독립을 선포했다.

069 **demanding** [dimǽndiŋ]
형 (일이) 부담이 큰, 힘든, 요구가 많은 참고 demand 수요, 요구(하다)
A TV producer is one of the **demanding** jobs.
TV프로듀서는 힘든 일 중 하나이다.

070 **difficulty**
[dífikʌ̀lti]

명 어려움, 곤경, 장애 형 difficult 어려운

I had much **difficulty** finding his office.
나는 그의 사무실을 찾는 데 많은 어려움을 겪었다.

071 **dumb**
[dʌm]

형 말문이 막힌, 벙어리의 참고 deaf 청각 장애가 있는

Animals also can be born deaf and **dumb**.
동물들도 청각과 발성기관에 장애를 갖고 태어날 수 있다.

072 **equipment**
[ikwípmənt]

명 장비, 용품 동 equip 장비를 갖추다

I paid $4,000 cash to purchase office **equipment**.
나는 사무용품을 구입하는 데 현금 4천 달러를 지불했다.

073 **fairly**
[fέərli]

부 상당히, 꽤; 공정하게

The book is **fairly** thick to read.
그 책은 읽기에 꽤 두껍다.

074 **improve**
[imprúːv]

동 개선하다, 향상시키다 명 improvement 개선 유 enhance 향상시키다

Eat almonds to **improve** your memory.
기억력을 향상시키려면 아몬드를 섭취하라.

075 **investigate**
[invéstəgèit]

동 수사〔조사〕하다 명 investigation 수사, 조사

The police carefully **investigated** the cause of the fire.
경찰이 그 화재의 원인을 신중하게 조사했다.

076 **manufacture**
[mæ̀njəfǽktʃər]

동 제조하다, 만들다 명 제조, 제작 참고 manufacturer 제조업자

The company **manufactures** car engines.
그 회사는 차량 엔진을 제조한다.

077 **mature**
[mətjúər]

형 성숙한, 잘 익은 동 성숙〔발달〕시키다 반 immature 미숙한

I always try to look **mature** and responsible.
나는 항상 성숙하고 책임감 있게 보이려고 노력한다.

078 **outcome**
[áutkʌ̀m]

명 결과, 성과, 결론 유 result 결과

We are still waiting for the final **outcome** of the policy.
우리는 여전히 그 정책의 최종 결과를 기다리고 있다.

079 **persuade**
[pəːrswéid]

동 설득하다, 납득시키다 명 persuasion 설득, 확신

The coach **persuaded** us that we were wrong.
그 코치는 우리가 잘못한 점에 관해 우리를 설득했다.

080 **treat**
[triːt]

동 대하다, 다루다; 대접하다

It is important to **treat** people with respect.
사람들을 존중하는 마음으로 대하는 것은 중요하다.

4B Complete the Phrases *빈칸에 알맞은 말을 넣어 어구를 완성하세요.*

1 mentally ______________ jobs (정신적으로 힘든 직업들)

2 ______________ for one's age (나이에 비해 성숙한)

3 ______________ one's hands (손뼉을 치다)

4 ______________ an experiment (실험을 수행하다)

5 have ______________ finding a job (취직하는 데 여러 어려움을 겪다)

6 ______________ your memory (기억력을 향상시키다)

7 ______________ to changing conditions (변화하는 상황에 적응하다)

8 ______________ independence (독립을 선언하다)

4C Complete the Sentences *[보기]에서 알맞은 단어를 골라 어법에 맞게 완성하세요.*

[보기]

characteristic aggressive dumb equipment adapt casually fairly

1 I know myself ______________ well, but I'd like to try it once.
나는 내 자신을 매우 잘 알고 있지만, 한 번 시도해 보고 싶다.

2 There are genetic ______________ which may affect a kid.
아이에게 영향을 끼칠 수 있는 유전적 특징들이 있다.

3 The native species ______________ to the changing climate to survive.
그 토착종은 살아남기 위해서 변화하는 기후에 적응했다.

4 Susie ______________ mentioned the possibility of writing a book.
Susie는 무심코 책을 쓸 가능성을 언급했다.

5 Despair has almost struck me ______________.
나는 절망감에 거의 말문이 막혔다.

6 You should use more ______________ advertising strategies.
당신은 보다 공격적인 광고 전략을 써야 한다.

7 We packed ______________ for all possible scenarios.
우리는 가능한 모든 시나리오에 대비한 장비를 꾸렸다.

4D Fill in the Blanks 빈칸에 공통으로 들어갈 단어를 문장에 맞게 고쳐 쓰세요.

1 • Every species needs to a_______________ to the environment.
모든 종들은 환경에 적응해야 한다.
• These practices helped humans a_______________ to harsh climates.
이러한 습관들은 인간이 가혹한 기후에 적응하도록 도움을 주었다.

2 • How can stem cells be used to t_______________ human disease?
줄기 세포는 인간의 질병을 치료하는 데 어떻게 사용될 수 있는가?
• Let me t_______________ you to dinner tonight.
오늘 저녁은 제가 대접할게요.

3 • We will c_______________ background checks on potential employees.
우리는 입사 지원자의 신원 조사를 할 것이다.
• Joseph refused to c_______________ the orchestra.
Joseph은 그 관현악단에서 지휘하는 것을 거절했다.

4 • Factory work can be physically d_______________.
공장에서 일하는 것은 신체적으로 힘들 수 있다.
• She has a busy and d_______________ job.
그녀는 바쁘고 요구가 많은 직업을 갖고 있다.

4E Choose Synonyms 문장의 밑줄 친 부분과 가장 유사한 뜻의 단어를 고르세요.

1 Most people are happy with the present <u>outcome</u> of the election.
대부분의 사람들은 현재의 선거 결과에 만족해 한다.
① condition ② input ③ result ④ symbol

2 The company intends to <u>manufacture</u> smaller and energy-efficient cars.
그 회사는 좀 더 작고 연비가 좋은 차를 생산하려고 한다.
① produce ② launch ③ export ④ repair

3 The girls in school like to <u>boast</u> about being popular.
학교에서 여학생들은 인기가 많은 것에 대해 자랑하는 것을 좋아한다.
① recognize ② award ③ support ④ brag

4 Every civilization has its own distinctive <u>characteristics</u>.
모든 문명사회에는 각각의 특징들이 존재한다.
① examples ② careers ③ features ④ possibilities

4F Reading Passage

공부한 단어가 포함된 글을 잘 읽고 다음 문제를 풀어 보세요.

Many parents seem to adopt the attitude "My child, right or wrong"— with terrible results. Being a parent means being **mature** enough to ⓐ help a child **adapt** to disappointment. Parents who can't accept when their child isn't No.1 send the message that when they are frustrated, they blame the source of frustration instead of ⓑ looking for a way to cope.

A better message parents can show is to teach children that while they cannot always control the **outcome** of every situation, they can ______________________. Children must learn to behave more politely than they feel. By doing so, they will not get hurt and will be able to deal with **difficulties**. Being polite is about more than simply saying "please" and "thank you." It's about not **boasting** or calling someone names behind their back, about winning fairly and losing graciously, and ⓒ **treating** everyone with respect.

Of course, all the training in the world won't **persuade** a child to ⓓ behave politely if his parents become **aggressive**, **demanding** and rude. That's why experts agree the best way for parents to **improve** a child's manners is to improve their own first. Parents need to be especially careful not to ⓔ say something **casually** that they may be alarmed to hear later in the mouths of their children. If we aren't practicing good manners, how can we expect our children to do so?

1 위 글의 제목으로 가장 적절한 것은?

① Children Teach Themselves
② Never Blame Your Children
③ Being Polite Is Not Always Good
④ Children Are the Best Teacher for Adults
⑤ Be a Model if You Are to Raise a Polite Kid

2 위 글의 빈칸에 들어갈 말로 가장 적절한 것은?

① accept as they are
② learn how to excuse
③ predict what they want
④ control how they respond
⑤ guess what makes them do wrong

English Only

3 Which one of the underlined ⓐ~ⓔ is NOT included in the underlined good manners?

① ⓐ ② ⓑ ③ ⓒ ④ ⓓ ⑤ ⓔ

서술형

4 According to the passage, what does being a parent mean? Write your answer in Korean.

Word 500 81~100
Reading 25 05

SUMMA CUM LAUDE

5A Word List

중학교 3학년 필수단어를 예문과 함께 공부하세요.

081 **attempt** [ətémpt]
명 (일에 대한) 시도 동 시도하다, 애써 해보다
To my surprise, he made no **attempt** to escape.
놀랍게도, 그는 도망갈 시도를 전혀 하지 않았다.

082 **chemistry** [kémistri]
명 화학 참고 chemist 약사, 화학자
The subject I like most is **chemistry**.
내가 가장 좋아하는 과목은 화학이다.

083 **chunk** [tʃʌŋk]
명 큰 덩어리, 상당한 양
The dog found a **chunk** of meat by chance.
그 개는 우연히 고깃덩어리를 발견했다.

084 **device** [diváis]
명 장치, 기구 동 devise 고안하다
There is no safety **device** on this weapon.
이 무기에는 어떤 안전장치도 없다.

085 **extracurricular** [èkstrəkəríkjələr]
형 과외의 참고 curriculum 교육과정
Most students participate in **extracurricular** activities.
대부분의 학생들이 과외 활동에 참여한다.

086 **loose** [lu:s]
형 느슨한, 헐거워진, 풀린 동 loosen 느슨하게 하다
The door knob has come **loose**.
문 손잡이가 헐거워졌다.

087 **memorize** [méməràiz]
동 암기하다 명 memorization 암기
Memorizing a poem helps students remember words.
시를 암기하는 것은 학생들이 단어를 기억하는 데 도움을 준다.

088 **occupation** [àkjəpéiʃən]
명 직업; 점유, 점거 유 career 직업, 경력
I'm thinking about changing my **occupation**.
나는 직업을 바꾸는 것에 대해 생각 중이다.

089 **operation** [àpəréiʃən]
명 수술(=surgery), 활동, 가동 동 operate 작동시키다; 수술하다
She underwent a successful **operation** yesterday.
그녀는 어제 성공적으로 수술을 받았다.

090 **panic**
[pǽnik]

㊔ 극심한 공포, 공황 상태 ㊕ 공황에 빠지다

My father was in a state of **panic** when I returned home.
내가 집에 돌아왔을 때 아버지는 공황 상태에 있었다.

091 **phrase**
[freiz]

㊔ 구(句), 어구, 구절

She read the **phrase** over and over again.
그녀는 그 구절을 계속해서 읽었다.

092 **planet**
[plǽnit]

㊔ 행성 [참고] the planet 지구

Jupiter is one of the **planets** of our solar system.
목성은 우리 태양계 행성 중 하나이다.

093 **portable**
[pɔ́ːrtəbl]

㊖ 휴대용의, 휴대가 쉬운

The equipment is easier to handle and **portable.**
그 장비는 더 다루기 쉽고 휴대하기 편하다.

094 **practice**
[prǽktis]

㊔ 연습; 실행; 관습 ㊕ 연습하다

To be a good musician, you have to **practice** a lot.
훌륭한 연주자가 되기 위해서는 무척 많이 연습해야 한다.

095 **property**
[prápərti]

㊔ 재산, 소유물, 부동산

We must protect our private **property** ourselves.
우리는 스스로 사유 재산을 보호해야 한다.

096 **reserve**
[rizə́ːrv]

㊕ 예약하다; 남겨두다, 보류하다

Why don't you **reserve** a table for dinner?
저녁 식사 자리를 예약하는 게 어때요?

097 **spelling**
[spéliŋ]

㊔ 철자법, 맞춤법 [동] spell 철자를 말하다(쓰다)

Check for **spelling** mistakes before you hand in your essay.
과제물을 제출하기 전에 맞춤법 검사를 하라.

098 **structure**
[strʌ́ktʃər]

㊔ 구조, 구조물, 건축물

You should know the **structure** of the building.
너는 그 건물의 구조를 알아야 한다.

099 **at once**

즉시, 동시에, 한꺼번에

Once you make a decision, start **at once**.
일단 결정을 했으면 즉시 시작하라.

100 **work on**

~에 애쓰다, 착수하다

We are **working on** a report on the city's water use.
우리는 그 도시의 물 사용에 관한 보고서 작업에 매진하고 있다.

5B Complete the Phrases

빈칸에 알맞은 말을 넣어 어구를 완성하세요.

1 a noun ______________ (명사구)

2 various ______________ activities (다양한 과외 활동)

3 the surface temperature of the ______________(행성의 표면 온도)

4 the ______________ of the human body (인체의 구조)

5 the world-famous ______________ contest (세계적으로 유명한 철자법 대회)

6 an ______________ to meet him in person (그를 직접 만나려는 시도)

7 ______________ electronic devices (휴대용 전자기기들)

8 a frozen ______________ of cheese (냉동 상태의 치즈 덩어리 하나)

5C Complete the Sentences

[보기]에서 알맞은 단어를 골라 어법에 맞게 완성하세요.

[보기]
work on chemistry device panic loose occupation planet

1 There are continuous demands for the latest digital ______________.
최신 디지털 장비들에 대한 끊임없는 수요가 있다.

2 I like ______________ because I want to understand a small part of our world.
나는 우리 세계의 작은 부분을 이해하고 싶기 때문에 화학을 좋아한다.

3 ______________ disorder patients are a vulnerable group.
공황 장애 환자들은 상처받기 쉬운 부류의 사람들이다.

4 He always wears ______________ trousers because they are comfortable.
그는 편하기 때문에 항상 헐렁한 바지를 입는다.

5 I need to ______________ my pronunciation more.
나는 발음 연습에 좀 더 매진할 필요가 있다.

6 Some ______________ have uniforms to convey their status.
몇몇 직종에는 각자의 지위를 나타내는 제복이 사용된다.

7 No generation has any right to pollute the ______________.
그 어떤 세대의 사람들도 지구를 오염시킬 권리를 갖고 있지 않다.

5D Fill in the Blanks

빈칸에 공통으로 들어갈 단어를 문장에 맞게 고쳐 쓰세요.

1
- The s_______________ of the temple is relatively simple.
  그 사원의 구조는 상대적으로 간단하다.
- The Eiffel Tower is a fairly famous s_______________ built in 1889.
  에펠탑은 1889년에 세워진 무척 유명한 구조물이다.

2
- We have to wait for the results of the o_______________.
  우리는 수술 결과를 기다려야 한다.
- The new factory will be in o_______________ by 2018.
  새로운 공장은 2018년에 가동될 것이다.

3
- You should r_______________ tickets on the website.
  당신은 웹사이트에서 티켓을 예약해야 한다.
- We r_______________ the right to reject your application.
  우리는 당신의 지원서를 거부할 권한을 갖고 있다.

4
- The meanings of the p_______________ are explained in detail in the report.
  그 어구들의 의미는 보고서에 상세하게 설명되어 있다.
- Some poets like to use colorful p_______________.
  몇몇 시인들은 화려한 어구들을 사용하기를 좋아한다.

5E Choose Synonyms

문장의 밑줄 친 부분과 가장 유사한 뜻의 단어를 고르세요.

1 You need to claim intellectual <u>property</u> rights for knowledge service.
당신은 지식서비스에 관한 지적 재산권을 주장할 필요가 있다.
① innovation ② development ③ possession ④ creativity

2 Their speedy attacks caused <u>panic</u> and disorder.
그들의 신속한 공격은 극심한 공포와 난동을 야기했다.
① miracle ② envy ③ merit ④ fear

3 Her <u>occupation</u> seems to be a highly respectable and rewarding one.
그녀의 직업은 높은 존경과 보상을 받는 것처럼 보인다.
① chance ② job ③ remark ④ vision

4 After the <u>operation</u>, he had to practice walking properly.
수술을 받은 후에, 그는 원활하게 걷는 것을 연습해야 했다.
① surgery ② position ③ examination ④ function

5F Reading Passage *공부한 단어가 포함된 글을 잘 읽고 다음 문제를 풀어 보세요.*

When you have many subjects or many things, it can help to break things into **chunks**. Let's say you have a test on 20 **spelling** words. Instead of thinking about all of the words **at once**, try breaking them down into five-word chunks and **working on** one or two different chunks each night.

Don't worry if you can't remember something on the first **attempt**. That's where the practice comes in. The more days you spend reviewing something, the more likely it is to stick in your brain. (ⓐ) There are also tricks called secret **devices** that can help you remember things. (ⓑ) When you're trying to **memorize** a list of things, make up a **phrase** that uses the first letter of each. (ⓒ) Think: My Very Excellent Mother Just Served Us Nachos to remember Mercury, Venus, Earth, Mars, Jupiter, Saturn, Uranus, and Neptune. (ⓓ) Your teacher can give you ideas, too. (ⓔ)

Another way to break it up is to study regularly instead of just the night before. You can always review your notes and read over the chapters you're working on. Or, if you're studying math, **chemistry**, or biology, do some **practice** problems.

1 위 글의 제목으로 가장 적절한 것은?

① Study Together, Do Better
② Smart Studying: Break It Up
③ Want to Study Well? Review!
④ Concentrate to Improve Memory
⑤ Home Is the Best Place to Study

2 주어진 문장이 들어갈 위치로 가장 적절한 곳은?

> For example, are you trying to learn the eight planets and their order from the sun?

① ⓐ ② ⓑ ③ ⓒ ④ ⓓ ⑤ ⓔ

English Only

3 According to the passage, which is NOT mentioned as a way to study?

① to study again
② to ask questions
③ to study regularly
④ to do practice problems
⑤ to make up a meaningful phrase

서술형

4 What is the strategy used to remember the eight planets's order from the sun? Arrange the words given in order.

> The strategy is to (up, a, phrase, make) ______________________ that uses the initial of each word.

Speedy Check-up 1

Lesson별로 모르는 단어에 체크한 후, 그 갯수를 /20 안에 쓰고 학습성과를 점검해 보세요.
모르는 단어는 다시 찾아 학습하세요.

Lesson 1 /20

- ▢ awkward
- ▢ calculate
- ▢ conflict
- ▢ creature
- ▢ deserve
- ▢ effective
- ▢ fable
- ▢ fever
- ▢ forbid
- ▢ frustrate
- ▢ method
- ▢ overweight
- ▢ prevent
- ▢ protest
- ▢ sight
- ▢ strike
- ▢ timid
- ▢ yell
- ▢ as though
- ▢ depend on

Lesson 2 /20

- ▢ abstract
- ▢ accuse
- ▢ blossom
- ▢ breathe
- ▢ cheerful
- ▢ cling
- ▢ desperate
- ▢ emergency
- ▢ erupt
- ▢ expert
- ▢ indeed
- ▢ injury
- ▢ miracle
- ▢ produce
- ▢ purchase
- ▢ recall
- ▢ recover
- ▢ replace
- ▢ strength
- ▢ worth

Lesson 3 /20

- ▢ aim
- ▢ authority
- ▢ contrast
- ▢ corridor
- ▢ guarantee
- ▢ launch
- ▢ opportunity
- ▢ permanent
- ▢ possibility
- ▢ principle
- ▢ pursuit
- ▢ quality
- ▢ relate
- ▢ religion
- ▢ shelter
- ▢ succeed
- ▢ surface
- ▢ therefore
- ▢ whisper
- ▢ be willing to

Lesson 4 /20

- ▢ adapt
- ▢ aggressive
- ▢ boast
- ▢ casually
- ▢ characteristic
- ▢ clap
- ▢ conduct
- ▢ declare
- ▢ demanding
- ▢ difficulty
- ▢ dumb
- ▢ equipment
- ▢ fairly
- ▢ improve
- ▢ investigate
- ▢ manufacture
- ▢ mature
- ▢ outcome
- ▢ persuade
- ▢ treat

Lesson 5 /20

- ▢ attempt
- ▢ chemistry
- ▢ chunk
- ▢ device
- ▢ extracurricular
- ▢ loose
- ▢ memorize
- ▢ occupation
- ▢ operation
- ▢ panic
- ▢ phrase
- ▢ planet
- ▢ portable
- ▢ practice
- ▢ property
- ▢ reserve
- ▢ spelling
- ▢ structure
- ▢ at once
- ▢ work on

Chapter 2

슈마 주니어®
중학 영어교과서
WORD MANUAL ③

Lesson 6

Word 500 101~120
Reading 25 06

SUMMA CUM LAUDE

6A Word List

중학교 3학년 필수단어를 예문과 함께 공부하세요.

101 **accompany** [əkʌ́mpəni]
동 동행하다, 동반하다
Children under 7 years of age must be **accompanied** by an adult.
7세 이하의 어린이들은 반드시 성인과 동행해야 한다.

102 **applause** [əplɔ́:z]
명 박수(갈채) 동 applaud 박수를 치다
He received **applause** from the audience.
그는 청중들로부터 박수갈채를 받았다.

103 **associate** [əsóuʃièit]
동 관련지어 생각하다, 연상하다 명 association 연관, 연상
Most people **associate** smoking with lung cancer.
대부분의 사람들은 흡연과 폐암을 연관시킨다.

104 **atmosphere** [ǽtməsfìər]
명 대기, 분위기 유 environment (주위의) 상황
This summer, the **atmosphere** is becoming more unstable.
올 여름에는 대기가 더욱 불안정해지고 있다.

105 **classify** [klǽsəfài]
동 분류하다, 구분하다 명 classification 분류, 구분
All books are **classified** according to subject.
모든 책은 주제에 따라 분류된다.

106 **comment** [kɑ́ment]
명 논평, 말, 언급 동 논평하다
He has made helpful **comments** on my paper.
그가 내 논문에 도움이 되는 논평을 해주었다.

107 **descendant** [diséndənt]
명 자손, 후손 반 ancestor 조상, 선조
We have borrowed the earth from our **descendants**.
우리는 지구를 후손들로부터 빌려 왔다.

108 **expression** [ikspréʃən]
명 표현, 표정 동 express 표현하다
Freedom of **expression** must not be limited in any way.
표현의 자유는 어떤 식으로든지 제한되어서는 안 된다.

109 **faithful** [féiθfəl]
형 충실한, 신뢰할 수 있는 명 faith 믿음, 신뢰
He was rescued by his **faithful** dog.
그는 자신의 충직한 개에게 구조되었다.

110 **focus** [fóukəs]

㊀ 집중하다, (~에) 초점을 맞추다(on)

This course **focuses** on fluency, not accuracy.
이 강좌는 정확성이 아닌 유창성에 초점을 맞춘다.

111 **ignore** [ignɔ́ːr]

㊀ 무시하다, 못 본 척하다 유 neglect 방치하다

If I had not **ignored** his advice, I would be successful now.
내가 그의 조언을 무시하지 않았더라면, 지금 나는 성공해 있을 것이다.

112 **participant** [pɑːrtísəpənt]

명 참가자 참고 participate in ~에 참여하다(=take part in)

The **participants** read the passage at their normal speed.
참가자들은 일반적인 속도로 그 문단을 읽었다.

113 **raw** [rɔː]

형 날것의, 가공되지 않은; 원자재의

Eating **raw** carrots is good for your health.
생당근을 먹는 것은 여러분의 건강에 좋다.

114 **reality** [riǽləti]

명 현실, 실제 상황 유 fact 사실

The first job of a leader is to face **reality**.
지도자가 첫 번째로 할 일은 현실을 직시하는 것이다.

115 **ridiculous** [ridíkjuləs]

형 말도 안 되는, 터무니없는 유 silly, stupid 어리석은

It is **ridiculous** to try to blame innocent people.
무고한 사람들을 비난하려고 하는 것은 어리석은 짓이다.

116 **ruin** [rúːin]

동 망치다(=spoil), 폐허로 만들다 명 붕괴, 파산

A late spring storm **ruined** our plan.
늦봄의 폭풍우가 우리 계획을 망쳤다.

117 **support** [səpɔ́ːrt]

동 지지〔지원〕하다, 후원하다 명 지지, 옹호

Over half of the citizens do not **support** the policy.
시민의 절반 이상이 그 정책을 지지하지 않는다.

118 **temperature** [témpərətʃər]

명 온도, 기온, (몸의) 신열

The **temperature** has risen by two degrees.
기온이 2도 올랐다.

119 **whereas** [wɛ̀ərǽz]

접 반면에, 그런데, 그러나 유 while

Some students like physics, **whereas** others don't.
몇몇 학생들은 물리를 좋아하는 반면에 다른 학생들은 그렇지 않다.

120 **according to**

~에 따르면, ~에 따라

Evaluation was done strictly **according to** the rules.
평가는 원칙에 따라 엄격하게 집행되었다.

6B Complete the Phrases
빈칸에 알맞은 말을 넣어 어구를 완성하세요.

1 ________________ eggs (날달걀)

2 a ________________ animal (충직한 동물)

3 virtual ________________ (가상현실)

4 a facial ________________ (얼굴 표정)

5 a direct ________________ (직계 후손)

6 a careless ________________ (부주의한 발언)

7 a rise in ________________ (기온 상승)

8 ________________ on the economy (경제에 초점을 맞추다)

6C Complete the Sentences
[보기]에서 알맞은 단어를 골라 어법에 맞게 완성하세요.

[보기]
associate classify ignore reality according to comment expression

1 The ________________ is that we can't afford to buy that.
우리의 현실은 그것을 살 형편이 되지 않는다.

2 We often ________________ summer with swimming and camps.
우리는 여름이라 하면 주로 수영과 캠프를 연상한다.

3 None of his ________________ make sense.
그의 발언 중 어떤 것도 타당하지 않다.

4 He accepted her ________________ of sympathy.
그는 그녀가 나타낸 연민의 표현을 받아들였다.

5 Obesity is now ________________ as a disease.
비만은 이제 병으로 분류된다.

6 ________________ the legend, Romulus disappeared in a storm.
전설에 따르면 Romulus는 폭풍우 속에서 사라졌다.

7 Jackson ________________ the decision and went out of the room.
Jackson은 그 결정을 무시하고 방 밖으로 나갔다.

6D Fill in the Blanks
빈칸에 공통으로 들어갈 단어를 문장에 맞게 고쳐 쓰세요.

1
- Our company's directors have s________________ me a lot.
  우리 회사의 임원들은 나를 많이 지원해 주었다.
- Some new information has s________________ the theory.
  몇몇 새로운 정보는 그 이론을 뒷받침한다.

2
- I always a________________ the playground with my adolescence.
  나는 항상 놀이터를 청소년기와 연관시킨다.
- You need to choose carefully the people you're going to a________________ with.
  당신은 교제할 사람들을 주의 깊게 선택해야 한다.

3
- Minors must be a________________ by a parent or legal guardian.
  미성년자는 부모 또는 법적 보호자가 동반되어야 한다.
- His daughter a________________ him on the trip.
  그의 딸이 여행에 그와 동행했다.

4
- The a________________ is becoming more and more polluted.
  대기는 점점 더 오염되고 있다.
- The restaurant offers a comfortable a________________ and great food.
  그 식당은 편안한 분위기와 훌륭한 음식을 제공한다.

6E Choose Synonyms
문장의 밑줄 친 부분과 가장 유사한 뜻의 단어를 고르세요.

1 Marilyn said she was sorry to have <u>ruined</u> my plans.
Marilyn은 나의 계획을 망친 것에 대해 사과했다.
① promised ② spoiled ③ corrected ④ attempted

2 A <u>faithful</u> friend is a strong shelter.
충실한 친구는 든든한 피난처이다.
① loyal ② talkative ③ handsome ④ clever

3 What they said is totally <u>ridiculous</u>.
그들이 말했던 것은 도저히 말도 안 되는 내용이다.
① sensible ② right ③ fortunate ④ stupid

4 She refused to <u>comment</u> until the investigation was complete.
그녀는 수사가 종결될 때까지 말하는 것을 거부했다.
① protest ② remark ③ conclude ④ approve

6F Reading Passage

공부한 단어가 포함된 글을 잘 읽고 다음 문제를 풀어 보세요.

Marcel Zeelenberg found a pattern in observations of **participants** on a Dutch **reality** television show. If you happened to be in the Netherlands in the mid-1990s, you might have watched an episode or two of *I Am Sorry*, in which ordinary people explained some **ridiculous** things they had done to someone **faithful** to them.

One guest regretted ignoring a friend during a difficult time, another regretted saying unpleasant things about a deceased friend at his funeral, still another felt bad about slapping a friend's face. After expressing their regret on television, these participants were then presented with the opportunity to apologize and give flowers to the person who had been hurt.

According to Zeelenberg, "This was usually followed by emotional scenes with lots of hugging, kisses, and tears **accompanied** by **applause** from the audience." Zeelenberg's team collected 82 **expressions** of regret that appeared on 18 different episodes, then **classified** these into regrets of inaction and action. They discovered that the inaction regrets had been becoming three and a half times longer than the action regrets. ______________, regrets of action **focus** on the short term, **whereas** regrets of inaction focus on the long term.

1 위 글의 내용과 일치하지 않는 것은?

① Zeelenberg는 TV쇼의 참가자들의 유형을 관찰했다.
② 어려운 시절 친구를 무시했던 것을 후회한 출연자도 있었다.
③ 출연자에게는 상처를 준 사람에게 사과할 수 있는 기회가 주어졌다.
④ Zeelenberg 팀은 후회의 항목을 2가지로 분류했다.
⑤ 행한 것에 대한 후회가 행하지 않은 것에 대한 것보다 더 길었다.

2 위 글의 빈칸에 들어갈 연결사로 가장 적절한 것은?

① Instead
② In short
③ However
④ Conversely
⑤ Nevertheless

English Only

3 Which person would probably not appear on the program *I Am Sorry*?

① someone who did homework for a friend
② someone who didn't help a friend in need
③ someone who said bad things about a friend
④ someone who stole some money from a friend
⑤ someone who broke a friend's cup

서술형

4 What do the participants do on *I Am Sorry*? Use words from the passage to complete the sentence below.

They ___________ bad things they did in the past and ___________ for what they did.

7A Word List

중학교 3학년 필수단어를 예문과 함께 공부하세요.

121 **appropriate** [əpróuprièit]
형 적절한, 적당한　유 suitable 적절한, 알맞은
I taught my son **appropriate** ways to express his emotions.
나는 아들에게 자신의 감정을 표현하는 적절한 방법을 가르쳤다.

122 **article** [ɑ́:rtikl]
명 (신문 · 잡지의) 글, 기사
Reading this **article** will help improve your writing.
이 글을 읽으면 작문 실력을 향상시키는 데 도움이 될 것이다.

123 **custom** [kʌ́stəm]
명 관습, 풍습　형 customary 통상[관습]적인
It is our **custom** to have dinner together.
저녁을 함께 먹는 것은 우리의 관습이다.

124 **describe** [diskráib]
동 서술하다, 묘사하다　명 description 묘사, 서술
She **described** her exprience in an email to her friends.
그녀는 친구들에게 보내는 이메일에 그녀의 경험을 자세히 묘사했다.

125 **detail** [dí:teil]
명 세부 사항, 정보　참고 in detail 상세하게
I told the police officer every **detail** about the accident.
나는 경찰관에게 사고에 관한 모든 세부 사항을 말했다.

126 **element** [éləmənt]
명 요소, 성분; 원소　유 component 구성 요소, 부품
Water is a key **element** in the body.
물은 우리 몸의 중요한 요소이다.

127 **entire** [intáiər]
형 전체의, 완전한　유 whole
I'm planning to travel the **entire** world.
나는 전 세계를 여행할 계획이다.

128 **ethical** [éθikəl]
형 윤리적인, 도덕적인　유 moral 도덕상의
The attitude of the tobacco industry has raised **ethical** issues.
담배 회사의 태도가 윤리적인 문제를 불러일으켰다.

129 **feature** [fí:tʃər]
명 특징, 특성　동 특징으로 삼다
The best **feature** of this hotel is the fantastic view.
이 호텔의 가장 큰 특징은 환상적인 전망에 있다.

130 **germ**
[dʒəːrm]

명 세균, 미생물 참고 in germ 초기 단계의

Germs are always around us and we are exposed to them every day.

세균은 우리의 주변에 항상 존재하며 우리는 매일 그것에 노출되어 있다.

131 **hopeless**
[hóuplis]

형 가망 없는, 절망적인 반 hopeful 희망에 찬

When it comes to reading a map, I'm totally **hopeless**.

지도 보는 것에 관해서라면, 나는 완전히 구제불능이다.

132 **individual**
[ìndəvídʒuəl]

명 개인 형 개인의, 각각의

Each **individual** is special and unique.

개인 각각은 특별하고 유일무이하다.

133 **institute**
[ínstətjùːt]

명 기관, 협회 동 세우다, 설립하다

The university established many research **institutes**.

그 대학은 많은 연구 기관을 세웠다.

134 **journalism**
[dʒə́ːrnəlìzm]

명 신문 · 잡지 편집(집필), 언론계

These days, it is quite hard to get a job in **journalism**.

요즘 언론계에 직장을 얻는 것은 꽤 어렵다.

135 **leak**
[liːk]

동 (액체 · 기체가) 새다 명 새는 곳, 누출 참고 leakage 누출(량)

The ceiling in the bathroom was **leaking**.

욕실 천장이 새고 있었다.

136 **pill**
[pil]

명 알약, 정제 유 tablet

I took a sleeping **pill** by mistake.

나는 실수로 수면제를 먹었다.

137 **politics**
[pálitiks]

명 정치, 정치학 형 political 정치적인

Some citizens are indifferent to **politics**.

몇몇 시민들은 정치에 무관심하다.

138 **recycle**
[rìːsáikl]

동 재활용하다, 재사용하다

Recycling paper helps protect trees.

종이를 재활용하는 것은 나무를 보호하는 데 도움이 된다.

139 **reflect**
[riflékt]

동 비추다, 반영(반사)하다 명 reflection 상(모습), 반영

The light **reflected** off the surface of your glasses.

빛이 당신의 안경 표면에 반사되었다.

140 **wonder**
[wʌ́ndər]

동 궁금해 하다, 생각하다 명 경탄, 경이

I **wondered** what would happen next.

나는 다음에 무슨 일이 일어날지 궁금했다.

7B Complete the Phrases *빈칸에 알맞은 말을 넣어 어구를 완성하세요.*

1 a newspaper ______________ (신문 기사)

2 have an interest in ______________ (정치에 관심을 갖다)

3 ______________ the educational policy (교육 정책을 반영하다)

4 ______________ of the book (책의 세부 사항들)

5 feel ______________ (절망감을 느끼다)

6 take a ______________ (약을 먹다)

7 ______________ waste (폐품을 재활용하다)

8 a key ______________ (핵심 요소)

7C Complete the Sentences *[보기]에서 알맞은 단어를 골라 어법에 맞게 완성하세요.*

[보기]

entire appropriate politics germ ethical journalism pill

1 This country has largely two-party ______________.
이 국가에는 크게 두 개의 정당 정치 체제가 있다.

2 I was told my choice of words was not ______________ for a high school essay.
내가 선택한 어휘들은 고등학교 과제물에 적절하지 않다는 말을 들었다.

3 Study says vitamin ______________ have no health benefits.
연구에 따르면 비타민 정제는 건강상에 이점이 없다고 한다.

4 Historian Mark Miller is a former ______________ professor.
역사학자 Mark Miller는 전직 언론학과 교수이다.

5 He has dedicated his ______________ life to helping others.
그는 그의 일생을 남을 돕는 데 전념했다.

6 Your fridge could be a breeding ground for ______________.
당신의 냉장고는 세균의 온상지일 수도 있다.

7 It is not ______________ to promote the interests of the firm now.
현재 그 회사의 이익을 홍보하는 것은 윤리적이지 않다.

7D Fill in the Blanks 빈칸에 공통으로 들어갈 단어를 문장에 맞게 고쳐 쓰세요.

1 • I w_______________ if you can give me a ride to the subway station.
네가 나를 지하철역까지 태워다 줄 수 있는지 궁금하다.
• I w_______________ what time the park opens.
나는 그 공원의 개장 시간이 궁금하다.

2 • This a_______________ was sent to us by a supporter.
이 글은 한 지지자에 의해서 우리에게 발송되었다.
• Writing a newspaper a_______________ can be a difficult task.
신문 기사를 작성하는 것은 어려운 작업일 수 있다.

3 • Last night the tank l_______________ about 300 tons of water.
어젯밤 물탱크에서 약 300톤의 물이 새어 나왔다.
• His secret letter was l_______________ to the press.
그의 비밀 편지는 언론에 유출되었다.

4 • She could see herself r_______________ in its surface.
그녀는 그것의 표면에 반영된 자신의 모습을 볼 수 있었다.
• His decision r_______________ the shared opinions of the countries participating.
그의 결정은 참석한 국가들의 공통된 의견들을 반영했다.

7E Choose Synonyms 문장의 밑줄 친 부분과 가장 유사한 뜻의 단어를 고르세요.

1 It is the <u>custom</u> for the bride to wear a white dress on her wedding day.
결혼식 날에 흰색 드레스를 입는 것은 관습이다.
① solution ② tradition ③ contribution ④ pollution

2 How much is an <u>appropriate</u> amount to ask for in a pay raise?
임금 인상에서 요구할 수 있는 적절한 금액은 얼마인가?
① legal ② competent ③ suitable ④ strange

3 Competition is an important <u>element</u> of the free-market system.
경쟁은 자유 시장 체제에서 중요한 요소이다.
① charity ② weight ③ component ④ balance

4 Reporters have an <u>ethical</u> obligation to report the truth.
기자들은 진실을 보도해야 하는 윤리적 의무를 지니고 있다.
① tragic ② moral ③ danger ④ practical

7F Reading Passage 공부한 단어가 포함된 글을 잘 읽고 다음 문제를 풀어 보세요.

Newspaper **articles** can never tell the **entire** truth: some **element** of lying is inherent in all **journalism** because it is impossible for one article to include all the **details** of the story. Journalists may also manipulate the order in which they present information to achieve more dramatic or other effects in their writing. Choosing details and the order to **describe** them is considered proper and ethical behavior for journalists. Editors can even **reflect** their paper's political bias when writing opinion pieces about elections and **politics**.

In book publishing, many companies do not always examine carefully the information authors write. (ⓐ) A best-selling book can make a lot of money, so some authors find it tempting to make up lies. (ⓑ) The writing seemed credible, so most **individuals** believed his story. (ⓒ) However, the writer later was unable to make a record of the facts in the books, and he was revealed as a fake. (ⓓ) Although the writer's tale was not **appropriate**, many people still found it meaningful. (ⓔ) Even these readers agree that they would rather not be left in the dark, **wondering** whether or not a story is true. They would rather be aware of any major alteration of facts that made a good story possible.

1 위 글의 제목으로 가장 적절한 것은?

① A Journalist Should Be Confident
② Lying Is Unavoidable in Journalism
③ Don't Write a Book to Earn Money
④ Editing Is Important in Book Publishing
⑤ Gather Lots of Information to Write an Article

2 글의 흐름으로 보아, 주어진 문장이 들어가기에 가장 적절한 곳은?

In one famous case, a writer invented a completely fictitious history about himself.

① ⓐ ② ⓑ ③ ⓒ ④ ⓓ ⑤ ⓔ

English Only

3 Which one is closest in meaning to the underlined make up in the second paragraph?

① I'm sorry I missed the test. May I make it up?
② They argue a lot, but they always kiss and make up.
③ Women make up only 30% of the student numbers.
④ She takes ages to make herself up in the mornings.
⑤ Judy's story is hard to believe. I'm sure she made it up.

서술형

4 Use words from the passage to complete the answer below.

What did the readers think about the story that was made up?
→ Even though the story was __________, many readers found it __________.

8A Word List

중학교 3학년 필수단어를 예문과 함께 공부하세요.

141 **annoy** [ənɔ́i]
동 짜증나게 하다, 귀찮게 하다 유 irritate
He **annoyed** me by asking me stupid questions.
그는 어리석은 질문을 해서 나를 짜증나게 했다.

142 **aspect** [ǽspekt]
명 측면, 면, 양상 유 feature 특징, 특색
This book covers all **aspects** of rural life.
이 책은 전원 생활의 모든 측면을 다룬다.

143 **behavior** [bihéivjər]
명 행동, 태도 동 behave 행동하다, 처신하다 유 conduct 품행
Students will be rewarded for good **behavior**.
학생들은 선행에 대한 보상을 받을 것이다.

144 **brief** [bri:f]
형 (시간이) 짧은, (말 · 글이) 간단한 부 briefly 잠시
The officer made a **brief** visit to the park.
담당 직원은 공원에 잠시 다녀갔다.

145 **comfort** [kʌ́mfərt]
명 안락, 편안 동 위로하다 형 comfortable 편안한
These sneakers are designed for **comfort** and convenience.
이 운동화는 편안함과 편리함에 중점을 두어 설계되었다.

146 **confident** [kάnfidənt]
형 자신감 있는 명 confidence 자신감
He looks very **confident** in every photo.
그는 모든 사진에서 무척 자신감이 있어 보인다.

147 **conform** [kənfɔ́:rm]
동 순응하다, 따르다 명 conformity 순응, 따름
Travelers need to **conform** to the local customs.
여행자는 그 지역의 관습을 따를 필요가 있다.

148 **disaster** [dizǽstər]
명 재난, 재해, 참사 형 disastrous 처참한
The nuclear accident was a man-made **disaster**.
그 원전 사고는 인간이 일으킨 재해였다.

149 **distinguish** [distíŋgwiʃ]
동 구별하다, 식별하다; 차이를 나타내다
The man failed to **distinguish** between right and wrong.
그 남자는 옳고 그름을 구별하는 데 실패했다.

150 **document**
[dɑ́kjumənt]

명 서류, 문서 동 기록하다

I was told to draw up a public **document** right away.
나는 당장 공문서를 작성하라는 말을 들었다.

151 **embrace**
[imbréis]

동 껴안다, (제안 등을) 받아들이다, 수용하다

Aunt Sophie **embraced** her warmly.
Sophie 이모는 그녀를 따뜻하게 안아주었다.

152 **financial**
[finǽnʃəl]

형 금융의, 재정의 명 finance 금융, 재정

At that time, I was in **financial** difficulties.
그 당시 나는 재정적인 어려움에 처해 있었다.

153 **independent**
[ìndipéndənt]

형 독립적인, 자립적인 명 independence 독립, 자립

Living away from home has made me more **independent**.
집을 떠나 사는 것이 나를 더욱 독립적으로 만들었다.

154 **influence**
[ínfluəns]

명 영향(력) 동 영향을 미치다 유 affect 영향을 주다

These products **influenced** the lives of many women.
이 제품들은 많은 여성들의 삶에 영향을 미쳤다.

155 **interrupt**
[ìntərʌ́pt]

동 방해하다, 중단시키다 명 interruption 방해, 중단

I'm so sorry, but I didn't mean to **interrupt** you.
정말 죄송합니다만 당신을 방해할 의도는 아니었어요.

156 **isolate**
[áisəlèit]

동 격리하다, 고립시키다 명 isolation 격리, 고립

Those who committed cruel crimes should be **isolated**.
흉악 범죄를 저지른 사람들은 격리되어야 한다.

157 **merit**
[mérit]

명 가치; 장점(주로 복수형) 반 demerit 단점

Every man has his or her **merits** and demerits.
모든 사람은 장점과 단점을 가지고 있다.

158 **obtain**
[əbtéin]

동 얻다, 입수하다, 달성하다 유 gain 얻다

You are not allowed to enter unless you **obtain** permission.
허가를 받지 않으면 들어갈 수 없습니다.

159 **sacrifice**
[sǽkrəfàis]

명 희생; 제물 동 희생하다

I owe my success to my mother's **sacrifice**.
나의 성공은 어머니의 희생 덕분이다.

160 **seldom**
[séldəm]

부 드물게, 좀처럼〔거의〕 ~ 않는 유 rarely 드물게

I **seldom** watch TV soap operas.
나는 TV 연속극을 거의 보지 않는다.

8B Complete the Phrases 빈칸에 알맞은 말을 넣어 어구를 완성하세요.

1 for a ______________ time (잠시 동안)

2 a ______________ crisis (재정 위기)

3 an important ______________ of life (인생에서 중요한 측면)

4 an ______________ country (독립국)

5 a natural ______________ (자연 재해)

6 offer a ______________ (제물을 바치다)

7 provide warmth and ______________ (따뜻함과 편안함을 제공하다)

8 abnormal ______________ (비정상적인 행동)

8C Complete the Sentences [보기]에서 알맞은 단어를 골라 어법에 맞게 완성하세요.

[보기]
seldom distinguish annoy document conform confident obtain

1 You have to attach copies of the relevant ______________.
당신은 관련 서류 사본을 첨부해야 한다.

2 I want the students to feel ______________.
나는 그 학생들이 자신감을 느끼기를 희망한다.

3 I ______________ go to the art museum.
나는 좀처럼 미술관에 가지 않는다.

4 You must ______________ approval of your research plan.
당신은 연구 계획의 승인을 받아야 한다.

5 It is hard to ______________ one twin from the other.
쌍둥이들 중 한 명과 다른 한 명을 구별하는 것은 어렵다

6 Write about the types of people who ______________ you the most.
당신을 가장 짜증나게 하는 사람들의 유형을 적으시오.

7 He was the only person who refused to ______________ to customs.
그는 관습에 따르기를 거부했던 유일한 사람이었다.

8D Fill in the Blanks 빈칸에 공통으로 들어갈 단어를 문장에 맞게 고쳐 쓰세요.

1 • It's hard to continue our work without the d_______________.
그 문서 없이 우리의 작업을 지속하는 것은 힘들다.
• Visitors receive a d_______________ as they enter the exhibit area.
방문객들은 전시회장에 들어갈 때 서류를 하나 받는다.

2 • The sound of car horns i_______________ my thoughts.
자동차 경적 소리가 나의 생각을 방해했다.
• My phone service was i_______________ because I owed the company 200 dollars.
나는 통신사에 200달러의 미납금액이 있었기 때문에 전화 서비스가 중단되었다.

3 • I'm going to visit his house to c_______________ him on his failure.
나는 그의 실패를 위로해 주려고 그를 찾아갈 예정이다.
• Tom and Jane took c_______________ from being together.
Tom과 Jane은 함께 있는 것에서 위안을 찾았다.

4 • We must thank the firefighters for their s_______________ and hard work.
우리는 소방관들의 희생과 노고에 감사해야 한다.
• Many soldiers went to war to s_______________ their lives for their country.
많은 군인들이 전쟁에 나가서 조국을 위해 그들의 생명을 희생했다.

8E Choose Synonyms 문장의 밑줄 친 부분과 가장 유사한 뜻의 단어를 고르세요.

1 It is really annoying to have to pick them up every time.
매번 그들을 데리러 가야 하는 것은 정말 귀찮은 일이다.
① shocking ② irritating ③ pleasing ④ touching

2 It is popularly believed that birth order influences personality.
출생 순서가 성격에 영향을 준다는 것은 일반적인 생각이다.
① resist ② protect ③ affect ④ realize

3 Violent TV scenes have a negative effect on children's behavior.
폭력적인 TV 장면들은 아이들의 행동에 부정적인 영향을 준다.
① conduct ② intelligence ③ health ④ emotion

4 He has a positive attitude and seldom complains about anything.
그는 긍정적인 태도를 갖고 있어서 좀처럼 불평을 하지 않는다.
① frequently ② shortly ③ hardly ④ typically

8F Reading Passage

공부한 단어가 포함된 글을 잘 읽고 다음 문제를 풀어 보세요.

We often look to others for cues on how we should behave. Most of us are followers, not leaders, traveling along the ⓐ beaten path with **comfort** and ease, **seldom** striking out in our own direction. We prefer to let others set the standard and then fall into line, careful not to make waves. TV comedies use laugh tracks for this very reason. Will you think something is ⓑ funnier if other people are laughing? A lot of people are betting you will.

This response is ⓒ absent in many other **aspects** of your life. When you allow your **behavior** to be **influenced** by the behavior of others, you **sacrifice** your own desires and needs to be **embraced**. **Independent** and **confident** people are less likely to be swayed by the majority if they feel it's not in their best interest. They know what they want and do not care if they stand alone. But you don't want to stick out or gain attention as an independent thinker. For you, this label is ⓓ **isolating**. You would rather **conform** to become part of the group.

It's for this reason that you often second-guess your own judgment based on ________________________. On the highway, if you see a lot of traffic going in the opposite direction, you ⓔ wonder if you are going the wrong way. You are the one who asks everyone else what they are ordering at the restaurant. You want to make sure that you **obtain** something that's "okay."

1 위 글의 요지로 가장 적절한 것은?

① Humans laugh to live.
② Humans like funny things.
③ Humans tend to follow others.
④ Humans love a good challenge.
⑤ Humans want to be independent.

2 위 글의 밑줄 친 부분 중, 문맥상 낱말의 쓰임이 적절하지 않은 것은?

① ⓐ ② ⓑ ③ ⓒ ④ ⓓ ⑤ ⓔ

English Only

3 Which one is closest in meaning to the underlined to make waves in the first paragraph?

① to make friends
② to go the right way
③ to make any decision
④ to accept no criticism
⑤ to cause some problems

서술형

4 Fill in the blank with four words in the passage.

______ ______ ______ ______

Lesson 9

SUMMA CUM LAUDE

9A Word List

중학교 3학년 필수단어를 예문과 함께 공부하세요.

161 **anywhere** [éniwὲər]

㊫ 어디든지(긍정문), 아무데도(부정문)

Since we can take a smartphone **anywhere**, we're always online.
우리는 어디에든 스마트폰을 갖고 다닐 수 있기 때문에 항상 온라인 상태이다.

162 **bloom** [blu:m]

㊏ 꽃이 피다, 개화하다 ㊔ 꽃, 개화(기)

When we plant lilies in spring, they'll **bloom** in summer.
봄에 백합을 심으면 여름에 꽃이 필 것이다.

163 **democracy** [dimάkrəsi]

㊔ 민주주의 형 democratic 민주적인

He said that justice takes over freedom in a **democracy**.
그는 민주주의에서 정의가 자유보다 우선한다고 말했다.

164 **exist** [igzíst]

㊏ 존재하다 명 existence 존재

How many non-native communities **exist** in London?
런던에 얼마나 많은 외국인 공동체가 있는가?

165 **fasten** [fǽsn]

㊏ 매다, 묶다, 고정하다 유 tie, bind 묶다

Please **fasten** your seat belt and stay in your seat.
안전띠를 매고 자리에 앉아 계십시오.

166 **fist** [fist]

㊔ 주먹 참고 palm 손바닥

The man hit the thief with his right **fist**.
그 남자는 오른손 주먹으로 그 도둑을 쳤다.

167 **float** [flout]

㊏ 뜨다, 띄우다 ㊔ 뜨는 물건 반 sink 가라앉다

An empty bottle will **float**.
빈병은 (물에) 뜰 것이다.

168 **holy** [hóuli]

㊒ 신성한, 경건한, 독실한 유 sacred 신성한

In India, cows are considered **holy**, so people leave them alone.
인도에서는 소가 신성하다고 여겨지기에 사람들은 그들을 내버려 둔다.

169 **intersection** [ìntərsékʃən]

㊔ 교차로, 교차 지점 동 intersect 교차하다

Turn right at the next **intersection**.
다음 교차로에서 우회전 하시오.

170 **involve** [inválv]

㊍ **포함하다; 관련[참여]시키다** 형 involved 수반된, 관련된

More than ten professors are **involved** in the research.
그 연구에 10명 이상의 교수들이 참여하고 있다.

171 **obvious** [ábviəs]

㊎ **분명[명백]한, 확실한** 유 clear, apparent 분명한

It is **obvious** that tablet computers have become a useful tool.
태블릿 컴퓨터가 유용한 도구가 되었다는 것은 명백하다.

172 **realize** [rí:əlàiz]

㊍ **깨닫다, 실현하다** 명 reality 현실

Do you **realize** that you often use English words?
영어 단어를 자주 사용하는 것을 깨닫고 있는가?

At last, the old man **realized** his childhood dream.
마침내, 그 노인은 어린 시절의 꿈을 실현했다.

173 **regard** [rigá:rd]

㊍ **여기다** ㊐ **관심; 존경** 참고 with regard to ~에 관해서는

Such acts are **regarded** as piracy of intellectual property.
그런 행동은 지적 재산권의 침해로 여겨진다.

174 **remark** [rimá:rk]

㊐ **논평** ㊍ **말하다, 주목하다** 유 comment, mention 언급, 논평

He made a number of **remarks** about the show.
그는 그 쇼에 대해 여러 가지 논평을 했다.

175 **represent** [rèprizént]

㊍ **나타내다, 대표하다, 보여주다** 참고 representative 대표자

It's an honor to **represent** all the students.
모든 학생들을 대표한다는 것은 영광입니다.

176 **root** [ru:t]

㊐ **뿌리, 기원** ㊍ **뿌리를 내리다** 참고 root for 응원하다

The strong **roots** of trees hold soil in place.
깊이 박힌 나무 뿌리는 흙을 제 자리에 고정시킨다.

177 **symbolize** [símbəlàiz]

㊍ **상징하다** 명 symbol 상징

The dolls **symbolize** wealth and good harvest.
그 인형들은 부유함과 풍작을 상징한다.

178 **unite** [ju:náit]

㊍ **연합하다, 통합시키다** 명 unification 통일, 연합

Horus was the god who **united** the two ancient Egypts.
Horus는 양측의 고대 이집트를 통일시킨 신이었다.

179 **unusual** [ʌ̀njú:ʒuəl]

㊎ **특이한, 드문** 유 extraordinary 비범한, 놀라운

Artists always come up with **unusual** ideas.
예술가들은 항상 특이한 아이디어를 생각해 낸다.

180 **keep one's fingers crossed**

좋은 결과(행운)를 빌다, 기도하다

I'll **keep my fingers crossed** for you!
당신의 행운을 빌어요!

9B Complete the Phrases

빈칸에 알맞은 말을 넣어 어구를 완성하세요.

1 the ________________ of unhappiness (불행한 마음의 근원)

2 to ________________ graduation as liberation (졸업을 해방으로 여기다)

3 to ________________ a fresh start for the couple (부부의 새로운 시작을 상징하다)

4 tiny ________________ing plants in the pond (연못에 떠다니는 작은 식물들)

5 the principles of ________________ (민주주의의 원칙)

6 the ________________(e)d political parties (연합한 정당들)

7 to ________________ the seat belt (안전벨트를 조여 매다)

8 roses in full ________________ (활짝 핀 장미들)

9C Complete the Sentences

[보기]에서 알맞은 단어를 골라 어법에 맞게 완성하세요.

[보기]

bloom democracy fist obvious remark unite unusual

1 "Arirang" is the song that can ________________ South Korea and North Korea.
아리랑은 한국과 북한을 통일할 수 있는 노래이다.

2 It is ________________ to find a movie produced in an African language.
아프리카어로 제작된 영화를 찾는 것은 흔치 않은 일이다.

3 Most roses begin to ________________ from late May.
대부분의 장미는 5월 하순부터 피기 시작한다.

4 In a ________________, every citizen should have the right to vote.
민주주의 (체제)에서는 모든 시민은 투표할 권리를 갖아야 한다.

5 When he is angry, he often makes a ________________.
그는 화가 날 때 자주 주먹을 쥔다.

6 I was ________________ that he wasn't prepared for the exam.
그가 시험 준비를 하지 않았다는 것이 분명해 보였다.

7 The author is known for making witty ________________.
그 작가는 재치있는 말들을 하는 것으로 유명하다.

9D Fill in the Blanks
빈칸에 공통으로 들어갈 단어를 문장에 맞게 고쳐 쓰세요.

1 • No one knew that they were i________________.
누구도 그들이 연관되어 있다는 것을 알지 못했다.
• When you are i________________ in interesting tasks, you concentrate more.
흥미로운 일을 할 때 좀 더 집중한다.

2 • "R________________" means any underground part of a plant.
뿌리는 식물에서 땅속에 묻힌 모든 부분을 의미한다.
• You'll do well and I'll be there to r________________ for you.
당신은 잘 해낼 것이고 나는 당신을 응원할 것이다.

3 • I am not a________________ near the level of the other players.
나는 다른 어떤 선수들의 수준 어디에도 미치지 못한다.
• I can't find my keys a________________.
나는 어디에서도 내 열쇠를 찾을 수 없다.

4 • She believes that ghosts really do e________________.
그녀는 정말로 귀신이 존재한다고 믿는다.
• Many versions of the story e________________, but they share the same plot.
다양한 형태의 이야기가 있지만 같은 줄거리를 공유한다.

9E Choose Synonyms
문장의 밑줄 친 부분과 가장 유사한 뜻의 단어를 고르세요.

1 Egyptians worshiped cats as <u>holy</u> animals.
이집트인은 고양이를 신성한 동물로 숭배했다.
① common ② unlucky ③ sacred ④ useful

2 Let's <u>keep our fingers crossed</u> that he can advance to the finals.
그가 결승전에 진출할 수 있도록 행운을 빌자.
① hire a helper ② find a solution ③ wish good luck ④ try hard together

3 Hosting cities of the Olympics use mascots to <u>represent</u> the event.
올림픽의 개최 도시는 그 행사를 상징하기 위해 마스코트를 사용한다.
① tell ② merchandise ③ hold ④ symbolize

4 Do you <u>realize</u> our team is far behind schedule for our group project?
당신은 우리 팀이 팀 프로젝트 일정에 상당히 뒤처졌다는 것을 깨달았는가?
① ignore ② notice ③ emphasize ④ suggest

9F Reading Passage

공부한 단어가 포함된 글을 잘 읽고 다음 문제를 풀어 보세요.

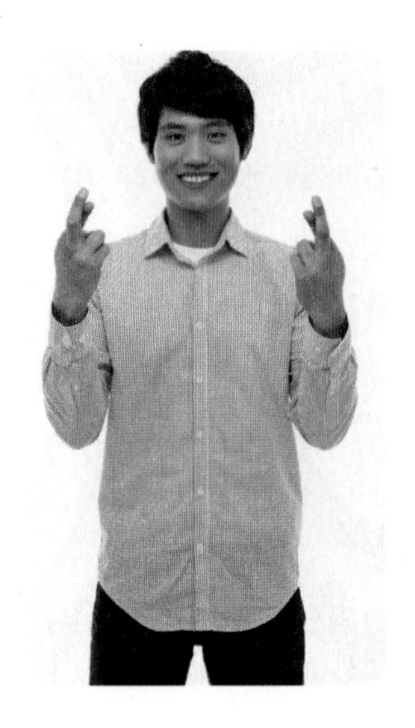

If you tell a friend, "**Keep your fingers crossed**", you're practicing a custom that required the intersecting and **fastening** of index fingers. It differed from the one that we know today, but ________________________. The gesture is **rooted** in the belief that a cross **represents** the **uniting** of two people; and that its point of **intersection** marked the place **holy** spirits **exist**. So it **involved** two people: one a wisher, and the other a supporter. A wish made on a cross was **regarded** as something anchored at the cross's intersection until that desire was **realized**. It was **remarked** in old books that the superstition was popular among many early European cultures. In crossing fingers for good luck, the index finger of a well wisher was placed over the index finger of the person expressing the wish. It is **obvious** that the ancient custom of the "crossed fingers" of friends was simplified to a wisher crossing his own fingers and finally to today's expression "I'll keep my fingers crossed."

* superstition 미신

1 위 글의 제목으로 가장 적절한 것은?

① Various Hand Signs for Luck
② Crossing Fingers: Different Meanings
③ Superstitions about Fingers and Bad Luck
④ Changes in the Gesture of Making a Wish
⑤ You Need a Supporter to Realize Your Wish

2 위 글의 빈칸에 들어갈 말로 가장 적절한 것은?

① was not widely practiced
② was considered as serious
③ symbolizes the same thing
④ influenced religious beliefs
⑤ spread in the European countries

English Only

3 What did the intersection of the cross symbolize?

① where the friendship existed
② where the wish was anchored
③ where a person's soul lived
④ where the devil was watching
⑤ where the promise was expressed

서술형

4 According to the passage, fill in the blanks to complete the summary.

In the past, the well wisher and the supporter crossed their __________ __________ to symbolize their united wish. However the custom changed over time and today a person can __________ his or her own fingers to make a wish.

Lesson 10

SUMMA CUM LAUDE

Word 500 181~200
Reading 25 10

10A Word List

중학교 3학년 필수단어를 예문과 함께 공부하세요.

181 **appear** [əpíər]

동 나타나다; ~인 듯하다 명 appearance 외모; 출현

The girls **appeared** with long red ribbons in their hair.

그 소녀들이 머리에 긴 빨간 리본을 달고 나타났다.

182 **dim** [dim]

형 어둑한, 흐릿한, 희미한 동 어둑하게 하다, 희미하게 하다

I could see a **dim** shape in the moonlight.

나는 달빛 속에서 흐릿한 형체를 볼 수 있었다.

183 **drought** [dràut]

명 가뭄, 부족, 결핍 참고 flood 홍수

After years of **drought**, water levels went down.

여러 해에 걸친 가뭄 끝에 수위가 낮아졌다.

184 **drown** [dràun]

동 물에 빠지다, 익사하다; 익사시키다

The lifeguard rushed to save the **drowning** boy.

구조 요원이 물에 빠진 소년을 구하러 서둘러 갔다.

185 **ethnic** [éθnik]

형 인종의, 민족의, 민족 전통의 명 ethnicity 민족성, 인종 유 racial 인종의

The **ethnic** origin of the group is not clear.

그 집단의 인종적 기원은 분명하지 않다.

186 **grip** [grip]

명 움켜쥠, 쥐는 방식; 통제 동 움켜쥐다; 사로잡다

You should adjust your **grip** on the racket.

당신은 라켓 잡는 방식을 조정해야 한다.

187 **height** [hait]

명 높이, 고도, 키 참고 width 폭, 너비

I remember that he was of medium **height**.

그는 보통 키였던 것으로 기억한다.

188 **leap** [li:p]

동 도약하다, (경기 · 가격 등이) 급격히 상승하다 명 도약

Suddenly, a frog **leaped** out of the water.

갑자기 개구리 한 마리가 물 밖으로 뛰어올랐다.

189 **particle** [pá:rtikl]

명 (아주 작은) 입자, 작은 조각

We can see dust **particles** in beams of light.

빛을 비추면 우리는 먼지 입자를 볼 수 있다.

190 **propose**
[prəpóuz]

동 제안하다; 청혼하다　명 proposal 제안, 신청; 청혼

Experts **proposed** that students should eat breakfast.
전문가들은 학생들이 아침을 먹어야 한다고 제안했다.

191 **purpose**
[pə́:rpəs]

명 목표, 목적　참고 on purpose 고의로, 의식적으로

The **purpose** of the meeting is to improve efficiency.
회의의 목적은 효율성 증대에 있다.

192 **rainfall**
[réinfɔ̀:l]

명 강우, 강수량　참고 snowfall 강설(량)

There will be more heavy **rainfall** during the week.
주중에 더 많은 비가 내릴 것이다.

193 **rescue**
[réskju:]

동 구조하다　명 구조

Some soldiers have been reported to **rescue** lost divers.
군인들이 실종된 다이버들을 구조한 것으로 보고되었다.

194 **resource**
[rí:sɔ:rs]

명 자원(주로 복수형); 수단

Our environment offers **resources** which depend on geography.
우리의 환경은 지리적 위치에 따른 자원을 제공한다.

195 **solution**
[səljú:ʃən]

명 해결책; 용액　동 solve 해결하다

The **solution** to back pain is a gentle massage.
요통의 해결책은 부드러운 마사지이다.

196 **spill**
[spil]

동 (실수로) 쏟아지다, 넘치다　명 넘친 것, 유출

spill-spilled(spilt)-spilled(spilt)

Some of the wine **spilled** on to the tablecloth.
약간의 포도주가 식탁보에 쏟아졌다.

197 **spoil**
[spɔil]

동 망치다, (흥미 따위를) 감소시키다　명 spoilage 손상, (음식물의) 부패

The sad news **spoiled** our evening party.
그 슬픈 소식은 우리의 저녁 파티를 망쳤다.

198 **starve**
[stɑ:rv]

동 굶주리다, 배고프다　명 starvation 기아, 굶주림

참고 starve to death 굶어 죽다.

So many people **starved** to death that year.
그해에 수많은 사람들이 굶어 죽었다.

199 **underwater**
[ʌ́ndərwɔ̀:tər]

형 물 밑의, 해저의　참고 underground 지하의

Taking **underwater** photos is a lot of fun.
수중 사진을 찍는 것은 정말 재미있다.

200 **be concerned with**

~와 관련 있다, ~에 관심이 있다

The report **is concerned with** safety issues.
그 보고서는 안전 문제와 관련되어 있다.

10B Complete the Phrases *빈칸에 알맞은 말을 넣어 어구를 완성하세요.*

1 six feet in ______________ (키가 6피트인)

2 to ______________ his trip (그의 여행을 망치다)

3 a product for multiple ______________(e)s (다목적 제품)

4 to ______________ juice on the skirt (치마에 주스를 쏟다)

5 a ______________ of two meters (2미터의 도약)

6 to watch ______________ creatures (수중 생물을 관찰하다)

7 the worst ______________ ever (사상 최악의 가뭄)

8 a ______________ street with few street lamps (가로등이 별로 없는 어두운 거리)

10C Complete the Sentences *[보기]에서 알맞은 단어를 골라 어법에 맞게 완성하세요.*

[보기]

height ethnic solution spill spoil underwater

1 I'd like to have a close-up look at seals swimming ______________.
나는 가까이에서 바다표범들이 물속에서 헤엄치는 것을 보고 싶다.

2 "Jangseungs" come in a variety of forms, and there is no ______________ standard.
장승은 다양한 형태로 존재하며 표준 높이가 없다.

3 The number of ______________ groups living in the country is more than 100.
그 나라에 사는 인종 집단의 수는 100개가 넘는다.

4 White paint was ______________ everywhere and the floor was a mess.
흰 물감이 온갖 군데로 쏟아졌고 바닥은 엉망이었다.

5 I'm going to see that movie tonight, so don't ______________ it for me.
오늘 밤에 그 영화를 볼 거니까 망치지 말아요.

6 The ______________ contains water, salt, and some acids.
그 용액은 물, 소금, 약간의 산을 함유하고 있다.

10D Fill in the Blanks 빈칸에 공통으로 들어갈 단어를 문장에 맞게 고쳐 쓰세요.

1 • The child almost d_______________ after falling into the river.
그 아이는 강에 떨어진 다음 거의 익사할 뻔 했다.
• His eyes d_______________ in tears
그의 눈은 눈물로 흠뻑 젖었다.

2 • He made it to her house and p_______________ to her.
그는 그녀의 집에 무사히 도착해서 청혼했다.
• The group p_______________ that the book should be banned.
그 단체는 그 책의 출판 · 판매가 금지되어야 한다고 제안했다.

3 • This area has an average monthly r_______________ of 20 millimeters.
이 지역의 월평균 강수량은 20밀리미터입니다.
• The large forests regulate r_______________ and store water.
큰 숲은 강우량을 조절하고 물을 저장한다.

4 • I'm s_______________, so let's grab a bite to eat.
배가 몹시 고프니 간단히 뭐 좀 먹자.
• The s_______________ citizens could no longer hold out.
굶주리는 시민들은 더 이상 버틸 수 없었다.

10E Choose Synonyms 문장의 밑줄 친 부분과 가장 유사한 뜻의 단어를 고르세요.

1 The trees near rivers moderate destructive flood and drought cycles.
강 근처의 나무들은 심각한 홍수와 가뭄의 주기를 완화시킨다.
① hurricane ② dryness ③ earthquake ④ storm

2 Our eyes grow dim as we age.
나이가 듦에 따라 눈이 침침해진다.
① scarce ② clear ③ radiant ④ weak

3 Our users may be concerned with the prices of the Internet service.
우리의 사용자들은 인터넷 서비스의 가격에 관심이 있을 것이다.
① be confused by ② be interested in ③ be indifferent to ④ be contributed to

4 We can use baking soda for other purposes.
우리는 베이킹 소다를 다른 용도로 사용할 수 있다.
① usages ② classes ③ treatments ④ suggestions

10F Reading Passage

공부한 단어가 포함된 글을 잘 읽고 다음 문제를 풀어 보세요.

The planet is getting hotter as a result of global warming. Experts warn that when the polar ice caps melt down, water will **spill** over and eventually **drown** villages in the lowlands and islands. However, some scientists are worried about something that is the ______________________: global dimming. Global dimming **is concerned with** solid particles such as ash and soot that pollute the air and reduce the amount of sunlight reaching the planet's surface.

It **appears** that global dimming is the **solution** to global warming, but it does harm to the planet as well. It has a cooling effect on the northern hemisphere, reducing ground and ocean temperatures and thus reducing **rainfall**. Experts **propose** that this could have had a significant effect on Africa. They believe that the global dimming contributed to the **droughts** that **gripped** the continent during the 1980s and made people **starve** to death.

* global dimming 지구 일조량 감소 soot 매연 hemisphere 반구

1 위 글의 요지로 가장 적절한 것은?

① 세계 일조량의 감소는 온난화의 해결책일 수 있다.
② 세계 일조량의 감소 추세가 점차 완화되고 있다.
③ 세계 일조량은 증가와 감소를 반복하고 있다.
④ 세계 일조량의 감소는 지구 사막화의 결과이다.
⑤ 세계 일조량이 줄어드는 것도 환경에 악영향을 줄 수 있다.

2 위 글의 빈칸에 들어갈 말로 가장 적절한 것은?

① positive reverse
② preview of crisis
③ complete opposite
④ causes of warming
⑤ unexpected benefits

English Only

3 According to the passage, which is true?

① Experts deny that the polar ice caps are melting.
② Solid particles in the air increase the amount of rainfall.
③ Global dimming has a warming effect on the northern hemisphere.
④ Experts warn that global dimming will threaten Africa.
⑤ Global dimming is expected to cause floods.

서술형

4 Use words from the passage to complete the answer below.

What's the negative effect of global dimming?
→ It cools down the northern hemisphere and reduces __________, causing __________.

Speedy Check-up 2

Lesson별로 모르는 단어에 체크한 후, 그 갯수를 [/20] 안에 쓰고 학습성과를 점검해 보세요.
모르는 단어는 다시 찾아 학습하세요.

Lesson 6 /20

▢ accompany	▢ comment	▢ ignore	▢ ruin
▢ applause	▢ descendant	▢ participant	▢ support
▢ associate	▢ expression	▢ raw	▢ temperature
▢ atmosphere	▢ faithful	▢ reality	▢ whereas
▢ classify	▢ focus	▢ ridiculous	▢ according to

Lesson 7 /20

▢ appropriate	▢ element	▢ hopeless	▢ pill
▢ article	▢ entire	▢ individual	▢ politics
▢ custom	▢ ethical	▢ institute	▢ recycle
▢ describe	▢ feature	▢ journalism	▢ reflect
▢ detail	▢ germ	▢ leak	▢ wonder

Lesson 8 /20

▢ annoy	▢ confident	▢ embrace	▢ isolate
▢ aspect	▢ conform	▢ financial	▢ merit
▢ behavior	▢ disaster	▢ independent	▢ obtain
▢ brief	▢ distinguish	▢ influence	▢ sacrifice
▢ comfort	▢ document	▢ interrupt	▢ seldom

Lesson 9 /20

▢ anywhere	▢ fist	▢ obvious	▢ root
▢ bloom	▢ float	▢ realize	▢ symbolize
▢ democracy	▢ holy	▢ regard	▢ unite
▢ exist	▢ intersection	▢ remark	▢ unusual
▢ fasten	▢ involve	▢ represent	▢ keep one's fingers crossed

Lesson 10 /20

▢ appear	▢ grip	▢ purpose	▢ spill
▢ dim	▢ height	▢ rainfall	▢ spoil
▢ drought	▢ leap	▢ rescue	▢ starve
▢ drown	▢ particle	▢ resource	▢ underwater
▢ ethnic	▢ propose	▢ solution	▢ be concerned with

:: Chapter 3

Lesson 11

SUMMA CUM LAUDE

Word 500 201~220
Reading 25 11

11A Word List

중학교 3학년 필수단어를 예문과 함께 공부하세요.

201 **affordable** [əfɔ́:rdəbl]
형 (가격이) 알맞은, 입수 가능한 동 afford ~의 여유가 있다
It is hard to find **affordable** houses in big cities.
대도시에서 비용이 적절한 주택을 찾는 것은 어렵다.

202 **aptitude** [ǽptitù:d]
명 소질, 적성 형 apt 적절한, ~하기 쉬운
The boy has an **aptitude** for computer programming.
그 소년은 컴퓨터 프로그래밍에 소질이 있다.

203 **combine** [kəmbáin]
동 결합시키다, 연결시키다 명 combination 결합, 배합
There is a wish to **combine** tradition and convenience.
전통과 편리함을 결합시키려는 소망이 있다.

204 **digital** [dídʒitl]
형 디지털 방식의 동 digitalize 디지털 방식으로 바꾸다
Is it a good idea to bring in **digital** learning?
디지털 방식의 학습을 도입하는 것이 좋은 생각일까?

205 **ensure** [inʃúər]
동 책임지다, 보장하다 유 guarantee 보장하다, 보증하다
This system can **ensure** that there are enough volunteer workers.
이 제도는 충분한 자원봉사 인력을 보장해 줄 수 있다.

206 **glue** [glu:]
명 접착제 동 붙이다 유 stick 붙이다 fix 고정시키다
I need to buy another **glue** stick.
나는 풀을 하나 더 사야 한다.

207 **intelligent** [intélədʒənt]
형 지적인, 영리한 명 intelligence 지능
Some animals are known to be as **intelligent** as humans.
일부 동물들은 인간만큼 영리하다고 알려져 있다.

208 **logical** [lɑ́dʒikəl]
형 논리적인, 논리학의 명 logic 논리
I enjoy solving **logical** problems, but I don't like math.
나는 논리적인 문제를 해결하는 것을 좋아하지만 수학은 싫어한다.

209 **passport** [pǽspɔ̀:rt]
명 여권; (어떤 일을 가능케 하는) 수단, 보증
He was stopped as he went through **passport** control.
그는 여권 심사대를 통과하다가 저지당했다.

210 **permit**
[pəːrmít]

동 허락〔허가〕하다　명 permission 허락, 허가

Mom **permitted** me to take the kitten home.
엄마는 내가 새끼 고양이를 집으로 데려가는 것을 허락했다.

211 **predict**
[pridíkt]

동 예측하다, 예언하다　명 prediction 예측, 예언

Look at the pictures and **predict** what will happen next.
그림을 보고 다음에 무엇이 일어날지 예측해 보시오.

212 **recognize**
[rékəgnàiz]

동 알아보다, 인정하다　명 recognition 인정, 인식

She had changed a lot, so I had a hard time **recognizing** her.
그녀는 많이 변해서 나는 그녀를 알아보기 힘들었다.

213 **reject**
[ridʒékt]

동 거절〔거부〕하다(=turn down)　명 rejection 거절

The proposal was hard to **reject**.
그 제안은 거절하기 힘들었다.

214 **rule**
[ruːl]

명 규칙, 지배　동 (국왕 · 정부 등이) 지배하다, 통치하다

A dynasty **ruled** over the region for 500 years.
한 왕조가 500년간 그 지역을 통치했다.

215 **security**
[sikjúəriti]

명 안전, 보안　참고 secure 안전한; 확보하다

For the **security** of passengers, baggage is carefully checked.
승객의 안전을 위해 수하물 검사가 철저하다.

216 **sheet**
[ʃiːt]

명 (침대에 까는) 시트, 얇은 판, (종이) 한 장

He put a large **sheet** of white paper on the wall.
그는 커다란 백지 한 장을 벽에 붙였다.

217 **surf**
[səːrf]

명 (해안에 밀려드는) 파도　동 파도타기를 하다

He's learning to **surf** during this vacation.
그는 이번 휴가 동안에 서핑을 배우고 있다.

218 **useless**
[júːslis]

형 쓸모없는　반 useful 유용한　유 worthless 가치 없는

I do not want to buy this **useless** machine.
이 쓸모없는 기계는 사고 싶지 않다.

219 **vital**
[váitl]

형 필수적인, 생명 유지와 관련된　유 critical 결정적인, 중요한

It is **vital** that the system is regularly maintained.
그 시스템을 정기적으로 점검하는 것은 필수적이다.

220 **turn out**

~인 것으로 밝혀지다, 나타나다

The plan looked great, but it **turned out** to be a failure.
그 계획은 멋져 보였지만 결국 실패했다.

11B Complete the Phrases *빈칸에 알맞은 말을 넣어 어구를 완성하세요.*

1 to sign the _______________ (여권에 서명하다)

2 a natural _______________ for the work (그 일을 위한 타고난 적성)

3 the _______________ thinking process (논리적인 사고 과정)

4 to _______________ a job offer (취업 제안을 거절하다)

5 to apply for a _______________ (허가를 신청하다)

6 to waste money on _______________ things (쓸모없는 것에 돈을 낭비하다)

7 _______________ life form living on other planets (타 행성의 지적 생명체)

8 to ensure _______________ of citizens (시민의 안전을 보장하다)

11C Complete the Sentences *[보기]에서 알맞은 단어를 골라 어법에 맞게 완성하세요.*

[보기]

aptitude intelligent logical predict sheet useless

1 He is the top student in the class because he is the most _______________.
그는 가장 영리한 학생이어서 그 학급에서 수석을 차지했다.

2 The teacher was talking to him about his _______________ test record.
선생님은 그의 적성 평가 결과에 대해 말하고 있었다.

3 Some people think that mathematics is difficult, boring, and _______________.
몇몇 사람들은 수학이 어렵고 지루하며 쓸모없다고 생각한다.

4 Experts _______________ that the population of developing countries will increase.
전문가들은 개발도상국의 인구가 늘어날 것이라고 예측한다.

5 No one saw the white _______________ of paper hung on the wall.
어느 누구도 벽에 걸린 흰 종이를 보지 못했다.

6 They say that left-brain people tend to be _______________.
좌뇌형 인간들이 논리적이라고 알려져 있다.

11D Fill in the Blanks *빈칸에 공통으로 들어갈 단어를 문장에 맞게 고쳐 쓰세요.*

1 • The s_______________ of the visiting group is the most important.
방문자 단체의 안전이 가장 중요하다.

• We will provide private meeting rooms because of the s_______________ concerns.
보안상의 문제 때문에 개별 회의실을 제공할 것입니다.

2 • In the end, he t____________________ to be a handsome knight in disguise.
결국 그가 잘생긴 기사로 변장한 것이 밝혀졌다.

• If only I had followed my dreams, life would have t____________________ differently.
나의 꿈을 따라갔다면 인생은 결국 달라졌을 것이다.

3 • First you have to put your personal information in your p_______________.
먼저 여권에 개인 정보를 적어야 한다.

• Education is a p_______________ to success.
교육이 성공의 방편이다.

4 • The r_______________ was that you could not speak with anyone.
누구와도 대화를 나눌 수 없다는 것이 규칙이었다.

• America was colony under the r_______________ of Great Britain.
미국은 대영제국의 지배하에 있던 식민지였다.

11E Choose Synonyms *문장의 밑줄 친 부분과 가장 유사한 뜻의 단어를 고르세요.*

1 Now there is an <u>affordable</u> way to get clean water using sunlight.
이제는 햇빛을 사용하여 적절한 비용으로 깨끗한 물을 얻을 수 있는 방법이 존재한다.
① costly ② reasonable ③ newest ④ urgent

2 Some researchers trained parrots to <u>combine</u> the words they have learned.
일부 연구자들은 앵무새들에게 그 동안 배운 단어들을 결합하는 훈련을 시켰다.
① memorize ② speak ③ connect ④ remember

3 These matters are <u>vital</u> to national defense.
이 사안들은 국가 방위에 있어 극히 중요하다.
① essential ② grateful ③ helpful ④ secure

4 Emerson, who was in charge of the government project, <u>rejected</u> Tesla's idea.
정부 프로젝트를 맡고 있던 Emerson은 Tesla의 방안을 거절했다.
① hid ② welcomed ③ discovered ④ turned down

11F Reading Passage

공부한 단어가 포함된 글을 잘 읽고 다음 문제를 풀어 보세요.

In a sense, the **digital** revolution in telecommunications has already started. The **intelligent** technology industry is booming. Moore's Law, a rule that states microprocessor power doubles every 18 months, continues to hold true. In the same way Gilder's Law — available bandwidth will triple every 12 months — makes the Internet **affordable**. The Internet connection has become a **vital** part of both work and personal life. Moreover, we can easily **predict** that ______________________ as it connects to the Internet. (ⓐ) Take the doorbell, for example. (ⓑ) When someone rings it and no one's at home, it turns out to be a **useless** device. (ⓒ) But if you **combine** the doorbell and the cell phone, you can answer the door on the other side of the town. (ⓓ) You can then decide whether to **permit** him to enter the house or not. (ⓔ) The new doorbell can **ensure** a higher level of **security** for you!

* bandwidth 대역폭(시간 내에 보낼 수 있는 정보량)

1 위 글의 요지로 가장 적절한 것은?

① 디지털화는 삶의 방식을 바꾼다.
② 디지털화는 개인들을 소외시킨다.
③ 젊을수록 디지털화에 민감하게 반응한다.
④ 디지털 기기가 사생활을 침해할 위험이 있다.
⑤ 디지털 기기는 과소비를 조장하는 경향이 있다.

2 위 글의 빈칸에 들어갈 말로 가장 적절한 것은?

① we show off our new electronic device
② the price of the electronic device drops
③ the value of the electronic device increases
④ we need to learn to use the electronic device
⑤ the complexity of the electronic device decreases

English Only

3 Where is the appropriate place for the sentence?

You recognize the 'ringer' via the video camera and talk to him.

① ⓐ ② ⓑ ③ ⓒ ④ ⓓ ⑤ ⓔ

서술형

4 Arrange the words given in order to complete the answer below.

What do Moore's Law and Gilder's Law infer?
→ People can (access, easier, have) ______________________ to the electronic devices and the Internet service (prices, at, lower) ______________ ______________.

Lesson 12

Word 500 221~240
Reading 25 12

SUMMA CUM LAUDE

12A Word List

중학교 3학년 필수단어를 예문과 함께 공부하세요.

221 **advantage** [ədvǽntidʒ]
명 이익, 장점 반 disadvantage 약점, 불리한 점
Don't give them time to think, surprise is your **advantage**.
그들에게 생각할 시간을 주지 마라, 기습은 당신에게 이익이 된다.

222 **amusement** [əmjúːzmənt]
명 재미, 오락, 놀이 동 amuse ~을 즐겁게 하다
The crowd smiled with **amusement**.
모인 사람들은 즐거워서 웃음을 지었다.

223 **celebration** [sèləbréiʃən]
명 기념 (행사), 축하 동 celebrate 축하하다
Big **celebrations** are planned for the summer holidays.
여름 휴가를 위한 큰 기념 행사들이 계획되어 있다.

224 **charm** [tʃɑːrm]
명 매력(=fascination) 동 매혹하다 형 charming 매력적인
She is a woman of great **charm** and personality.
그녀는 매우 매력적이고 성격이 좋은 여자이다.

225 **consult** [kənsʌ́lt]
동 상담(상의)하다 참고 consultant 상담가, 자문위원
Always **consult** your doctor for questions on medical problems.
의료문제에 관해 의문이 있으면 항상 당신의 의사와 상의하라.

226 **crawl** [krɔːl]
동 기어가다, 서행하다 명 포복, 서행
There's a spider **crawling** on the wall behind you.
당신의 뒤편 벽에 거미가 한 마리 기어가고 있다.

227 **determine** [ditə́ːrmin]
동 결정(결심)하다, 알아내다 명 determination 결정
Childhood experiences **determine** a person's character.
유년시절의 경험이 한 사람의 성격을 결정한다.

228 **endanger** [indéindʒər]
동 위험에 빠뜨리다, 위태롭게 만들다
Lots of animals are **endangered** by human activity.
많은 동물들이 인간의 활동으로 인해 위험에 처해 있다.

229 **exposure** [ikspóuʒər]
명 노출, 폭로 동 expose 노출하다, 폭로하다
Exposure to sunlight helps a person improve his health.
햇빛에의 노출은 사람의 건강을 향상시키는 데 도움이 된다.

230 **hibernate** [háibərnèit]

동 동면하다, 겨울잠을 자다 명 hibernation 동면, 겨울잠

Bats, skunks, and snakes all **hibernate** in winter.

박쥐, 스컹크, 뱀은 모두 겨울에 동면을 한다.

231 **ideal** [aidí:əl]

형 이상적인, 가장 알맞은 명 이상

This book is **ideal** for children ages 4 to 12.

이 책은 4세에서 12세의 아이들에게 이상적이다.

232 **legend** [lédʒənd]

명 전설, 전설적인 인물 형 legendary 전설적인, 아주 유명한

According to **legend**, it was here that the story had begun.

전설에 따르면 그 이야기가 시작된 곳은 바로 여기였다.

233 **otherwise** [ʌ́ðərwàiz]

부 그렇지 않다면(=if not); 그 외에는, 다른 점에서

Close the door, **otherwise** someone will go inside.

문을 닫으시오, 그렇지 않으면 누군가가 안으로 들어갈 것이다.

234 **principal** [prínsəpəl]

형 주요한, 주된 명 (교)장

Learning to solve problems is the **principal** reason for studying math.

문제를 해결하는 방법을 배우는 것이 수학을 공부하는 주요한 이유이다.

235 **recipe** [résəpì:]

명 요리법, 비결 참고 ingredients 재료

I bought a **recipe** book for my wife.

나는 내 아내를 위해 요리책 한 권을 샀다.

236 **resemble** [rizémbl]

동 ~을 닮다, ~와 비슷하다 명 resemblance 닮음, 유사함

He closely **resembles** his elder brother.

그는 그의 형과 매우 닮았다.

237 **rob** [rɑb]

동 빼앗다, 강탈하다 명 robbery 강도 (사건)

The store was **robbed** of more than 5,000 dollars.

그 가게는 5천 달러 이상의 돈을 빼앗겼다.

238 **shadow** [ʃǽdou]

명 그림자, 어둠, 그늘

I noticed my dog was chasing my **shadow**.

나의 개가 내 그림자를 따라오고 있다는 것을 알아차렸다.

239 **translate** [trænsléit]

동 번역하다, 통역하다(=interpret) 명 translation 번역, 통역

She **translated** the e-mail into Spanish.

그녀는 전자 우편을 스페인어로 번역했다.

240 **just around the corner**

가까운, 곧 ~인, 임박한

The midterm exams are **just around the corner**.

이제 곧 중간고사가 시작이다.

12B Complete the Phrases *빈칸에 알맞은 말을 넣어 어구를 완성하세요.*

1 various _______________ (다양한 조리법들)

2 suppliers of _______________ equipment (놀이 장비 공급 업체)

3 a _______________ of a strange animal (이상한 동물의 그림자)

4 _______________ water ways in Britain (영국의 주요한 수로)

5 a living _______________ of hip-hop (살아 있는 힙합의 전설)

6 _______________ each other (서로서로 닮다)

7 _______________ harmony and balance (이상적인 조화와 균형)

8 a comparative _______________ (비교상의 이점)

12C Complete the Sentences *[보기]에서 알맞은 단어를 골라 어법에 맞게 완성하세요.*

[보기]

determine celebration crawl otherwise rob hibernate endanger

1 The thief _______________ me of all my belongings.
그 도둑이 나의 모든 소지품을 털어갔다.

2 Tonight's game will _______________ the winners.
오늘 저녁의 경기가 승자를 결정할 것이다.

3 Hurry up, _______________ you will lose the chance.
서두르라, 그렇지 않으면 당신은 그 기회를 놓칠 것이다.

4 This site provides an _______________ mammals list.
이 사이트는 멸종 위기에 빠진 포유동물의 목록을 제공한다.

5 Easter is the most important _______________ of the church.
부활절은 그 교회의 가장 중요한 기념행사이다.

6 They _______________ primarily in deep caves with large rooms.
그들은 주로 큰 공간이 있는 깊은 동굴에서 동면을 한다.

7 The boy _______________ through the brush and followed his father.
그 소년은 덤불 사이로 기어 들어가서 그의 아버지를 따라갔다.

12D Fill in the Blanks
빈칸에 공통으로 들어갈 단어를 문장에 맞게 고쳐 쓰세요.

1 • The system is an i______________ way to deal with crime.
그 시스템은 범죄에 대응할 수 있는 이상적인 방법이다.
• The priest pursued the i______________ of a perfect man.
그 성직자는 완전한 사람의 이상적인 모습을 추구했다.

2 • Why don't you c______________ an expert on the disease?
그 질병과 관련해 전문가의 상담을 받는 것이 어떠한가?
• I was told to c______________ with him about a business matter.
나는 사업 문제에 관해 그와 상담하라는 말을 들었다.

3 • E______________ to radiation can result in chronic sickness.
방사선 노출은 만성질환을 일으킬 수 있다.
• Long-term e______________ to air pollution can lead to lung problems.
대기 오염에 장기적으로 노출되면 폐 질환을 일으킬 수 있다.

4 • Living in the countryside has a lot of a______________.
시골에 거주하는 것에는 많은 장점이 있다.
• These are a______________ of buying books online.
책을 온라인으로 구매하는 것의 장점들은 이러한 것들입니다.

12E Choose Synonyms
문장의 밑줄 친 부분과 가장 유사한 뜻의 단어를 고르세요.

1 I think she can <u>translate</u> this passage for you.
그녀는 당신을 위해 이 글을 번역해 줄 수 있다고 생각합니다.
① frighten ② compose ③ ignore ④ interpret

2 These animals were a <u>principal</u> source of food for humans.
이 동물들은 인간을 위한 주요 식량 자원이었다.
① scary ② primary ③ plentiful ④ formal

3 We have to <u>determine</u> whether we start right now or not.
우리는 지금 바로 시작할지 안 할지를 결정해야 한다.
① decide ② request ③ delay ④ obtain

4 The story has been the source of <u>amusement</u> and laughter.
그 이야기는 재미와 웃음의 원천이었다.
① pity ② opinion ③ shock ④ fun

12F Reading Passage

공부한 단어가 포함된 글을 잘 읽고 다음 문제를 풀어 보세요.

Punxsutawney, Pennsylvania, is the home of Punxsutawney Phil, the most famous of the furry weather forecasters who walk slowly forth from their holes every February 2 to predict how long winter will stay. In early February, this tiny town **resembles** a large city. (ⓐ) And on February 2, named Groundhog Day, leaders of the community gather on Gobbler's Knob to **consult** with Phil, who **crawls** out of his hole and either sees his **shadow** or doesn't. (ⓑ) As the tradition goes, if Phil sees his shadow, that means that winter is still hanging around, for another six weeks; if Phil doesn't see his shadow, the **legend** says, then spring is **just around the corner**.

No one is sure just when this tradition began. (ⓒ) It is first mentioned in the 18th Century, possibly connected with the **celebration** of Candlemas, which occurred halfway between the first day of winter and the first day of spring. (ⓓ) And although the dates are not the same, the belief that the weather on Candlemas **determined** how soon spring would come was **translated** to the groundhog, or woodchuck, who was a **hibernating** animal who usually chose early February to end his hibernation. (ⓔ) It's all an excuse to get together and celebrate a "holiday" and **exposure** for the small, **otherwise** ordinary town of Punxsutawney.

1 위 글의 제목으로 가장 적절한 것은?

① Winter Is Getting Longer
② No More Cruelty to Animals
③ The Origin of Groundhog Day
④ Spring: The Season of New Life
⑤ Only Summer and Winter on Earth

2 글의 흐름으로 보아, 주어진 문장이 들어가기에 가장 적절한 곳은?

Nowadays, however, it doesn't matter whether Phil is even right.

① ⓐ ② ⓑ ③ ⓒ ④ ⓓ ⑤ ⓔ

English Only

3 According to the passage, which is NOT true?

① Punxsutawney Phil predicts the weather.
② Punxsutawney is crowded with people on February 2.
③ No one knows for sure when Groundhog Day started.
④ The celebration of Candlemas started on the first day of winter.
⑤ A groundhog is an animal that spends the winter sleeping.

서술형

4 Fill in the blanks to complete the sentence.

> According to the tradition, if Phil sees his shadow and returns to his hole, it means __________ more weeks of winter. If Phil does not see his shadow, spring is about to __________.

Lesson 13

SUMMA CUM LAUDE

Word 500 241~260
Reading 25 13

13A Word List

중학교 3학년 필수단어를 예문과 함께 공부하세요.

241 **acid** [ǽsid]
㊔(화학) 산 ㊒산성의, (맛이) 신 유 sour 신
The gas goes into the atmosphere and falls to the earth as **acid** rain.
그 가스는 대기로 들어가서 산성비로 땅에 떨어진다.

242 **backbone** [bǽkbòun]
㊔등뼈, 척추 유 spine 척추
The **backbone** reaches from the base of the skull to the tailbone.
등뼈는 두개골의 아래쪽부터 꼬리뼈에 이른다.

243 **bubble** [bʌ́bl]
㊔비눗방울, 거품 ㊗부글부글 끓다
My nephew loves blowing **bubbles** in the playground.
내 조카는 놀이터에서 비눗방울 부는 것을 정말로 좋아한다.

244 **clone** [kloun]
㊗복제하다 ㊔복제 (생물)
These scientists have been trying to **clone** a tiger for years.
이 과학자들은 여러 해 동안 호랑이를 복제하려고 노력해 왔다.

245 **damage** [dǽmidʒ]
㊔손상, 피해 ㊗손상을 입히다
They cause too much **damage** to our environment.
그들은 우리의 환경에 너무 많은 손상을 유발한다.

246 **destination** [dèstənéiʃən]
㊔목적지, 행선지, 도착지
The park is a favorite **destination** for family picnics.
그 공원은 사람들이 가족 소풍 장소로 가장 선호하는 곳이다.

247 **disabled** [diséibld]
㊒장애를 가진; 무능력해진 유 handicapped 장애가 있는
This parking space is reserved for the **disabled**.
이 주차 공간은 장애인 전용이다.

248 **dissolve** [dizɑ́lv]
㊗녹다, 사라지다, 녹이다 유 melt
This sugar **dissolves** more easily in cold water.
이 설탕은 찬물에 더 잘 녹는다.

249 **emotion** [imóuʃən]
㊔감정, 정서 ㊒ emotional 감정적인
Elephants are able to express a wide range of **emotions**.
코끼리들은 넓은 범위의 감정을 표현할 수 있다.

250 **lifelong** [láiflɔ̀ːŋ]

㊐ 일생의, 평생의 유 long-lasting 오래 지속되는

Mickey Jackson and Ted Jones were **lifelong** rivals.
Mickey Jackson과 Ted Jones는 평생의 맞수였다.

251 **liquid** [líkwid]

명 액체 형 액체의

Pour the **liquid** into a saucepan and boil it.
그 액체를 소스 냄비에 넣고 끓이시오.

252 **lump** [lʌmp]

명 덩어리, 응어리; 혹

I had a **lump** in my chest, but it disappeared naturally.
가슴에 혹이 있었지만 저절로 사라졌다.

253 **necessary** [nésəsèri]

형 필요한 명 필수품 유 essential 필수적인

You have to get the **necessary** shots in advance.
필요한 사진을 미리 찍어야 합니다.

254 **nutrient** [njúːtriənt]

명 영양소 형 nutritious 영양분이 있는

Plants can produce **nutrients** with water and sunlight.
식물은 물과 햇빛으로 영양소를 만들 수 있다.

255 **organ** [ɔ́ːrgən]

명 (몸의) 기관, 장기 형 organic 유기체의, 유기농의

These sounds are controlled by an **organ** on the forehead.
이 소리들은 이마에 있는 기관에 의해 제어된다.

256 **react** [riːǽkt]

동 반응하다 명 reaction 반응

How did the spectators in the stadium **react** to his dance?
경기장의 관객들은 그의 춤에 어떻게 반응했는가?

257 **refresh** [rifréʃ]

동 상쾌하게 하다, 재충전하다

Traveling **refreshes** your body and mind.
여행은 신체와 정신을 상쾌하게 한다.

258 **stomach** [stʌ́mək]

명 위, 복부, 배 동 먹다, (모욕 등을) 참다

Sally woke up with a terrible pain in her **stomach**.
Sally는 배에 심한 통증을 느끼며 깼다.

259 **swallow** [swɑ́lou]

동 (음식물을) 삼키다, 넘기다 명 한 입; 제비

John could hardly **swallow** his toast.
John은 그의 토스트를 거의 삼킬 수가 없었다.

260 **break down**

고장 나다; 실패하다; 나누다; 분해하다〔되다〕

The old bus **broke down** on the highway.
그 오래된 버스는 고속도로에서 고장이 났다.

Paper cannot completely **break down** underground.
종이는 땅 속에서 완전히 분해될 수 없다.

13B Complete the Phrases 빈칸에 알맞은 말을 넣어 어구를 완성하세요.

1 a ______________ of oxygen (산소 방울)

2 to ______________ one's memory (누군가의 기억을 새롭게 하다)

3 change from a solid to a ______________ (고체에서 액체로 변하다)

4 a ______________ companion (평생의 동반자)

5 a parking space for the ______________ (장애인 전용 주차 공간)

6 a sense ______________ (감각 기관)

7 ______________ rain due to environmental pollution (환경오염으로 인한 산성비)

8 the world's first ______________ of a turtle (세계 최초의 거북 복제)

13C Complete the Sentences [보기]에서 알맞은 단어를 골라 어법에 맞게 완성하세요.

[보기]

break down clone damage dissolve lifelong organ stomach

1 The flood badly ______________ all the town.
그 홍수는 마을 전체에 심한 피해를 주었다.

2 The boxer got punched in the ______________, and he fell down.
그 선수는 주먹으로 복부를 맞고 쓰러졌다.

3 The first successful ______________ was Dolly the sheep.
최초의 성공적인 (유전자) 복제는 Dolly라는 이름의 양이다.

4 He ______________ sugar in a hot cup of coffee.
그는 뜨거운 한 잔의 커피에 설탕을 녹였다.

5 His role as a pioneer in pop art comes out of ______________ interests.
팝아트의 선구자로서 그의 역할은 일생에 걸친 관심에서 나온다.

6 The chimpanzee doesn't have the language ______________ like humans.
침팬지는 인간과 같은 언어 기관을 갖고 있지 않다.

7 While paper bags will ______________ quickly, they still take up space.
종이 가방은 신속하게 분해할 수 있지만 여전히 공간을 차지한다.

13D Fill in the Blanks *빈칸에 공통으로 들어갈 단어를 문장에 맞게 고쳐 쓰세요.*

1 • Regular training can prepare you to r_______________ appropriately.
규칙적인 훈련은 적절하게 반응하도록 여러분을 준비시킬 수 있다.
• When there is an emergency, we have to r_______________ immediately.
비상 상황에는 즉각적으로 반응해야 한다.

2 • L_______________ gas emits less greenhouse gases than coal.
액화 가스는 석탄보다 온실 가스를 덜 배출한다.
• The plant will absorb a lot of l_______________.
그 식물은 많은 액체를 흡수하기 마련이다.

3 • Wetlands provide animals with n_______________ and oxygen.
습지는 동물들에게 영양소와 산소를 제공한다.
• No single food can supply the variety of n_______________ needed for good health.
한 가지 식품으로는 건강 유지에 필요한 다양한 영양소를 절대 공급받을 수 없다.

4 • The b_______________ is another word for the spine.
등뼈는 척추의 다른 말이다.
• The mountains form the b_______________ of the country.
그 산맥은 국가의 근간을 이룬다.

13E Choose Synonyms *문장의 밑줄 친 부분과 가장 유사한 뜻의 단어를 고르세요.*

1 It takes 200 to 500 years for a soda can to <u>break down</u> naturally.
음료수 캔이 자연적으로 분해되는 데 200에서 500년이 걸린다.
① decay ② produce ③ fall ④ build

2 The report includes all the <u>necessary</u> information.
그 보고서는 모든 필요한 정보를 포함한다.
① brilliant ② needed ③ useless ④ recent

3 The city was heavily <u>damaged</u> during the war.
그 도시는 전쟁에서 큰 피해를 받았다.
① adopted ② concerned ③ covered ④ harmed

4 The painting brings about mixed <u>emotions</u>.
그 그림은 뒤섞인 감정을 불러일으킨다.
① reviews ② actions ③ feelings ④ memories

13F Reading Passage 공부한 단어가 포함된 글을 잘 읽고 다음 문제를 풀어 보세요.

Keep a piece of bread in your mouth for a few minutes and after a short while you'll notice a sweet taste. (ⓐ) That is the beginning of digestion, as enzymes in your saliva begin to **dissolve** the food. (ⓑ) The next step is when you **swallow** the food. (ⓒ) In the **stomach**, a pool of **acid**, enzymes, and other fluids **break** the food **down** further. (ⓓ) Luckily, your stomach has a special lining that keeps the chemicals from **damaging** it. The food is in the **liquid** form now and is pushed into the 5m coiled-up small intestine. (ⓔ) When the food arrives, the small intestine **reacts** by pouring more digestive juices before at last everything is pushed out of the small intestine. By now the body has absorbed the **necessary nutrients** to keep it fit. The next **destination** is the large intestine. There, any remaining water is sucked out of the food and it goes down as a **lump** of waste. Air **bubbles** in the food leak out of your body. It's time for you to go to the bathroom!

* enzymes 효소 saliva 침 intestine 창자 lump 덩어리

1 위 글의 주제로 가장 적절한 것은?

① the roles of chemicals in the body
② the function of air bubbles in foods
③ the process of digestion in the body
④ ways the sugars in foods are used
⑤ the components of fluids in the stomach

2 글의 흐름으로 보아, 주어진 문장이 들어가기에 가장 적절한 곳은?

That acid would be strong enough to dissolve iron nails.

① ⓐ ② ⓑ ③ ⓒ ④ ⓓ ⑤ ⓔ

English Only

3 What helps you taste something sweet soon after you chew a piece of bread?

① acids
② water
③ nutrients
④ enzymes
⑤ air bubbles

서술형

4 Complete the sentence with words from the passage.

The small intestine adds __________ __________ to the food and it absorbs the __________ necessary to keep the body healthy before it pushes the food to the large intestine.

Word 500 261~280
Reading 25 14

SUMMA CUM LAUDE

14A Word List

중학교 3학년 필수단어를 예문과 함께 공부하세요.

261 **affect** [əfékt]
㉿ 영향을 미치다 유 influence
My family's opinion did not **affect** my decision.
가족의 의견은 나의 결정에 영향을 미치지 않았다.

262 **charity** [tʃǽrəti]
명 자선(구호) 단체, 자선 참고 fund 기금
This **charity** raises money for children who need medical help.
이 자선 단체는 의료적 도움이 필요한 아이들을 위한 돈을 모금하고 있다.

263 **commit** [kəmít]
동 (범죄를) 저지르다; 헌신하다 명 commitment 전념, 헌신
He must have **committed** a serious crime against the country.
그는 국가에 반하는 중대한 범죄를 저질렀음에 틀림없다.

264 **complex** [kɔ́mpleks]
형 복잡한 명 복합 건물, 단지
Solving **complex** problems takes time and effort.
복잡한 문제를 푸는 데는 시간과 노력이 든다.

265 **connection** [kənékʃən]
명 연결, 연관성 동 connect 연결하다
Police deny that this case has any **connection** with drugs.
경찰은 이 사건에 관해 마약과의 연관성을 강하게 부인하고 있다.

266 **contact** [kɑ́ntækt]
명 연락, 접촉 동 연락하다
Let me know how we can keep in **contact** with you.
우리가 당신과 연락하며 지낼 수 있는 방법을 알려주세요.

267 **donation** [dounéiʃən]
명 기부, 기증 동 donate 기증하다, 기부하다
I make a regular **donation** to charity.
나는 정기적으로 자선 단체에 기부를 한다.

268 **evidence** [évidəns]
명 증거, 흔적, 증언 참고 proof 증거물, 증명
There is no **evidence** that he committed a crime.
그가 범행을 저질렀다는 증거는 없다.

269 **harmful** [hɑ́:rmfəl]
형 해로운, 유해한 반 harmless 해가 없는
Energy drinks may be **harmful** to children's dental health.
에너지 음료는 아이들의 치아 건강에 해로울 수 있다.

270 **heritage** [héritidʒ]

명 (국가 · 사회의) 유산

It is a part of the cultural **heritage** in Korea.
그것은 한국 문화유산의 한 부분이다.

271 **informal** [infɔ́:rməl]

형 허물없는, 비공식의, (옷이) 평상복인 반 formal 공식적인

I delivered a speech at an **informal** meeting.
나는 비공식 모임에서 연설을 했다.

272 **progress** [prágres]

명 전진, 증진, 진행 동 진보하다, 발전하다

According to the report, negotiations are in **progress** now.
보고서에 따르면 현재 협상이 진행 중이다.

273 **refuse** [rifjú:z]

동 거절(거부)하다 명 refusal 거절 유 reject 거절하다

The buyer **refused** to accept the package because it was damaged.
구매자는 상품이 파손되었기 때문에 그 소포의 인수를 거부했다.

274 **relationship** [riléiʃənʃip]

명 관계, 관련성 참고 association 연계, 유대

It is crucial to maintain positive human **relationships**.
긍정적인 인간관계를 유지하는 것은 매우 중요하다.

275 **reveal** [riví:l]

동 밝히다, 폭로하다, 드러내다 반 hide 숨기다

I didn't know who **revealed** my personal secret.
나는 누가 내 사적인 비밀을 폭로했는지 몰랐다.

276 **reward** [riwɔ́:rd]

명 보상, 보수, 상 ; 사례금 동 보상(보답)하다

The girl got **reward** for her efforts.
그녀는 자신의 노력에 대해 보상을 받았다.

277 **significant** [signífikənt]

형 중요한, 의미 있는, 커다란 명 significance 중요성, 의미

Cost is a highly **significant** factor in production.
비용은 생산에서 매우 중요한 요소이다.

278 **similarity** [sìməlǽrəti]

명 유사성, 닮은 점 형 similar 유사한, 비슷한

There are **similarities** and differences between the two groups.
두 집단 사이에는 유사점과 차이점이 있다.

279 **specifically** [spisífikəli]

부 분명히, 명확하게, 구체적으로 말하면

I **specifically** told you to bring your umbrella.
나는 분명히 당신에게 우산을 가져오라고 말했다.

280 **unselfish** [ʌ̀nsélfiʃ]

형 사심이 없는, 이기적이 아닌 반 selfish 이기적인

I'm thankful to them for being generous and **unselfish**.
나는 그들이 관대하고 사심이 없음에 감사한다.

14B Complete the Phrases *빈칸에 알맞은 말을 넣어 어구를 완성하세요.*

1 convincing ______________ (신빙성 있는 증거)

2 ______________ machinery (복잡한 기계 장치)

3 the ______________ effects of caffeine (카페인의 해로운 영향)

4 the ______________ of science (과학의 진보)

5 human ______________ in the workplace (직장에서의 인간 관계)

6 a financial ______________ (재정적인 보상)

7 ______________ conversations with colleagues (동료와의 비공식적 대화)

8 a kind and ______________ person (친절하고 사심이 없는 사람)

14C Complete the Sentences *[보기]에서 알맞은 단어를 골라 어법에 맞게 완성하세요.*

[보기]

charity relationship donation heritage similarity specifically

1 There are additional ways to raise money for our ______________ concert.
우리의 자선 음악회를 위한 자금을 모을 특별한 방법이 있다.

2 A decision was finally made regarding organ ______________.
마침내 장기 기증에 관한 결정이 이루어졌다.

3 The man criticized her more ______________ for her unethical behavior.
그 남자는 그녀의 비윤리적인 행동에 대해 더욱 구체적으로 비판했다.

4 I have a very close ______________ with my neighbors.
나는 이웃 사람들과 매우 친밀한 관계를 유지하고 있다.

5 There are some ______________ between the two.
그 둘 사이에는 몇 가지 유사점이 있다.

6 The government cares little about preserving this artistic ______________.
정부는 이 예술적 유물을 보전하는 것에 거의 신경을 쓰지 않는다.

14D Fill in the Blanks *빈칸에 공통으로 들어갈 단어를 문장에 맞게 고쳐 쓰세요.*

1
- Recently I have lost c_______________ with some of my friends.
  최근 나는 몇몇 친구들과의 연락이 끊어졌다.
- These days we can c_______________ people anytime, anywhere.
  요즘 우리는 언제 어디서든 사람들과 연락을 할 수 있다.

2
- He has c_______________ no crime and poses no danger to children.
  그는 어떠한 범행도 한 적이 없으며 아이들에게 위험하지 않다.
- She c_______________ herself to protecting the endangered animals.
  그녀는 멸종 위기에 처한 동물들을 보호하기 위해 자신을 헌신했다.

3
- Campus life is lively and i_______________ with lots of social activities.
  대학 생활에는 사교적인 활동이 많으며 활기차고 비격식적이다.
- After the meeting, an i_______________ discussion will be held.
  회의가 끝난 후 비공식 토의가 열릴 것이다.

4
- Your writing has shown a s_______________ improvement.
  당신의 작문 실력은 커다란 향상을 보이고 있다.
- This is considered to be one of his s_______________ works.
  이것은 그의 중요한 작품들 중에 하나라고 여겨진다.

14E Choose Synonyms *문장의 밑줄 친 부분과 가장 유사한 뜻의 단어를 고르세요.*

1 This study revealed the <u>connections</u> between aging and memory loss.
이 연구는 노화와 기억 상실의 관련성을 밝혀냈다.
① relationship ② exception ③ instruction ④ conclusion

2 The city is going to focus on the <u>progress</u> and improvements it has made.
그 도시는 그간 이루어온 발전과 개선에 중점을 둘 것이다.
① experiment ② compliment ③ development ④ amusement

3 They <u>refused</u> to participate in health improvement programs.
그들은 건강 증진 프로그램에 참가하는 것을 거부했다.
① hoped ② rejected ③ reflected ④ confused

4 There are too many <u>complex</u> sentences in this book.
이 책에는 복잡한 문장이 너무나 많이 쓰여 있다.
① complicated ② awful ③ cruel ④ necessary

14F Reading Passage 공부한 단어가 포함된 글을 잘 읽고 다음 문제를 풀어 보세요.

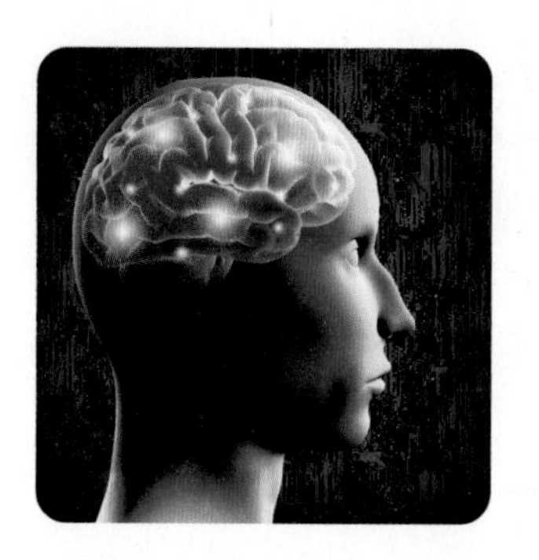

Bill Harbaugh and his team at the University of Oregon looked **specifically** at the **connection** between the brain and economic decisions. In one of their experiments to **reveal** the seemingly **complex relationship**, the researchers tried seeing if people's **donations** to **charity** were **affected** by neurons. Nineteen women were given $100 to play a charity game on the computer. ⓐ They could choose to donate or not to a charity and each decision led to other situations where they could gain or lose money. At the end of the game, the subjects were able to keep all the money that was left in ⓑ their accounts.

As the subjects played the game, the scientists scanned their brains. ⓒ They looked at the brain's "pleasure center," which controls how good people feel. When most subjects donated money to a charity, ⓓ their pleasure centers lit up on the brain scan. Some even lit up when ⓔ they were taxed on their donations. Both results suggest that the brain's pleasure center is **rewarded** for **unselfish** acts. In addition, the more people donated, the more their pleasure centers lit up. For some, the pleasure center lit up more when the computer gave the charity extra money than when they received extra money to keep for themselves. The scientists point out that this was the first neural **evidence** for pure altruism, meaning that altruism may indeed have a(n) ______________ connection.

* neuron 신경 세포 altruism 이타주의

1 위 글의 주제로 가장 적절한 것은?

① various ways to improve brain memory
② the impact of selfishness on one's health
③ the relationship between altruism and biology
④ the bad effects of playing a game on the computer
⑤ the importance of behaving according to the situation

2 위 글의 빈칸에 들어갈 말로 가장 적절한 것은?

① local
② illegal
③ biological
④ economic
⑤ controlling

English Only

3 Which one refers to something different from the rest among ⓐ~ⓔ?

① ⓐ ② ⓑ ③ ⓒ ④ ⓓ ⑤ ⓔ

서술형

4 According to the passage, what does pure altruism mean?

Pure altruism means that people __________ __________ when they __________ something to others for no specific reason.

Lesson 15

Word 500 281~300
Reading 25 15

SUMMA CUM LAUDE

15A Word List

중학교 3학년 필수단어를 예문과 함께 공부하세요.

281 **concentrate** [kάnsəntrèit]
동 모으다; 집중하다 명 concentration 집중
It's hard to **concentrate** in class recently.
최근 수업 시간에 집중하는 것이 어렵다.

282 **consist** [kənsíst]
동 이루어져 있다 참고 be made up of ~로 이루어져 있다
A high jump **consists** of three phases: approach, take-off, and flight.
높이뛰기는 세 가지 부문으로 이루어져 있다: 접근, 도약, 그리고 날기이다.

283 **degree** [digríː]
명 온도, 정도; 학위 유 grade 등급, 정도
Global temperatures warmed roughly 1 **degree** during the last 100 years.
지난 100년간 지구 온도가 약 1도 상승했다.

284 **dispute** [dispjúːt]
동 논쟁하다, 다투다 명 논쟁, 싸움
Their physical appearance has always been a matter of **dispute**.
그들의 외모는 항상 논쟁거리였다.

285 **earthquake** [ə́ːrθkwèik]
명 지진 참고 quake 흔들림, 지진
The city might be destroyed by a fire or by **earthquake**.
그 도시는 화재나 지진으로 파괴되었을 것이다.

286 **experiment** [ikspérəmənt]
동 실험하다, 시험 삼아 해 보다 명 실험
He burned his arm while **experimenting** with chemicals.
그는 화학약품으로 실험을 하다가 팔을 데었다.

287 **extend** [iksténd]
동 연장하다, 확장하다 명 extension 연장
Why don't you **extend** the due date of return?
반납 기한을 연장하는 게 어떤가요?

288 **forecast** [fɔ́ːrkæ̀st]
명 예측, 예보 동 예측하다, 예보하다
Here is your weather **forecast** for this week.
이번 주 일기예보입니다.

289 **harmony** [hάːrməni]
명 조화, 화음 참고 sympathy 공감
The color green means **harmony** and freshness.
초록색은 조화와 신선함을 의미한다.

290 **horizon** [həráizən]

명 **수평선, 지평선; (지식 등의) 범위, 시야(주로 복수형)**

The moon moved toward the **horizon**, out to sea.
달은 바다 쪽으로 수평선을 향해 움직였다.

291 **indicate** [índikèit]

동 **나타내다, 보여주다** 명 indication 표시, 암시

Russians wear a ring on the right hand to **indicate** they have a partner.
러시아 사람들은 배우자가 있음을 나타내기 위해 오른손에 반지를 낀다.

292 **landscape** [lǽndskèip]

명 **풍경, 조망; 풍경화** 유 view 전망

The names of some cities reflect the natural features of the **landscape**.
몇몇 도시의 이름은 그 지역 풍경의 특성을 반영한다.

293 **material** [mətíəriəl]

명 **재료, 물질** 형 **물질의**

Artists use metal, paint, and other **materials**.
예술가들은 금속, 페인트, 그리고 다른 재료들을 사용한다.

294 **route** [ruːt]

명 **길, 도로; 노선; 항로**

There are hundreds of pirate attacks on shipping **routes**.
해상 수송로에서 해적의 습격이 수백 건 있다.

295 **sunset** [sʌ́nsèt]

명 **일몰, 해질녘, 저녁노을** 반 sunrise 일출

I will make sure to go and see the **sunset** on the beach.
나는 꼭 그 해변의 일몰을 보러 갈 것이다.

296 **technology** [teknάlədʒi]

명 **기술** 형 technological 기술적인

Computer **technology** is becoming more widely used at home.
컴퓨터 기술은 가정에서 더욱 많이 사용되기 시작했다.

297 **temporary** [témpərèri]

형 **일시적인, 임시의** 반 permanent 영구적인, 오래가는

At first, any hearing loss is **temporary**.
처음에는 어떤 청력 손상이든 일시적이다.

298 **viewpoint** [vjúːpɔ̀int]

명 **관점, 견해** 유 perspective 전망, 시각

I see things a little differently, so I have a different **viewpoint**.
나는 사물을 약간 다르게 보기 때문에 다른 관점을 갖고 있다.

299 **a series of**

일련의(하나로 이어지는), 계속되는

Spiders use **a** complex **series of** signals for mating.
거미들은 짝짓기를 위해 일련의 복잡한 신호를 사용한다.

300 **make sense**

타당하다, 말이 되다, 의미가 통하다

His story doesn't **make sense**, so I think it's a lie.
그의 이야기는 말이 안 되는 것으로 보아 거짓말인 것 같다.

15B Complete the Phrases *빈칸에 알맞은 말을 넣어 어구를 완성하세요.*

1 to get a ______________ job (임시직을 구하다)

2 to ______________ one's visa (비자 유효기간을 연장하다)

3 the effects of the ______________ (지진의 영향)

4 a new ______________ in education (교육에 있어 새로운 실험)

5 flooring ______________ such as wood (나무와 같은 바닥재)

6 the ______________ between the two countries (두 나라 사이의 분쟁)

7 a certificate of an academic ______________ (학위 증서)

8 a ______________ in oil (유화로 그린 풍경화)

15C Complete the Sentences *[보기]에서 알맞은 단어를 골라 어법에 맞게 완성하세요.*

[보기]

dispute earthquake experiment forecast harmony landscape route

1 There was an ______________ in my hometown yesterday, so I'm worried.
어제 나의 고향 마을에 지진이 발생해서 걱정스럽다.

2 He has repeated the ______________ and gotten the same result.
그는 그 실험을 되풀이했고 같은 결과를 얻었다.

3 The suggestion sounds brilliant, but they're open to ______________.
그 제안은 훌륭한 생각이지만 논쟁의 여지가 많다.

4 The artist thinks that gardens are important in the British ______________.
그 화가는 정원이 영국의 풍경에 있어 중요한 부분이라고 생각한다.

5 In order to live in ______________, we should respect other cultures.
조화를 이루고 살려면 다른 문화를 존중해야 한다.

6 The weather ______________ says it's very likely to rain in the evening.
일기 예보에서 저녁에 비가 올 가능성이 높다고 한다.

7 The sailors knew that this ______________ was a risky one.
그 선원들은 이 항로가 위험하다는 것을 알고 있었다.

15D Fill in the Blanks 빈칸에 공통으로 들어갈 단어를 문장에 맞게 고쳐 쓰세요.

1 • The drummer bent his head as he tried to c______________ on his performance.
드럼 연주자는 연주에 집중하려 하며 머리를 숙였다.

• It's difficult for me to c______________ when I listen to classical music.
나는 고전 음악을 들을 때 집중하기 힘들다.

2 • Their logos c______________ of circles in blue, white, and black.
그들의 로고는 청색, 흰색, 흑색의 원으로 이루어져 있다.

• The clubs c______________ of students who are interested in physics.
그 동아리들은 물리에 관심이 있는 학생들로 이루어져 있다.

3 • We saw the sun sink below the h______________.
우리는 해가 수평선으로 지는 것을 보았다.

• As she becomes an adult she is expanding her h______________.
그녀는 성인이 되면서 시야를 넓히고 있다.

4 • Modern t______________ is replacing traditional ways of life.
현대 기술은 전통적인 생활 방식을 대체하고 있다.

• Your homes have changed a lot due to t______________.
여러분의 집은 기술로 인해 많이 변해왔다.

15E Choose Synonyms 문장의 밑줄 친 부분과 가장 유사한 뜻의 단어를 고르세요.

1 Write your opinion on extending break time.
쉬는 시간을 늘리는 것에 대한 자신의 의견을 쓰시오.

① shortening ② lengthening ③ replacing ④ starting

2 Can you guess what the different colors on this map indicate?
이 지도상의 다양한 색이 나타내는 것이 무엇인지 추측할 수 있는가?

① originate ② form ③ hide ④ mean

3 All the materials were recycled after each project ended.
각각의 프로젝트가 끝나면 모든 재료들은 재활용되었다.

① components ② ideas ③ slides ④ money

4 These temporary changes can have a great influence on your life.
이런 일시적인 변화들이 인생에 큰 영향을 끼칠 수 있다.

① permanent ② spiritual ③ habitual ④ short-term

15F Reading Passage 공부한 단어가 포함된 글을 잘 읽고 다음 문제를 풀어 보세요.

There is a theory that our sun is a part of a Binary Solar system that **consists** of two suns and their planets. If we had two suns, the **landscape** would be very different and we would see a **sunset** twice a day! Well, our solar system actually orbits around this other solar system, so we can see only ⓐ one sun that rises on the **horizon**. The orbit, or the **route** that the other solar system moves is ⓑ bound to our own solar system and they meet each other every 25,920 years. So we can ⓒ **forecast** the next "encounter" with the second sun. Our **technology** can prove whether our sun has a ⓓ companion. Through **a series of experiments**, NASA has gathered evidence of the other sun, but it hasn't been ⓔ concealed because of the **disputes** it could create. The other sun is really far and from our **viewpoint**, it's only a small brown star. To a certain **degree**, it makes sense. It is known that about 80% of the stars in the galaxy are binary stars, and they are all in a perfect **harmony**.

* binary 둘의 orbit 궤도를 돌다

1 위 글의 제목으로 가장 적절한 것은?

① Will Our Sun Explode Someday?
② Do We Really Have Two Suns?
③ NASA: Causes of Disputes
④ What Is a System with Two Suns like?
⑤ Worshipping the Sun: A Common Religion

2 위 글의 밑줄 친 부분 중, 문맥상 낱말의 쓰임이 적절하지 않은 것은?

① ⓐ ② ⓑ ③ ⓒ ④ ⓓ ⑤ ⓔ

English Only

3 What's the writer's attitude toward the theory that argues that there are two Suns?

① approving
② skeptic
③ critical
④ indifferent
⑤ analytic

서술형

4 Complete the answer with words from the passage.

Why does NASA hide the evidence of the two sun theory?
→ They are afraid of the __________ it could __________.

Speedy Check-up 3

Lesson별로 모르는 단어에 체크한 후, 그 갯수를 /20 안에 쓰고 학습성과를 점검해 보세요.
모르는 단어는 다시 찾아 학습하세요.

Lesson 11 /20

- ☐ affordable
- ☐ aptitude
- ☐ combine
- ☐ digital
- ☐ ensure
- ☐ glue
- ☐ intelligent
- ☐ logical
- ☐ passport
- ☐ permit
- ☐ predict
- ☐ recognize
- ☐ reject
- ☐ rule
- ☐ security
- ☐ sheet
- ☐ surf
- ☐ useless
- ☐ vital
- ☐ turn out

Lesson 12 /20

- ☐ advantage
- ☐ amusement
- ☐ celebration
- ☐ charm
- ☐ consult
- ☐ crawl
- ☐ determine
- ☐ endanger
- ☐ exposure
- ☐ hibernate
- ☐ ideal
- ☐ legend
- ☐ otherwise
- ☐ principal
- ☐ recipe
- ☐ resemble
- ☐ rob
- ☐ shadow
- ☐ translate
- ☐ just around the corner

Lesson 13 /20

- ☐ acid
- ☐ backbone
- ☐ bubble
- ☐ clone
- ☐ damage
- ☐ destination
- ☐ disabled
- ☐ dissolve
- ☐ emotion
- ☐ lifelong
- ☐ liquid
- ☐ lump
- ☐ necessary
- ☐ nutrient
- ☐ organ
- ☐ react
- ☐ refresh
- ☐ stomach
- ☐ swallow
- ☐ break down

Lesson 14 /20

- ☐ affect
- ☐ charity
- ☐ commit
- ☐ complex
- ☐ connection
- ☐ contact
- ☐ donation
- ☐ evidence
- ☐ harmful
- ☐ heritage
- ☐ informal
- ☐ progress
- ☐ refuse
- ☐ relationship
- ☐ reveal
- ☐ reward
- ☐ significant
- ☐ similarity
- ☐ specifically
- ☐ unselfish

Lesson 15 /20

- ☐ concentrate
- ☐ consist
- ☐ degree
- ☐ dispute
- ☐ earthquake
- ☐ experiment
- ☐ extend
- ☐ forecast
- ☐ harmony
- ☐ horizon
- ☐ indicate
- ☐ landscape
- ☐ material
- ☐ route
- ☐ sunset
- ☐ technology
- ☐ temporary
- ☐ viewpoint
- ☐ a series of
- ☐ make sense

A Royal Guard at Buckingham Palace

Chapter 4

Lesson 16

Word 500 301~320
Reading 25 16

SUMMA CUM LAUDE

16A Word List

중학교 3학년 필수단어를 예문과 함께 공부하세요.

301 **awful** [ɔ́:fəl]

형 끔찍한, 지독한 부 awfully 끔찍하게

Our dog got sprayed by a skunk, and he smelled **awful**.
우리 개는 스컹크의 분비물을 맞아서 지독한 냄새가 났다.

302 **bark** [bɑːrk]

동 (짐승이) 짖다, 소리를 지르다 명 짖는 소리

Whenever the dog sees a stranger, it **barks** loudly.
그 개는 낯선 사람을 볼 때마다 큰 소리로 짖는다.

303 **blame** [bleim]

동 비난하다 명 비난 유 criticize 비판(비난)하다

Land art is often **blamed** for destroying nature.
랜드 아트는 자연을 훼손하는 것 때문에 자주 비난받는다.

304 **cruel** [krúːəl]

형 잔인한 명 cruelty 잔인함

Western dragons are described as mean and **cruel**.
서양의 용들은 심술궂고 잔인하게 묘사된다.

305 **increase** [inkríːs]

동 증가하다 명 증가 반 decrease 감소하다; 감소

A restaurant owner came up with ideas to **increase** sales.
음식점 주인은 매출을 높이기 위한 방안을 생각해 냈다.

306 **infection** [infékʃən]

명 감염, 전염병 참고 poison 독, 독물

Doctors found no evidence of **infection**.
의사들은 감염의 증거를 찾지 못했다.

307 **invasion** [invéiʒən]

명 침입, 침략, 침해 동 invade 침략하다

Europeans suffered from the Viking's **invasions**.
유럽인들은 바이킹의 침략으로 고생했었다.

308 **mammal** [mǽməl]

명 포유동물

A large number of birds, **mammals**, and fish live in wetlands.
습지에는 많은 수의 새, 포유동물, 물고기가 산다.

309 **mankind** [mæ̀nkáind]

명 인류, 인간 유 the human race 인류

Diversity is important both in **mankind** as well as other animals.
다양성은 다른 동물만큼이나 인간에게도 중요하다.

310 **palm** [pɑːm]

㊐ 손바닥, 야자과 나무 [참고] sole 발바닥

She showed the fortune-teller her **palm**.
그녀는 점성술사에게 손바닥을 보여주었다.

311 **physical** [fízikəl]

㊒ 육체의, 물질의; 실질의 [참고] mental 정신의

I have studied issues relating to **physical** and mental health.
나는 신체적, 정신적 건강과 관련된 것들을 연구해 왔다.

312 **smooth** [smuːð]

㊒ 매끄러운 ㊍ 매끄럽게 하다

She hopes to make their transition to a new country **smooth**.
그녀는 새로운 국가로의 이주가 매끄럽게 되기를 희망했다.

313 **spread** [spred]

㊍ 펼치다, 퍼뜨리다 ㊐ 확산, 전파 spread-spread-spread

The reporter **spread** false information.
그 기자는 잘못된 정보를 퍼뜨렸다.

314 **suffer** [sʌ́fər]

㊍ 겪다, 고통받다 [참고] suffer from ~로 인해 고생하다, 고통 받다

It has **suffered** huge losses in recent years.
그것은 최근 몇 년 동안 심한 손실을 겪어 왔다.

Many amusement parks **suffer from** declining visitors.
다수의 놀이공원들은 관람객이 줄어들어서 고통을 겪는다.

315 **threaten** [θrétn]

㊍ 위협하다 [명] threat 위협

Angry customers **threatened** not to shop at the store.
성난 소비자들은 그 가게에서 물건을 사지 않겠다고 위협했다.

316 **wander** [wɑ́ndər]

㊍ (천천히) 돌아다니다, 헤매다, 길을 벗어나다

There were a lot of students **wandering** around the park.
그 공원에는 돌아다니는 학생들이 많았다.

317 **wildlife** [wàildláif]

㊐ 야생 동물(주로 포유류, 조류, 어류)

Plans to protect **wildlife** are in fact plans to protect man.
야생 동물을 보호하는 계획은 사실 인간을 보호하는 계획이다.

318 **yawn** [jɔːn]

㊍ 하품하다, 크게 벌어지다 ㊐ 하품

The monkey was opening his mouth as if he was **yawning**.
그 원숭이는 하품하듯이 입을 벌렸다.

319 **to death**

죽을 만큼, 죽도록, 극도로

I've watched the movie twice, so I was bored **to death**.
나는 그 영화를 이미 두 번 봤기 때문에 극도로 지루했다.

320 **be susceptible to**

~에 민감한, 감염되기 쉬운 [유] be sensitive to ~에 민감한

Cotton **is** more **susceptible to** frost damage than other plants.
목화는 다른 작물보다 서리 피해에 민감하다.

16B Complete the Phrases *빈칸에 알맞은 말을 넣어 어구를 완성하세요.*

1 to ______________ from the flu (독감으로 고생하다)

2 to ____________________ disease (질병에 감염되기 쉽다)

3 ______________ habitats in the area (그 지역의 야생동물 서식지)

4 the year of the Viking ______________ (바이킹 침략의 해)

5 to reply with a ______________ (하품을 하며 대답하다)

6 love for all ______________ (모든 인류에 대한 사랑)

7 a(n) ______________ snowstorm (지독한 눈보라)

8 to ______________ for the result (결과에 대해 비난하다)

16C Complete the Sentences *[보기]에서 알맞은 단어를 골라 어법에 맞게 완성하세요.*

[보기]

cruel invasion spread threaten wander wildlife yawn

1 The disease ______________ out of control.
그 병은 통제불능 상태로 퍼졌다.

2 Men wear colorful clothes to ______________ their enemies.
사람들은 적군을 위협하기 위해 화려한 옷을 착용한다.

3 Spam messages and advertisement calls are a(n) ______________ of privacy.
스팸 메시지와 광고 전화는 사생활 침해이다.

4 My mind continued to ______________, until I fell asleep.
잠들기 전까지 나의 마음은 여러 생각으로 방황했다.

5 Fish ______________, cough, and even burp just like humans.
물고기도 사람들처럼 하품하고, 기침하고, 심지어는 트림을 한다.

6 Many people work together to save rainforests and their ______________.
많은 사람들이 열대우림과 야생동물을 지키기 위해 함께 일한다.

7 When his wife died, Bill was heartbroken over this ______________ fate.
그의 아내가 죽었을 때, Bill은 잔인한 운명에 가슴이 찢어지는 아픔을 느꼈다.

16D Fill in the Blanks 빈칸에 공통으로 들어갈 단어를 문장에 맞게 고쳐 쓰세요.

1 • Sea m_______________ such as dolphins and seals are sociable.
돌고래나 바다표범과 같은 바다 포유동물들은 사교성을 갖고 있다.
• The front legs show how whales are connected with land m____________.
한 쌍의 앞다리는 고래가 육상 포유동물들과 어떠한 관련이 있는지 보여준다.

2 • People often b_______________ others for their own mistakes.
사람들은 자신의 실수에 대해 자주 다른 사람들을 비난한다.
• I b_______________ this year's poor harvest on the weather.
나는 올해의 수확량이 형편없는 것에 대해 날씨를 탓한다.

3 • I was worried to d_______________ when my sister didn't answer the phone all day.
내 여동생이 하루 종일 전화를 받지 않아서 몹시 걱정이 되었다.
• I was scared to d_______________ as soon as I got on the ride.
나는 놀이기구에 타자마자 엄청난 두려움을 느꼈다.

4 • An i_______________ in the number means the energy has doubled.
그 숫자가 증가하는 것은 에너지가 두 배가 된 것을 의미한다.
• The i_______________ in the number of species leads to diversity.
종의 수가 증가하는 것은 다양성을 초래한다.

16E Choose Synonyms 문장의 밑줄 친 부분과 가장 유사한 뜻의 단어를 고르세요.

1 Since the actors were awful, I was disappointed with the musical.
배우들이 엉망이어서 그 뮤지컬에 실망했다.
① new ② creative ③ competent ④ terrible

2 As an instructor barked orders, the boys marched.
한 교관이 큰 소리로 명령을 내리자 소년들이 행진했다.
① protected ② showed ③ shouted ④ withdrew

3 Farmers are struggling to cope with an invasion of grasshoppers.
농부들은 메뚜기의 습격에 대처하느라 고생하고 있다.
① war ② usage ③ failure ④ attack

4 You should be in shape because you have to do demanding physical work.
육체 노동이 필요한 일을 해야 하므로 몸을 균형잡힌 상태로 유지해야 한다.
① mental ② bodily ③ skillful ④ psychological

16F Reading Passage 공부한 단어가 포함된 글을 잘 읽고 다음 문제를 풀어 보세요.

Marmots are members of the squirrel family, and they are about the size of a cat. Having large, round eyes and a small mouth and nose, they look cute and ⓐ innocent. But they can be an **awful** enemy of **mankind**. A kind of marmot found on the Mongolian grasslands **is** genetically ⓑ **susceptible to** a lung **infection** caused by the Yersinia pestis, commonly known as bubonic plague. The disease **threatens** humans and makes them cough **to death**. In **wildlife**, marmots ⓒ treat it around by coughing on their neighbors, infecting fleas, rats, and humans. The bacteria are then ⓓ transferred to the other creatures. The sick marmots **wander** the area, infecting others. The "marmot invasions" are ⓔ blamed for all the great plagues that swept through Eastern Asia to Europe. When marmots and humans **suffer** from the plague, they have a high fever and the lymph glands **increase** in size and become black. Mongolians enjoy marmot meat, but they will never eat a marmot's armpits because "they contain the soul of a dead hunter."

* bubonic plague 림프절 흑사병 armpit 겨드랑이

1 위 글의 요지로 가장 적절한 것은?

① 마멋에 대한 태도는 문화마다 다르다.
② 마멋의 서식지는 주의해서 관찰해야 한다.
③ 마멋이 옮기는 질병을 예방할 필요가 있다.
④ 마멋은 질병으로 인해 멸종 위기에 빠져 있다.
⑤ 마멋은 전염성 질병을 옮기므로 위험할 수 있다.

2 위 글의 밑줄 친 부분 중, 문맥상 낱말의 쓰임이 적절하지 않은 것은?

① ⓐ ② ⓑ ③ ⓒ ④ ⓓ ⑤ ⓔ

English Only

3 Which is NOT true about the marmot?

① One kind of marmot lives in the Mongolian grasslands.
② When the marmot suffers from bubonic plague, it coughs.
③ The marmot's disease can threaten humans.
④ The sick marmot's glands will swell.
⑤ Mongolians love to eat the meat from the armpits of marmots.

서술형

4 Fill in the blanks to complete the answer.

How can the great plagues that swept through Eastern Asia to Europe be explained?
→ The marmot __________, which is the bubonic plague that marmots __________ is responsible for the disaster.

Lesson 17

SUMMA CUM LAUDE

Word 500 321~340
Reading 25 17

17A Word List

중학교 3학년 필수단어를 예문과 함께 공부하세요.

321 **accurate** [ǽkjurət]
형 정확한, 정밀한, 오차가 없는 명 accuracy 정확성
Most scenes in sci-fi movies are not very **accurate**.
공상 과학 영화에서 대부분의 장면들이 아주 정밀하지는 않다.

322 **appreciate** [əpríːʃièit]
동 진가를 알아보다, 인식하다; 고마워하다 명 appreciation 평가, 감상
I will teach you how to **appreciate** these works of art.
이 예술 작품들을 어떻게 감상할지에 대해 가르쳐 주겠습니다.

323 **athlete** [ǽθliːt]
명 운동선수, 건장한 사람 형 athletic 운동의
The **athlete** is called a "human bullet."
그 운동선수는 "인간 탄환"으로 불린다.

324 **breeze** [briːz]
명 산들바람, 쉬운 일 동 산들바람이 불다
The warmth of the air was moved by the **breeze**.
산들바람 때문에 공기의 온기가 이동했다.

325 **compare** [kəmpɛ́ər]
동 비교하다, 비유하다 명 comparison 비교, 대조
Comparing and contrasting helps you recognize differences.
비교와 대조는 차이점을 인식하는 것에 도움이 된다.

326 **complicated** [kάmpləkèitid]
형 복잡한 명 complication 복잡함
I just can't stand all these **complicated** calculations.
나는 이 모든 복잡한 계산을 견딜 수 없을 뿐이다.

327 **contribute** [kəntríbjuːt]
동 기여하다, 기부하다; (~의) 원인이 되다 명 contribution 기여, 공헌
Movies have **contributed** to the development of science.
영화는 과학의 발전에 기여해 왔다.

328 **defeat** [difíːt]
동 이기다, 무산[좌절]시키다 명 패배
Harry's team **defeated** us and became the new champion.
Harry의 팀이 우리를 이기고 새로운 챔피언이 되었다.

329 **divide** [diváid]
동 나누다 명 division 분할
Our brain is **divided** into two parts.
우리의 뇌는 두 부분으로 나뉜다.

330 **judge**
[dʒʌ́dʒ]

명 재판관, 판사, 심판 동 ~에게 판결을 내리다.

When the **judge** came in, all the people stood up.
재판관이 들어오자 모든 사람들이 일어섰다.

331 **knowledge**
[nálidʒ]

명 지식, 인식, 견문, 정보 형 knowledgeable 지식이 있는

Our **knowledge** can't clearly explain the origin of the universe.
우리의 지식으로는 우주의 기원에 대해 명확하게 설명할 수 없다.

332 **obey**
[oubéi]

동 복종〔순종〕하다; (법 등을) 지키다 명 obedience 복종
반 defy 반항〔저항〕하다

The pets may be so nervous that they'll not **obey** their owners.
그 애완동물들은 너무 신경질적이어서 주인들에게 복종하지 않을 것이다.

333 **performance**
[pərfɔ́ːrməns]

명 실행; 성과; 공연 동 perform 실행하다; 공연하다

What is the most impressive **performance** you've ever seen?
여태까지 본 공연 중 가장 인상적인 것이 무엇인가?

334 **pitcher**
[pítʃər]

명 투수; 주전자 동 pitch (힘껏) 내던지다

He is the best **pitcher** ever in the history of baseball.
그는 야구 역사상 가장 뛰어난 투수이다.
Mom brought us a **pitcher** of orange juice.
엄마는 우리에게 오렌지 주스 한 통을 가져다주었다.

335 **recreation**
[rèkriéiʃən]

명 휴양, 오락 유 leisure 여가

These areas are used for **recreation** such as hiking or biking.
이 곳은 휴양 지역으로, 걷거나 자전거를 탈 수 있다.

336 **scout**
[skaut]

동 정찰하다; 스카우트〔발굴〕하다 명 스카우트 (조직), 정찰병

We **scouted** for a place to park.
우리는 주차할 곳을 찾아다녔다.

337 **sore**
[sɔːr]

형 아픈, 슬픈 유 painful 고통스러운

My feet were **sore** and my head ached.
나는 발이 아프고 두통이 있었다.

338 **statistics**
[stətístiks]

명 통계(표), 통계 자료(복수 취급); 통계학(단수 취급)

Statistics show that the number of births increased.
통계는 출생자 수가 증가한 것을 보여준다.

339 **keep track of**

~에 대해 파악하고 있다 반 lose track of

You should **keep track of** where you spend money.
항상 돈을 어디에 쓰는지에 대해 알고 있어야 한다.

340 **on the basis of**

~을 기반으로, ~에 근거하여

The members are selected **on the basis of** their qualities.
회원들은 능력에 근거하여 선발되었다.

17B Complete the Phrases 빈칸에 알맞은 말을 넣어 어구를 완성하세요.

1 ________________(e)d with the previous year (작년과 비교하여)

2 to ________________ expenses (비용을 계속 파악하다)

3 to consult the ________________ (심판관에게 충고를 구하다)

4 to be generally ________________ (대개 정확하다)

5 to ________________ the class into five groups (학급을 다섯 집단으로 나누다)

6 to remove a(n) ________________ from the game (경기에서 투수를 교체하다)

7 a natural ________________ who runs very fast (달리기가 무척 빠른 타고난 운동선수)

8 to develop a(n) ________________ system (복잡한 시스템을 개발하다)

17C Complete the Sentences [보기]에서 알맞은 단어를 골라 어법에 맞게 완성하세요.

[보기]

accurate athlete compare contribute divide pitcher scout

1 The police found that the cameras could ________________ to lower crime rates.
경찰은 카메라가 범죄율을 낮추는 데 기여할 수 있다는 것을 발견했다.

2 ________________ from around the world will be competing at the Olympics.
전 세계의 선수들이 올림픽에 참가하여 경쟁할 것이다.

3 The waiter ________________ the pie into eight pieces for the guests.
종업원은 손님들을 위해 파이를 8조각으로 나누었다.

4 There are a lot of diet and exercise tips but they are not always ________________.
다이어트와 운동에 관한 도움말이 많이 있지만 항상 정확한 것은 아니다.

5 They sent Ben to ________________ the trails ahead of them.
그들은 앞에 놓인 길을 정찰하기 위해 Ben을 보냈다.

6 The birth rate in Korea is not high ________________ to many countries.
많은 나라와 비교했을 때 한국의 출산률은 높지 않다.

7 Fans chanted the name of the other team's ________________ out of respect.
팬들은 존경심을 느끼며 상대 팀의 투수 이름을 반복하여 외쳤다.

17D Fill in the Blanks 빈칸에 공통으로 들어갈 단어를 문장에 맞게 고쳐 쓰세요.

1 • The weather will be pleasant with a little bit of a b________________ in the morning.
오늘의 날씨는 쾌적하겠고 아침에는 약간의 미풍이 불겠습니다.
• The exam was a b________________, so I passed it easily.
시험이 쉬워서 쉽게 통과했다.

2 • I tried skating, but I was left with nothing but a s________________ bottom.
나는 스케이트를 타 보려 노력했지만 엉덩이만 아팠을 뿐이다.
• My throat is s________________ and I have a fever.
나는 목이 아프고 열이 난다.

3 • The actor's talents are not a________________.
그 배우의 재능이 진가를 인정받지 못하고 있다.
• Your sincere support is greatly a________________.
당신의 진심어린 지지에 정말 감사합니다.

4 • During the approach, the a________________ runs toward the bar at a high speed.
도움닫기 하는 동안, 선수는 가로대를 향해 빠른 속도로 달린다.
• The a________________ wanted to run for his country.
그 선수는 자신의 국가를 위해 뛰고 싶어 했다.

17E Choose Synonyms 문장의 밑줄 친 부분과 가장 유사한 뜻의 단어를 고르세요.

1 These complicated problems are far beyond our ability to deal with.
이런 복잡한 문제들은 우리가 처리할 수 있는 범위를 훨씬 더 벗어나 있다.
① significant ② complex ③ repeated ④ changing

2 Statistics show that the population of the country is declining.
통계는 그 나라의 인구가 줄어들고 있음을 보여준다.
① a math test ② news broadcast ③ surveyed figures ④ an academic subject

3 The young tennis player defeated the champion in three sets.
그 어린 테니스 선수는 세 세트 만에 챔피언을 이겼다.
① beat ② called ③ competed ④ recognized

4 The novel is historically accurate.
그 소설은 역사적인 사실과 일치한다.
① anxious ② brilliant ③ correct ④ generous

17F Reading Passage

공부한 단어가 포함된 글을 잘 읽고 다음 문제를 풀어 보세요.

Statistics are very important to baseball, perhaps more than any other sport. Since the game of baseball has a very (A) [structured / unexpected] flow to it, it's easy to predict the results of games. Experts say that an **accurate** calculation of probabilities is possible. You may feel it's (B) [simple / complicated], but once you learn to use the **knowledge**, it is a **breeze** to **keep track of** the statistics. Traditionally, statistics like batting average for batters (the number of hits **divided** by the number of at bats) and earned run average (the number of runs given up by a **pitcher** per nine innings) are considered important.

These statistics are designed to be a better (C) [compliment / evaluation] of a player's field **performance**. Team managers and coaches **appreciate** how each player **contributed** to his team **on the basis of** the statistics. Baseball scouts study player statistics in order to **compare** the players that have different abilities. Statistics are used to set a strategy to **defeat** the rival teams. For example, managers often use statistics to base their decisions during the game, such as choosing who to put in the lineup, or which relief pitcher to bring in.

1 위 글의 빈칸 (A), (B), (C)에 들어갈 말로 가장 적절한 것은?

	(A)	(B)	(C)
①	structured	– simple	– compliment
②	unexpected	– simple	– compliment
③	structured	– complicated	– compliment
④	unexpected	– complicated	– evaluation
⑤	structured	– complicated	– evaluation

2 위 글의 내용과 일치하지 않는 것은?

① 전문가들은 정확한 확률의 계산이 가능하다고 말한다.
② 선수의 기여도는 통계에 근거해 평가된다.
③ 스카우터들은 선수들의 능력 비교를 위해 통계를 사용한다.
④ 상대 팀을 이기기 위한 전략에 통계가 사용된다.
⑤ 구원 투수는 당일의 몸상태에 따라 결정된다.

English Only

3 According to the passage, what record is considered important?

① earned out average
② relief pitching numbers
③ pitching average per inning
④ batting average for batters
⑤ total throw numbers for pitchers

서술형

4 Complete the answer with words from the passage.

Who uses statistics in the sport of baseball?
→ Team m__________, c__________, and baseball s__________ use them.

Lesson 18

Word 500 341~360
Reading 25 18

SUMMA CUM LAUDE

18A Word List

중학교 3학년 필수단어를 예문과 함께 공부하세요.

341 **achievement** [ətʃíːvmənt]
명 성취, 업적 동 achieve 성취하다, 업적을 달성하다
Harry was always modest about his **achievements**.
Harry는 자신의 업적에 대해 항상 겸손하다.

342 **amount** [əmáunt]
명 양, 총계 동 (양이) ~에 달하다
We want volunteers to give a set **amount** of time every week.
우리는 매주 정해진 시간을 할애할 자원봉사자들이 필요하다.

343 **available** [əvéiləbl]
형 사용 가능한, 구할 수 있는 유 accessible 접근 가능한
Locally produced food is **available** at lower prices.
(근처) 지역에서 생산된 식품은 더 저렴한 가격으로 구할 수 있다.

344 **convert** [kənvə́ːrt]
동 전환하다, 바꾸다 명 conversion 변환, 전환
Special sensory cells **convert** vibrations to electrical signals.
특별한 감각 세포가 진동을 전기 신호로 바꾼다.

345 **decorate** [dékərèit]
동 꾸미다, 장식하다 명 decoration 꾸미기, 장식
The room was **decorated** with flowers and plants.
그 방은 꽃과 식물들로 장식되었다.

346 **flour** [flàuər]
명 밀가루, 고운 가루
If the dough is too moist, add some **flour**.
반죽에 물기가 많다면 밀가루를 좀 넣으시오.

347 **function** [fʌ́ŋkʃən]
명 (사람 · 사물의) 기능, 직무; 함수 동 작용[작동]하다
Function is the most important factor when I choose shoes.
내가 신발을 고를 때에는 기능이 가장 중요한 요소이다.

348 **honor** [ɑ́nər]
명 명예, 존경, 경의 동 존경하다, (약속 등을) 지키다
I'd like to say how much I appreciate this **honor**.
이 영광에 대해 얼마나 감사해 하는지 말씀드리고 싶습니다.

349 **identify** [aidéntəfài]
동 (신원 등을) 확인하다, 알아보다
She **identified** the dog as her lost pet.
그녀는 그 개가 자신이 잃어버린 애완견이라는 것을 확인했다.

350 **ingredient** [ingrí:diənt]

명 성분, 재료, 구성요소

Pork is an important **ingredient** in our food.
돼지고기는 우리 음식에 있어서 중요한 재료이다.

351 **mention** [ménʃən]

동 말하다, 언급하다 명 언급, 진술

I haven't **mentioned** it to William yet.
나는 그것에 관해 아직까지 William에게 말한 적이 없다.

352 **odd** [ɑd]

형 이상한, 특이한; 홀수의

There's something **odd** about his story.
그의 이야기는 어딘가 이상한 데가 있다.

353 **revolution** [rèvəlú:ʃən]

명 혁명, 회전 형 revolutionary 혁명적인

This new theory will cause a **revolution** in education.
이 새로운 이론은 교육에 혁명을 일으킬 것이다.

354 **rinse** [rins]

명 헹구기 동 헹구다 참고 dip 담그다

He washed the dishes and then **rinsed** them thoroughly.
그는 접시를 닦은 후 꼼꼼하게 헹궈냈다.

355 **sew** [sou]

동 꿰매다, 바느질하다 sew-sewed-sewed(sewn)
참고 stitch 바늘의 한 땀; 바느질하다

She designs her own dresses and **sews** in her free time.
그녀는 여가 시간에 자신의 옷을 디자인하고 바느질을 한다.

356 **spectator** [spékteitər]

명 관중, 관찰자 유 audience 청중

Two boxers went to the ring and **spectators** cheered them.
두 명의 권투 선수가 링으로 나왔고 관중들이 그들을 응원했다.

357 **theory** [θíəri]

명 학설, 이론, 의견 참고 belief (옳다고 믿는) 신념

The scientist examined an earlier study to prove his **theory**.
그 과학자는 그의 학설을 입증하기 위해 이전의 연구를 검토했다.

358 **trousers** [tráuzərz]

명 바지 유 pants (주로 미국에서)

I wear short **trousers** when I go running.
나는 조깅을 하러 갈 때 반바지를 입는다.

359 **catch on**

유행하다, 인기를 얻다

The new game really **caught on** and he earned a lot of money.
새로운 게임은 큰 인기를 얻었고 그는 많은 돈을 벌었다.

360 **keep A from -ing**

A가 ~하지 못하게 하다

The noisy neighbors **keep me from sleeping** well every night.
시끄러운 이웃들 때문에 밤마다 푹 잘 수가 없다.

18B Complete the Phrases 빈칸에 알맞은 말을 넣어 어구를 완성하세요.

1 to confirm the ______________ of relativity (상대성 이론을 확인하다)

2 to be held in ______________ (존경받다)

3 to ______________ the file to a different format (파일을 다른 형식으로 변환하다)

4 a court ______________ with a sketchbook (스케치북을 든 재판 방청인)

5 to ______________ pieces together (조각들을 꿰매다)

6 a notable academic ______________ (주목할 만한 학술적 성취)

7 to mix water and ______________ to make dough
(반죽을 만들기 위해 물과 밀가루를 섞다)

8 to ______________ his fingerprints (그의 지문을 확인하다)

18C Complete the Sentences [보기]에서 알맞은 단어를 골라 어법에 맞게 완성하세요.

[보기]

amount decorate flour revolution rinse theory

1 They will ______________ the gate with flowers, fruits, and green leaves.
그들은 정문을 꽃, 과일, 초록색 잎으로 장식할 것이다.

2 The biggest problem is the huge ______________ of energy we use daily.
가장 큰 문제는 우리가 매일 사용하는 어마어마한 양의 에너지이다.

3 Rice ______________ and beans are used to make the cake.
그 케이크를 만드는 데 쌀가루와 콩이 사용된다.

4 One ______________ claims that it was written during the Silla Dynasty.
한 학설에서는 그것이 신라 왕조 때에 쓰여 졌다고 주장한다.

5 ______________ the cups under running water for at least two minutes.
그 컵들을 최소한 2분 동안 흐르는 물에 헹구시오.

6 ______________ means a complete change in the way of doing things.
혁명이란 행동 방식의 완전한 변화를 의미한다.

18D Fill in the Blanks 빈칸에 공통으로 들어갈 단어를 문장에 맞게 고쳐 쓰세요.

1 • Did you m_______________ why the movie is interesting?
그 영화가 흥미로운 이유를 언급했는가?
• He made no m_______________ of her latest work.
그는 그녀의 최근 작품에 대해 언급하지 않았다.

2 • When people eat at o_______________ times, they risk gaining weight.
불규칙적으로 음식을 먹으면 체중이 증가할 위험이 있다.
• One, three, five and seven are o_______________ numbers.
1, 3, 5, 7은 홀수이다.

3 • Some teenagers don't h_______________ the simple rules in schools.
몇몇 십대들은 학교의 기본적인 규칙을 지키지 않는다.
• These firefighters deserve to be treated with h_______________.
이 소방관들은 존경을 받을 자격이 있다.

4 • The architect seeks the balance between beauty and f_______________.
그 건축가는 미와 기능의 균형을 추구한다.
• This f_______________ is important in both mathematics and physics.
이 함수는 수학과 물리학 양쪽 모두에서 중요하다.

18E Choose Synonyms 문장의 밑줄 친 부분과 가장 유사한 뜻의 단어를 고르세요.

1 She was proud of her achievement and donated money to a charity.
그녀는 자신의 업적에 대해 자랑스러워하며 한 자선단체에 돈을 기부했다.
① research ② invention ③ contribution ④ accomplishment

2 The system can ensure that there are enough volunteer workers available.
그 제도는 활용 가능한 자원봉사자를 충분히 확보할 수 있게 한다.
① ordinary ② sufficient ③ accessible ④ competent

3 He kept talking, and it kept me from asking any questions.
그는 계속 말을 했고, 그것은 내가 질문하는 것을 막았다.
① forced me to ask ② made me think of
③ lead to a series of ④ prevented me from asking

4 The first ingredient in conversation is truth, the next good sense, and the third good humor.
대화의 첫 번째 요소는 진실함이고, 다음은 좋은 분별력이며, 세 번째는 좋은 유머 감각이다.
① secret ② challenge ③ success ④ component

18F Reading Passage

공부한 단어가 포함된 글을 잘 읽고 다음 문제를 풀어 보세요.

What we wear **identifies** us. For example, salespeople wear a suit and a tie. Baseball players wear a cap. Then, what about cooks? All kinds of hats are **available**, in **theory**, but they usually wear either ugly hair nets or **odd** white caps with long tops. Can there possibly be a ______________________ for the shape of the chef's caps?

As early as the Romans, master chefs were rewarded for their **achievements** by receiving special headware. For them, laurel-**decorated** caps were the **honor**.

In France up until the seventeenth century, chefs were awarded different colored caps depending on their ranks. During the early eighteenth century, Talleyrand's chef required his entire staff to wear white hats. He **mentioned** in his cookbook that the hat was designed to **keep** the cook's hair **from entering** food while mixing **ingredients**, such as **flour** and butter. But this original cap was flat. The high hat gradually **caught on** because it could provide some ventilation for the head, as chefs frequently work under extremely hot conditions. The large **amount** of heat produced by the cook's head could go up and then out of the hat, cooling the head.

* laurel-decorated 월계수로 장식된 ventilation 환기

1 위 글의 제목으로 가장 적절한 것은?

① Caps: Indicators of Identity
② High Caps: Exhibition of Pride
③ Cap Designs Favored by Chefs
④ The History of the High Chef Cap
⑤ Changes in Colors of Chefs' Caps

2 위 글의 빈칸에 들어갈 말로 가장 적절한 것은?

① clear rule
② rank order
③ logical function
④ decorative idea
⑤ selection standard

English Only

3 According to the passage, which is NOT true?

① Romans gave chefs laurel-decorated caps.
② In France, chef wore different colored caps.
③ Talleyrand's chef believed that white caps were good.
④ Talleyrand's chef asked his staff to wear long caps.
⑤ Long white caps gained popularity among cooks.

서술형

4 Fill in the blanks to complete the sentences. Use words from the passage.

At first, chef hats were ___________, but they later got long tops. The long tops allowed air to move in and ___________ down the cook's head by allowing the ___________ produced during cooking to escape.

Lesson 19

SUMMA CUM LAUDE

Word 500 361~380
Reading 25 19

19A Word List

중학교 3학년 필수단어를 예문과 함께 공부하세요.

361 **attack** [ətǽk]
동 공격하다 명 공격, (증상의 갑작스러운) 도짐(발발)
They believed that devils would **attack** sick people.
그들은 악마가 아픈 사람들을 공격한다고 믿었다.

362 **capable** [kéipəbl]
형 ~할 수 있는(of), 유능한 명 capability 능력
I'm quite **capable** of taking care of the patients.
나는 그 환자들을 잘 돌볼 수 있다.

363 **continent** [kántənənt]
명 대륙, 육지 참고 island 섬
English was used only on a couple of **continents**.
영어는 두서너 개의 대륙에서만 사용되었다.

364 **environment** [inváiərənmənt]
명 (주변의, 자연의) 환경
The working **environment** at my new office is great.
새 사무실의 근무 환경은 매우 좋다.

365 **gene** [dʒiːn]
명 유전자, 유전 인자 형 genetic 유전의
The cause of color blindness is a particular **gene**.
색맹의 원인은 특정한 유전자에 있다.

366 **habitat** [hǽbitæ̀t]
명 서식지, 거주지, 산지
Koala bears' natural **habitat** is a eucalyptus forest.
코알라의 본래 서식지는 유칼립투스 숲이다.

367 **motion** [móuʃən]
명 운동, 동작; (안건의) 발의, 동의 동 몸짓을 해 보이다
Motion sensors can be effective ways to control lighting.
동작 감지 센서는 조명을 제어하는 데 효과적인 방법이다.

368 **organization** [ɔ̀ːrgənizéiʃən]
명 조직, 단체 동 organize 조직하다
I regularly donate money to an **organization** that helps poor people.
나는 가난한 사람들을 돕는 단체에 정기적으로 돈을 기부한다.

369 **population** [pɑ̀pjuléiʃən]
명 인구, 주민(수), (동식물의) 개체수
Let's talk about the growing multicultural **population** in Korea.
한국의 늘어나는 다문화 인구에 대해 이야기해 봅시다.

370 **possess**
[pəzés]

동 소유하다 명 possession 소유, 재산

Many versions of Arirang **possess** regional characteristics.
다양한 형식의 여러 아리랑은 지역적인 특징을 갖고 있다.

371 **protect**
[prətékt]

동 보호하다 명 protection 보호

We have an umbrella to **protect** us from the rain.
우리에게는 비를 막아 줄 우산이 있다.

372 **solid**
[sálid]

형 고체의, 견고한, 튼튼한 명 고체

The movie was a big hit thanks to its **solid** plot.
그 영화는 탄탄한 줄거리 덕분에 크게 성공했다.

373 **southern**
[sʌ́ðərn]

형 남쪽[남부]에 있는, 남향의 유 southerly 남쪽의

It's a unique floor painting in **southern** India.
그것은 남부 인도의 독특한 바닥 그림이다.

374 **species**
[spíːʃiːz]

명 종(생물 분류의 기초 단위), 종류

We have wiped out **species** of animals from the Earth.
우리는 지구에서 동물 종들을 말살해 왔다.

375 **surround**
[səráund]

동 둘러싸다, 에워싸다 참고 surroundings 주위 환경

Surrounded by the audience, he performed his magic.
청중들에게 둘러싸여서 그는 마술 공연을 했다.

376 **traffic**
[trǽfik]

명 교통(량), 통행 참고 vehicle 차량, 운송 수단

New highways will solve many **traffic** problems.
신설된 여러 고속도로가 다수의 교통 문제를 해결할 것이다.

377 **transportation**
[træ̀nspərtéiʃən]

명 운송, 수송, 교통 수단 동 transport 수송하다

Camels are important for **transportation** in the village.
낙타는 그 마을에서 중요한 운송 수단이다.

378 **worldwide**
[wə́ːrldwàid]

형 세계적인 참고 global 세계적인 international 국제적인

I hope that this food can become known **worldwide**.
나는 이 음식이 세계적으로 알려질 수 있으면 좋겠다.

379 **zone**
[zoun]

명 지역, 지대, 구역 동 (장소를) 지역으로 나누다

Industrial **zones** are marked in red.
공업 지대는 빨간 색으로 표시되어 있다.

380 **in contrast**

대조적으로, 그에 반해서

In contrast to her silent sister, Sally is talkative.
조용한 여동생과는 대조적으로, Sally는 수다스럽다.

19B Complete the Phrases *빈칸에 알맞은 말을 넣어 어구를 완성하세요.*

1 to catch ________________ attention (세계적인 관심을 끌다)

2 the effort to reduce ________________ congestion (교통 체증을 줄이려는 노력)

3 ________________ that decide the color of hair (머리카락 색을 결정하는 유전자들)

4 to prevent ________________ explosion (인구 폭발을 방지하다)

5 a no-parking ________________ (주차 금지 구역)

6 to hire a ________________ salesperson (유능한 판매원을 고용하다)

7 to find a rare ________________ of bird (희귀한 종의 새를 발견하다)

8 to ________________ a landed property (부동산을 소유하다)

19C Complete the Sentences *[보기]에서 알맞은 단어를 골라 어법에 맞게 완성하세요.*

[보기]

continent organization protect southern surround solid

1 We're going to use the paper bags designed by a non-profit ________________.
우리는 비영리단체가 디자인한 종이 가방을 사용할 것이다.

2 South Africa is located at the ________________ tip of the African Continent.
남아프리카 공화국은 아프리카 대륙의 남쪽 끝에 위치한다.

3 They believe that the picture can ________________ their child from having nightmares.
그들은 그 그림이 아이가 악몽을 꾸는 것을 막아 줄 수 있다고 믿는다.

4 Parents start feeding their babies ________________ foods before they are four months old.
부모들은 아기들이 4개월이 되기 전에 고체형 식품을 먹이기 시작한다.

5 It's widely believed that there was once only one ________________ on the Earth.
한때 지구상에 한 개의 대륙만 있었다는 것이 널리 알려져 있다.

6 Green trees and red flowers ________________ the brick house.
초록색 나무와 붉은 꽃들이 그 벽돌집을 둘러싸고 있다.

19D Fill in the Blanks
빈칸에 공통으로 들어갈 단어를 문장에 맞게 고쳐 쓰세요.

1
- I'm quite c_______________ of taking care of myself.
  나는 충분히 혼자서 살아갈 능력이 있다.
- The woman proved herself highly c_______________ as a business leader.
  그 여자는 사업체의 지도자로서 굉장히 유능하다는 것을 입증했다.

2
- He made a m_______________ with his right hand.
  그는 오른손으로 동작을 취했다.
- The chairperson put the m_______________ to the committee.
  의장은 그 의제를 위원회에 회부했다.

3
- Wicked wizards and witches began to a_______________ good ones.
  사악한 마법사와 마녀들이 선한 마법사와 마녀들을 공격하기 시작했다.
- While swimming, I was suddenly seized by an a_______________ of cramps.
  수영을 하다가 갑자기 쥐가 나서 움직일 수 없었다.

4
- The Buddhist p_______________ has increased during the last decade.
  불교도의 수는 지난 10년 동안 증가했다.
- Seoul has a problem with the pigeon p_______________.
  서울에는 비둘기 개체 수 문제가 있다.

19E Choose Synonyms
문장의 밑줄 친 부분과 가장 유사한 뜻의 단어를 고르세요.

1 I do not possess an audio set like the one he has.
나는 그가 가진 것과 같은 오디오 세트를 갖고 있지 않다.
① purchase ② rent ③ own ④ provide

2 He tried to protect Sally from the attack.
그는 공격으로부터 Sally를 보호하려고 애썼다.
① claim ② deny ③ propose ④ defend

3 One of the most serious problems today is the worldwide shortage of water.
오늘날의 가장 심각한 문제 중 하나는 세계적인 물 부족이다.
① global ② national ③ definite ④ previous

4 Antarctic animals include penguins and many species of whales.
남극의 동물들은 펭귄과 많은 종의 고래들을 포함한다.
① varieties ② averages ③ solids ④ extinction

19F Reading Passage 공부한 단어가 포함된 글을 잘 읽고 다음 문제를 풀어 보세요.

Birds are **capable** of both walking and flying. But there are more birds that fly than flightless birds on this planet. Whether a **species** of bird chooses to fly or walk depends on its **environment**. Flying requires more energy than walking. (A)______________, a bird without fear of **attack** by predators in its native habitat will eventually be flightless. (ⓐ) Australia, a small **continent** far from the other continents, has many flightless birds. (ⓑ) And many other flightless birds have been reported on the islands in the Pacific and the Indian Ocean. (ⓒ) There, nature "chose" the **genes** that are better for walking. (ⓓ) Usually, where a land is **surrounded** by water and the **population** of its predators decreases, birds developed the ability to walk. (ⓔ) More birds are hoppers than walkers. **Worldwide**, birds that walk or run like an ostrich or flamingo **possess** long legs and live in wide open spaces. (B)______________, most tree-living birds are hoppers, because it is easier to move from branch to branch by hopping than by walking or flying.

* predator 포식 동물 ostrich 타조 flamingo 홍학

1 위 글의 요지로 가장 적절한 것은?

① 날개가 퇴화된 새들은 다시 날 수 없다.
② 날지 못하는 새들은 멸종 위기를 겪고 있다.
③ 새들은 천적이 없으면 이동하지 않으려 한다.
④ 새들은 에너지를 덜 소모하는 이동 방법을 선택한다.
⑤ 새들의 진화는 나는 것에서 걷는 것으로 이루어진다.

2 위 글의 빈칸 (A), (B)에 들어갈 말로 가장 적절한 것은?

	(A)		(B)
①	However	……	In contrast
②	However	……	In conclusion
③	Therefore	……	In contrast
④	Therefore	……	In addition
⑤	In fact	……	In addition

English Only

3 Where is the appropriate place for the sentence?

> In fact, 'walking' is not a proper expression to describe the motion of birds.

① ⓐ ② ⓑ ③ ⓒ ④ ⓓ ⑤ ⓔ

서술형

4 Fill in the blanks to complete the answer. Use words from the passage.

What makes a species of bird choose to fly or walk?
→ ___________ plays the most important role. In detail, where there are few predators, birds tend not to ___________. If there are trees, they will jump around branches, and if there are few trees, they will ___________ or run on the ground.

Lesson 20

Word 500 381~400
Reading 25 20

SUMMA CUM LAUDE

20A Word List

중학교 3학년 필수단어를 예문과 함께 공부하세요.

381 **affair** [əfέər]

명 (공적으로 중요한) 일, 업무, 사건

You can get information on this **affair** from the website.
그 웹사이트에서 이 사건에 관한 정보를 얻을 수 있다.

382 **agent** [éidʒənt]

명 대리인; 직원, 요원 참고 agency 대리점; 정부 기관

A travel **agent** booked her hotels and flights.
여행사 직원이 그녀의 호텔과 비행편을 예약해 주었다.

383 **benefit** [bénəfit]

명 이익, 수당, 복지 혜택 동 이익이 되다

There are more **benefits** than risks.
위험 요소보다 이익이 더 많다.

384 **conductor** [kəndʌ́ktər]

명 지휘자; (전기나 열의) 전도체 동 conduct 지휘하다

He was appointed principal **conductor** of the orchestra.
그는 교향악단의 수석 지휘자로 임명되었다.

Metal is a good **conductor** of electricity.
금속은 좋은 전기 전도체이다.

385 **confuse** [kənfjúːz]

동 혼동[혼란] 시키다 명 confusion 혼동, 혼란

The man is **confused** about the woman's suggestion.
그 남자는 그 여자의 제안에 대해 혼란스러워 했다.

386 **courage** [kə́ːridʒ]

명 용기 형 courageous 용기 있는

Her story gave me **courage** to reach for my dream.
그녀의 이야기는 나의 꿈을 이루겠다는 용기를 주었다.

387 **detective** [ditéktiv]

명 탐정, 형사 유 investigator 수사관

The **detective** opened the door of the suspect's house.
그 탐정은 그 용의자 집의 문을 열었다.

388 **disguise** [disgáiz]

동 변장하다, 위장하다 명 변장, 분장

She **disguised** herself in a wig and glasses.
그녀는 가발과 안경을 써서 변장했다.

389 **emperor** [émpərər]

명 황제 참고 empire 제국 monarch 군주

Napoleon became the **emperor** of France in 1804.
나폴레옹은 1804년에 프랑스의 황제가 되었다.

390 **employ**
[implɔ́i]

동 고용하다, 사용하다 명 employment 고용

The principal **employed** the man to guard the gate.
사장은 정문을 경비하도록 그 남자를 고용했다.

391 **establish**
[istǽbliʃ]

동 설립하다, 수립하다 명 establishment 설립, 창시

The school was **established** by two pioneers of the country.
그 학교는 두 명의 국가 선구자들에 의해 창립되었다.

392 **faint**
[feint]

형 희미한, 약한, (가능성이) 적은 유 dim (빛이) 어둑한

There is still a **faint** hope that the boy may be cured.
아직 그 소년이 완치될 수 있는 작은 희망이 있다.

393 **friendship**
[fréndʃìp]

명 우정, 친선 참고 affection 애정, 호의

Their paintings show the **friendship** between the two artists.
그들의 회화 작품들은 두 예술가의 우정을 보여준다.

394 **government**
[gʌ́vərnmənt]

명 정부 동 govern 다스리다, 통치하다

The **government** must protect the rights of citizens.
정부는 시민의 권리를 수호해야 한다.

395 **illusion**
[ilú:ʒən]

명 환상, 환각; (사람 · 상황에 대한) 오해 (착각)

We should distinguish **illusion** from reality.
우리는 환상과 현실을 구분해야 한다.

396 **immigrant**
[ímigrənt]

명 (입국) 이민자 형 이민자의 동 immigrate 이민을 오다

The city has a large **immigrant** population.
그 도시는 이민자의 수가 무척 많다.

397 **impress**
[imprés]

동 (깊은) 인상을 주다, 감명을 주다 형 impressive 인상적인
명 impression 인상

Which scenes in the movie **impressed** you most?
그 영화에서 어떤 장면이 가장 깊은 인상을 주었는가?

398 **military**
[mílitèri]

형 군대의, 군인의 참고 the army, navy, air force 육 · 해 · 공군

Benefits are given to those who have finished **military** service.
군 복무를 마친 사람들에게 혜택이 주어진다.

399 **primary**
[práimèri]

형 주요한, 첫째의 참고 secondary 부차적인

Water is the **primary** factor that controls the environment.
물은 환경을 조절하는 첫 번째 요소이다.

400 **bring about**

야기하다, 초래하다, (어떤 일이) 일어나게 하다

A simple walk can **bring about** positive emotional changes.
간단히 산책하는 것으로 긍정적인 감정 변화를 가져올 수 있다.

20B Complete the Phrases *빈칸에 알맞은 말을 넣어 어구를 완성하세요.*

1 an ______________ worker (이민 온 근로자)

2 an expert on foreign ______________ (외교 문제 전문가)

3 to have a ______________ hope (희미한 희망을 갖다)

4 to ______________ her reputation (그녀의 명성을 확립하다)

5 my ______________ goal in life (나의 인생에서 주요한 목표)

6 for the ______________ of (~의 이익을 위해)

7 to gather ______________ to apologize (사과하기 위해 용기를 내다)

8 a ______________ officer in uniform (제복을 입은 군 장교)

20C Complete the Sentences *[보기]에서 알맞은 단어를 골라 어법에 맞게 완성하세요.*

[보기]

conductor benefit courage detective government illusion

1 The ______________ officials said that it would take a few months for the town to recover.
정부 관료들은 그 마을을 복구하려면 두세 달이 걸릴 것이라고 말했다.

2 She's under the ______________ that she is a genius.
그녀는 자신이 천재라는 착각에 빠져 있다.

3 One thousand roses are buried with Elsa in honor of her ______________.
Elsa의 용기를 기리는 차원에서 천 송이의 장미가 그녀와 함께 묻혔다.

4 The ______________ bowed to the audience and everyone applauded.
지휘자는 관객에게 고개 숙여 인사했고 관객들은 모두 박수를 쳤다.

5 The new plan may ______________ many students.
새로운 계획은 많은 학생들을 이롭게 할 것이다.

6 They hired a private ______________ to find their missing dog.
그들은 없어진 개를 찾기 위해 사설 탐정을 고용했다.

20D Fill in the Blanks 빈칸에 공통으로 들어갈 단어를 문장에 맞게 고쳐 쓰세요.

1 • The new solution will c_______________ matters further.
새 해결책은 이 문제들을 더 혼란스럽게 만들 것이다.
• The lights of towers and tall buildings c_______________ birds.
탑과 고층 건물로부터 나오는 빛이 새들을 혼란스럽게 한다.

2 • I'm directly concerned in the a_______________.
나는 그 일에 직접적으로 연관되어 있다.
• As this is a family a_______________, children are encouraged to attend.
이것은 가족과 연관된 일이므로 어린이들도 참여하는 것을 권장한다.

3 • I was i_______________ with his presentation in English class.
나는 그가 영어 시간에 한 발표에 감명 받았다.
• The warriors' painted bodies i_______________ and threatened their enemies.
색칠을 한 전사들의 몸은 적에게 깊은 인상을 주고 위협을 가했다.

4 • They worked with a travel a_______________ to plan their vacation.
그들은 휴가 계획을 세우는 데 여행사 직원의 도움을 받았다.
• The actor hired a new a_______________ to look at scripts.
그 배우는 대본을 검토할 새로운 대리인을 고용했다.

20E Choose Synonyms 문장의 밑줄 친 부분과 가장 유사한 뜻의 단어를 고르세요.

1 We could hear their voices growing <u>fainter</u> as they walked down the road.
그들이 길을 걸어 내려가자 그들의 목소리가 점차 희미하게 들리는 것을 알 수 있었다.
① faster ② sadder ③ louder ④ quieter

2 Forty wig makers were <u>employed</u> to make wigs for the people in the palace.
궁전의 사람들을 위한 가발을 만들기 위해 40명의 가발 제작자들이 고용되었다.
① retired ② hired ③ blamed ④ praised

3 The <u>primary</u> difference between the two is the size of the battery.
두 제품 사이의 가장 주요한 차이점은 전지의 크기이다.
① unbelievable ② familiar ③ urgent ④ main

4 I never dreamed that his speech would <u>bring about</u> these results.
나는 그의 연설이 이러한 결과들을 가져올 줄은 꿈에도 몰랐다.
① cause ② switch ③ inform ④ explain

20F Reading Passage

공부한 단어가 포함된 글을 잘 읽고 다음 문제를 풀어 보세요.

Spies are frequently used in the world of international **affairs**. For example, Chevalier D'Eon, a French **agent employed** by King Louis XV in 1756, arranged a secret treaty with the Empress of Russia for the **benefit** of his country. As no foreign man could have the opportunity to meet the empress, D'Eon had the **courage** to disguise ⓐ himself as a woman and secure the meeting and negotiate the treaty.

The French Emperor Napoleon, apart from being a great military tactician was also a master in the art of espionage, as ⓑ he proved during the war against Austria. In 1804 he sent his top spy, Karl Schulmeister, to Vienna where Schulmeister told the story that ⓒ he had been expelled from France. He **established** a **friendship** with the Austrian army chief, Marshall Mack. He was so **impressed** with Schulmeister's knowledge of French military matters ⓓ he made him a **government** official — Chief of Intelligence for the Austrians. ⓔ He didn't have ______________________ Schulmeister. In this position, Schulmeister was able to **confuse** Mack with false **illusion** of the strength of Napoleon's army, eventually **bring about** the defeat of the Austrian army.

* espionage 간첩 행위

1 위 글의 제목으로 가장 적절한 것은?

① Spy War: Hidden but Fierce
② Great Spies and Their Achievements
③ Napoleon: A Great Artist in Spy War
④ Obstacles Spies Face during Missions
⑤ Politics Affected by the Available Information

2 위 글의 빈칸에 들어갈 말로 가장 적절한 것은?

① huge jealousy of
② different ideas on
③ a hint of suspicion on
④ some bad feelings about
⑤ few competitions against

English Only

3 Which of the underlined references(ⓐ~ⓔ) is NOT correct?

① himself: Chevalier D'Eon
② he: Napoleon
③ he: Karl Schulmeister
④ he: the emperor of Austria
⑤ He: Marshall Mack

서술형

4 Fill in the blanks to complete the summary. Use words from the passage.

> There are two famous spies. The first one, Chevalier D'Eon went to Russia and made a __________ with the empress. The second one, Karl Schulmeister, went to Austria and became a __________ __________ and gave them __________ information about Napoleon's army for the benefit of France.

Speedy Check-up 4

Lesson별로 모르는 단어에 체크한 후, 그 갯수를 ☐/20 안에 쓰고 학습성과를 점검해 보세요.
모르는 단어는 다시 찾아 학습하세요.

Lesson 16 ☐/20

☐ awful	☐ infection	☐ physical	☐ wander
☐ bark	☐ invasion	☐ smooth	☐ wildlife
☐ blame	☐ mammal	☐ spread	☐ yawn
☐ cruel	☐ mankind	☐ suffer	☐ to death
☐ increase	☐ palm	☐ threaten	☐ be susceptible to

Lesson 17 ☐/20

☐ accurate	☐ complicated	☐ knowledge	☐ scout
☐ appreciate	☐ contribute	☐ obey	☐ sore
☐ athlete	☐ defeat	☐ performance	☐ statistics
☐ breeze	☐ divide	☐ pitcher	☐ keep track of
☐ compare	☐ judge	☐ recreation	☐ on the basis of

Lesson 18 ☐/20

☐ achievement	☐ flour	☐ mention	☐ spectator
☐ amount	☐ function	☐ odd	☐ theory
☐ available	☐ honor	☐ revolution	☐ trousers
☐ convert	☐ identify	☐ rinse	☐ catch on
☐ decorate	☐ ingredient	☐ sew	☐ keep A from -ing

Lesson 19 ☐/20

☐ attack	☐ habitat	☐ protect	☐ traffic
☐ capable	☐ motion	☐ solid	☐ transportation
☐ continent	☐ organization	☐ southern	☐ worldwide
☐ environment	☐ population	☐ species	☐ zone
☐ gene	☐ possess	☐ surround	☐ in contrast

Lesson 20 ☐/20

☐ affair	☐ courage	☐ establish	☐ immigrant
☐ agent	☐ detective	☐ faint	☐ impress
☐ benefit	☐ disguise	☐ friendship	☐ military
☐ conductor	☐ emperor	☐ government	☐ primary
☐ confuse	☐ employ	☐ illusion	☐ bring about

Chapter 5

숨마 주니어®
중학 영어교과서
WORD MANUAL ③

21A Word List

중학교 3학년 필수단어를 예문과 함께 공부하세요.

401 **attitude** [ǽtitjùːd]
명 (사람 · 사물에 대한) 태도, 마음가짐
How can we encourage a change in **attitudes**?
우리는 어떻게 하면 태도의 변화를 촉진할 수 있을 것인가?

402 **cast** [kæst]
동 던지다; 배역을 정하다 명 던지기; 깁스 cast-cast-cast
He **cast** the book down on to the chair angrily.
그는 화가 나서 책을 의자 위로 집어 던졌다.

403 **childhood** [tʃáildhùd]
명 어린 시절 참고 adolescence 청소년기
What was the most memorable thing about your **childhood**?
어린 시절에 있어서 가장 기억할 만한 일은 무엇인가?

404 **compromise** [kámprəmàiz]
명 타협, 절충 동 양보하다, 타협하다; (명예 등을) 손상하다
There is no room for **compromise**.
타협의 여지가 없다.

405 **creative** [kriːéitiv]
형 창조적인 명 creation 창조
You cannot copy any **creative** work without permission.
어떤 창작물도 허가 없이 복제할 수 없다.

406 **encourage** [inkə́ːridʒ]
동 격려하다, 장려하다 명 encouragement 격려, 장려
We were **encouraged** by the success of this project.
우리는 이 작업에 성공함으로써 힘을 얻었다.

407 **greedy** [gríːdi]
형 욕심 많은, 탐욕스러운 명 greed 욕심, 탐욕
I took more of the profit, but he never considered this **greedy**.
내가 소득에서 더 많이 가져갔지만 그는 이것을 욕심이 과하다고 여기지 않았다.

408 **nod** [nɑd]
명 끄덕임, 승낙 동 끄덕이다, 승낙하다
A **nod** of the head by a Bulgarian means "No."
불가리아 인이 고개를 끄덕이는 것은 '아니오'를 의미한다.

409 **obstacle** [ábstəkl]
명 장애, 장애물 유 difficulty 곤란, 어려움
This is the biggest **obstacle** in his life.
이것은 그이 삶에서 가장 큰 장애물이다.

410 **opinion** [əpínjən]

명 의견, 견해 [참고] opinionated 자기 의견을 고집하는

In your **opinion**, what is the biggest problem?
당신의 견해로는 가장 큰 문제가 뭐라고 생각하나요?

411 **overcome** [òuvərkʌ́m]

동 극복하다 overcome-overcame-overcome

How could you ever **overcome** the difficulties you faced?
맞닥뜨린 어려움들을 어떻게 극복할 수 있었는가?

412 **pretend** [priténd]

동 ~인 척하다, 가장하다, 속이다

He **pretended** to be embarrassed and told a lie.
그는 당황한 척 하면서 거짓말을 했다.

413 **profit** [prɑ́fit]

명 이익, 이윤 동 이익을 얻다[주다]

Korea has gained great economic **profit** from Korean dramas.
한국은 드라마로 거대한 경제적 이익을 거둬 왔다.

414 **satisfactory** [sæ̀tisfǽktəri]

형 만족한, 만족스러운 동 satisfy 만족시키다 명 satisfaction 만족

She didn't get a **satisfactory** explanation.
그는 만족할만한 설명을 듣지 못했다.

415 **scratch** [skrætʃ]

동 긁다, 할퀴다 명 긁힌 자국, 긁기

The woman **scratched** herself on a nail.
그 여자는 못에 긁혔다.

416 **setback** [sétbæ̀k]

명 좌절, 차질 [참고] disappointment 실망

His team suffered a **setback** when the coach resigned.
코치가 사임했을 때 그의 팀은 차질을 겪었다.

417 **shoot** [ʃuːt]

동 쏘다; (영화 · 사진을) 촬영하다 명 발사; 촬영 shoot-shot-shot

He was **shot** in the leg during the war.
그는 전쟁에서 다리에 총상을 입었다.

418 **struggle** [strʌ́gl]

동 투쟁하다, 분투하다, 노력하다 명 분투, 노력

The man on the rope **struggled** to maintain his balance.
줄 위에 선 그 남자는 균형을 유지하려고 애썼다.

419 **wisdom** [wízdəm]

명 지혜, 상식, 현명함 형 wise 지혜로운

Learn the **wisdom** of combining the old and the new.
오래된 것과 새로운 것을 결합시키는 지혜를 배우라.

420 **had it rough**

고생하다 유 have a rough time

Craftsmen **had it rough** during the Industrial Revolution.
수공예가들은 산업 혁명기에 힘든 시간을 보냈다.

21B Complete the Phrases *빈칸에 알맞은 말을 넣어 어구를 완성하세요.*

1 ______________ for money and power (돈과 권력에 탐욕스러운)

2 to ______________ to be happy (행복한 척 하다)

3 to return a good ______________ (상당한 이익을 가져오다)

4 the goddess of ______________ (지혜의 여신)

5 one of his ______________ dreams (그의 어린 시절 꿈들 중 하나)

6 to develop ______________ powers (창의력을 개발하다)

7 to ______________ through the storm (폭풍을 뚫고 힘들게 가다)

8 to ______________ donation to the charity (자선 단체에 기부를 권장하다)

21C Complete the Sentences *[보기]에서 알맞은 단어를 골라 어법에 맞게 완성하세요.*

[보기]

attitude childhood creative greedy opinion pretend

1 Ben has been my closest friend since ______________.
Ben은 어린 시절부터 나의 가장 친한 친구였다.

2 I feel like we need to have more ______________ ideas for our project.
우리의 프로젝트를 위해 더 많은 창조적인 아이디어가 필요하다고 느낀다.

3 The hybrid car shows our engineers' imagination and open ______________.
하이브리드 자동차는 우리 기술자들의 상상력과 열린 태도를 보여준다.

4 What will you do if your child has ______________ that are contrary to yours?
당신의 아이가 당신과 다른 의견들을 가진다면 어떻게 하겠는가?

5 I try not to show my emotions and ______________ that I am OK.
나는 감정을 보이지 않고 괜찮아 보이도록 노력한다.

6 The ______________ old man wanted more money and treasure.
그 욕심 많은 노인은 더 많은 돈과 보물을 원했다.

21D Fill in the Blanks

빈칸에 공통으로 들어갈 단어를 문장에 맞게 고쳐 쓰세요.

1 • He s_______________ at the mosquito bites on his arm.
그는 팔에 있는 모기 물린 곳들을 긁었다.
• The dog s_______________ its ear.
그 개는 자기 귀를 긁었다.

2 • I want to o_______________ the fear of doing something by myself.
나는 혼자 일을 해 나가는 것에 대한 두려움을 극복하고 싶다.
• You have the ability to o_______________ a setback.
당신에게는 좌절을 극복할 능력이 있다.

3 • I made many s_______________ing mistakes and ended up scoring only 3 points.
나는 슈팅할 때 실수를 많이 해서 결국 3점 밖에 득점하지 못했다.
• They may even s_______________ scenes for several films on the same day.
그들은 심지어 한 날에 여러 다른 영화 장면을 촬영할지도 모른다.

4 • The secret of a happy marriage is c_______________.
행복한 결혼 생활의 비밀은 타협에 있다.
• Some people refuse to c_______________ when faced with a hard situation.
어떤 사람들은 어려운 상황에 직면하면 양보하기를 거부한다.

21E Choose Synonyms

문장의 밑줄 친 부분과 가장 유사한 뜻의 단어를 고르세요.

1 They composed a special song to encourage the athletes.
그들은 선수들을 격려하기 위해 특별한 노래를 작곡했다.
① cheer ② reserve ③ legalize ④ analyze

2 The supplier may have to raise the price of the product to make a profit.
공급자는 이윤을 남기기 위해 제품의 가격을 올려야 할 것이다.
① raise ② margin ③ partner ④ contract

3 The officer's reply to my question was not satisfactory.
내 질문에 대한 그 담당자의 대답은 만족스럽지 않았다.
① immediate ② sufficient ③ confusing ④ disappointing

4 You might not agree with this, but students have it rough in our society.
이 생각에 동의할지 모르겠지만 학생들은 우리 사회에서 힘든 시간을 보낸다.
① work very hard ② have a hard time
③ want outside help ④ behave as they want

21F Reading Passage 공부한 단어가 포함된 글을 잘 읽고 다음 문제를 풀어 보세요.

Sylvester Stallone **had it rough** in his **childhood**. He didn't have it much better as an adult. Not able to earn a steady income, and having to sell his dog for $25.00 to help turn on his electricity, he was faced with many **obstacles**. But he didn't lose faith in himself and **struggled** through the obstacles. It was only 2 weeks after selling his dog that he wrote the Rocky script in nearly 20 hours straight from **scratch**. ⓐ He sent it to many studios. Finally, being rejected over 1,500 times, Stallone was given a **nod** by United Artists for $125,000, but only if Stallone would not star in it. They thought ⓑ he was too **greedy**. But Stallone would not accept unless ⓒ he starred in it. Finally, they **compromised**. The **casting** director called him: ⓓ He said they would allow him to play the role of Rocky, but would only pay him $35,000 and a percentage of the **profits**. ⓔ He accepted and the **shooting** started. Rocky cost $1,000,000 to make, but it grossed over $200,000,000! The Rocky series earned over a billion dollars. Success comes after **setbacks**. What matters is your **attitude**.

1 위 글에서 Stallone에 대한 필자의 태도로 가장 적절한 것은?

① skeptic
② jealous
③ neutral
④ satisfactory
⑤ complimenting

2 위 글의 밑줄 친 ⓐ~ⓔ 중 가리키는 대상이 <u>다른</u> 하나는?

① ⓐ ② ⓑ ③ ⓒ ④ ⓓ ⑤ ⓔ

English Only

3 According to the passage, which is NOT true?

① Stallone had to sell his dog.
② Stallone worked on the Rocky script for two years.
③ Stallone's script was not accepted at first.
④ United Artists wanted another actor to play Rocky.
⑤ United Artists offered Stallone a percentage of the profit.

서술형

4 Complete the answer with words from the passage.

Why did Stallone refuse to accept United Artists's first offer of $125,000?
→ Because he wanted to ____________ ____________ the movie.

22A Word List

중학교 3학년 필수단어를 예문과 함께 공부하세요.

421 **adopt** [ədɑ́pt]

동 채택하다, 입양하다 명 adoption 채택, 입양

The scientists **adopted** a new approach to the problem.
과학자들은 그 문제에 관한 새로운 접근법을 채택했다.

422 **ancestor** [ǽnsestər]

명 선조, 조상 반 descendant 후손

Our **ancestors** arrived in this valley 1,000 years ago.
우리 선조들은 천 년 전에 이 계곡에 도착했다.

423 **artificial** [ɑ̀:rtəfíʃəl]

형 인조의, 인공적인, 모조의 반 natural 자연(천연)의

The room was decorated with **artificial** trees.
방은 모조 나무로 장식되었다.

424 **coal** [koul]

명 석탄 참고 oil 석유 natural gas 천연가스

It was very dark in the **coal** mine.
석탄 광산 내부는 굉장히 어두웠다.

425 **commercial** [kəmə́:rʃəl]

형 상업적인 명 광고 방송

Commercial fishing is prohibited in this area.
이 지역에서는 상업적인 어획이 금지된다.

I like the background music of this **commercial**.
나는 이 광고 방송의 배경 음악을 좋아한다.

426 **communicate** [kəmjú:nəkèit]

동 의사소통하다, 전달하다 명 communication 의사소통

To **communicate** with French people, speak French.
프랑스 사람들과 의사소통 하려면 프랑스어를 하라.

427 **electricity** [ilèktrísəti]

명 전기, 전력 참고 electric 전기의, 전기를 이용하는

The woman's idea is about saving **electricity**.
그 여자의 제안은 전기 절약에 관한 것이다.

428 **erase** [iréis]

동 지우다, 없애다 참고 eraser 지우개

The file will be **erased** from the hard disk.
그 파일은 하드디스크에서 삭제될 것이다.

429 **exchange** [ikstʃéindʒ]

동 교환하다 명 교환, 환전 참고 in exchange for ~대신의, 교환으로

They'll have meetings to **exchange** ideas for the project.
그들은 그 작업에 관한 의견을 교환하기 위해 회의를 할 것이다.

430 **foolish**
[fú:liʃ]

형 어리석은, 미련한 유 stupid, silly 어리석은

It was **foolish** to believe that he was serious.
그가 진심이었다고 믿은 것은 어리석은 것이었다.

431 **preserve**
[prizə́:rv]

동 보존하다, 보호하다 유 protect 지키다

What can we do to **preserve** our traditions?
우리는 전통을 지키기 위해 무엇을 할 수 있을까?

432 **refer**
[rifə́:r]

동 문의하다, 알아보도록 하다; 나타내다

You can **refer** to the following offices.
여러분은 다음의 여러 사무실에 문의할 수 있습니다.

433 **rubber**
[rʌ́bər]

명 고무; 지우개

Coffee and **rubber** play an important role in the economy.
커피와 고무는 경제에 있어 중요한 역할을 한다.

434 **skyscraper**
[skáiskreipər]

명 고층 건물, 마천루

Skyscrapers were being built in the center of the city.
그 도시의 중심부에 고층 건물들이 건설되고 있었다.

435 **steam**
[sti:m]

명 (수)증기 동 증기로 찌다

He wiped the **steam** from the mirrors.
그는 거울의 수증기를 닦아냈다.

436 **string**
[striŋ]

명 끈, 줄, 일련 동 끈에 묶다

Money, **string**, and a pencil are placed on the party table.
돈, 줄, 그리고 연필이 잔칫상에 놓여 있다.

437 **thought**
[θɔ:t]

명 생각, 사상 참고 consideration 사려, 숙고

The **thought** just crossed my mind that he had the key.
그가 열쇠를 갖고 있다는 생각이 내 마음을 스쳐갔다.

438 **trial**
[tráiəl]

명 재판; 실험; 시도 동 try 노력하다; 시도하다

He is awaiting **trial** for fraud.
그는 사기 혐의로 재판을 기다리고 있다.

439 **volunteer**
[vɑ̀ləntíər]

동 자원하다 명 자원 봉사자 형 voluntary 자발적인

He **volunteered** to teach math at the community center.
그는 지역 문화원에서 수학을 가르치는 것에 자원했다.

440 **a large number of**

수많은, 다수의 유 plenty of, a great deal of

A large number of birds live in the rainforest.
열대우림에는 많은 새들이 산다.

22B Complete the Phrases *빈칸에 알맞은 말을 넣어 어구를 완성하세요.*

1 to ______________ in a house-building project (집 짓는 프로젝트에 자원하다)

2 to laugh at the ______________ idea (어리석은 생각을 비웃다)

3 currency ______________ facilities in the airport (공항의 환전 시설)

4 to ______________ strawberries in sugar (딸기를 설탕에 넣어서 보존하다)

5 to ______________ a resolution (결의를 채택하다)

6 to generate ______________ (전기를 발생시키다)

7 a shop that carries ______________ fur coats (인조 모피 코트를 취급하는 가게)

8 to ______________ with others online (다른 사람들과 온라인으로 의사소통 하다)

22C Complete the Sentences *[보기]에서 알맞은 단어를 골라 어법에 맞게 완성하세요.*

[보기]

ancestor electricity exchange preserve rubber skyscraper volunteer

1 Urgent action is required to ______________ these forests.
이 숲을 보존하기 위해서는 긴급 조치가 필요하다.

2 This is a device that automatically turns off unused ______________ at home.
이것은 집에서 사용하지 않는 전기를 자동으로 차단하는 기구이다.

3 For our school festival, we need more ______________.
우리 학교 축제를 위해서는 더 많은 자원봉사자들이 필요하다.

4 It is illegal to parachute off a ______________ in this city.
초고층빌딩에서 낙하산을 타고 뛰어내리는 것은 이 도시에서 불법이다.

5 When stretched, a ______________ band produces an elastic force.
고무줄이 늘어나게 되면 탄성력이 생긴다.

6 Workers build products or offer services in ______________ for salaries.
근로자들은 급여를 받는 대가로 제품을 생산하거나 서비스를 제공한다.

7 We need to revive the traditions of our ______________.
우리는 선조들의 전통을 되살릴 필요가 있다.

22D Fill in the Blanks *빈칸에 공통으로 들어갈 단어를 문장에 맞게 고쳐 쓰세요.*

1 • The G s______________ on the violin suddenly broke.
그 바이올린의 G현이 갑자기 끊어졌다.
• He took two soda cans and connected them with a red s______________.
그는 두 개의 음료수 캔을 가져와서 그것을 빨간 줄로 연결했다.

2 • Many fans criticize their music for being too c______________ now.
많은 팬들은 지금 그들의 음악이 너무 상업적이라고 비판한다.
• During the c______________, a bag of popcorn appeared five times.
광고방송 중에 팝콘 한 봉지가 다섯 번 등장했다.

3 • Everything was black as if I were in a c______________ mine.
마치 탄광 안에 있는 듯 모든 것이 캄캄했다.
• In the 19th century, the trains used c______________, not oil as their fuel.
19세기에는 석유가 아닌 석탄을 기차 연료로 사용했다.

4 • These old engines are driven by s______________.
이 오래된 엔진들은 증기로 움직인다.
• Boil the water and s______________ the fish for 30 minutes.
물을 끓이고 생선을 30분간 쪄라.

22E Choose Synonyms *문장의 밑줄 친 부분과 가장 유사한 뜻의 단어를 고르세요.*

1 I have used my artificial limb since I was 7 years old.
나는 7살 때부터 의족을 사용해왔다.
① natural ② well-made ③ awkward ④ man-made

2 A new school of thought emerged; known as Sil-hak that highlighted practicality.
실학이라 알려진 실용을 강조하는 새로운 학파의 사상이 나타났다.
① reaction ② argument ③ ideology ④ consideration

3 Comics have been a convenient way to communicate social information.
만화는 사회적 정보를 전달하는 편리한 수단이 되어 왔다.
① block ② receive ③ deliver ④ complain

4 The two people were arrested but not brought to trial.
두 사람은 체포되었지만 재판에 회부되지 않았다.
① jail ② court ③ labor ④ investigation

22F Reading Passage 공부한 단어가 포함된 글을 잘 읽고 다음 문제를 풀어 보세요.

The enigma machine **refers** to a portable device run by **electricity** for **exchanging** secret messages. It encoded the message into a **string** of letters and then decoded at the other end of the line. An **ancestor** of the computer, it resembled a typewriter keyboard.

Its **commercial** use was not recorded, but it was (A) [adopted / destroyed] by the German army in World War II. The Germans were **foolish** enough to believe that the Allies would never be able to break the machine's codes. But it was very (B) [easy / difficult] to **communicate** with each other: Each day's settings for a machine had to be sent between encoder and decoder. After a day, the settings would be **erased** and the records would not be **preserved**. But these settings were often (C) [valued / captured] by the Allies. Even more, the codes, as well as the machine were stolen and cracked, leaking important information. One of the machines was intercepted in Poland and sent to Britain. With the help of Polish mathematicians who **volunteered** to break the codes, experts in the UK succeeded in breaking the codes of a large number of intercepted Nazi messages and gained vital military intelligence from them.

* the Allies (1, 2차 세계대전의) 연합군 encode 암호를 만들다 decode 암호를 풀다

1 위 글의 주제로 가장 적절한 것은?

① 암호 기계를 작동하는 복잡한 기술
② 20세기 암호 기계의 기본 구조
③ 2차 세계 대전에서 사용된 암호 기계의 장점
④ 군사적 목적으로 암호 기계가 발명된 이유
⑤ 2차 세계 대전에 쓰인 암호 기계의 사용상의 어려움

2 위 글 (A), (B), (C)에 들어갈 말로 가장 적절한 것은?

	(A)		(B)		(C)
①	adopted	……	easy	……	valued
②	destroyed	……	difficult	……	valued
③	adopted	……	difficult	……	captured
④	destroyed	……	easy	……	captured
⑤	adopted	……	difficult	……	valued

English Only

3 According to the passage, what was erased daily?

① the message of the codes
② the passwords for the mission
③ the machine's setting for the letters
④ the identity of the encoder and decoder
⑤ the places that sent and received the codes

서술형

4 Use words from the passage to complete the summary.

The enigma machine makes codes, and it was a__________ by the Germans during World War II. The settings were changed every day, making it rather difficult to use the machine. But the Allies could b__________ the c__________ and i__________ secret messages.

23A Word List

중학교 3학년 필수단어를 예문과 함께 공부하세요.

441 **academic** [ækədémik]
형 학업의, 학교의 명 학과, 학문(주로 복수형)
The two universities were rivals in **academic** achievements.
두 대학은 학문적 성취에 있어서 경쟁 상대였다.

442 **chairperson** [tʃέərpə̀ːrsn]
명 의장, 회장 참고 chair 의장직, 의장
The **chairperson** presented a new idea to settle the conflict.
의장은 분쟁을 조정하기 위해 새로운 아이디어를 제시했다.

443 **criticize** [krítisàiz]
동 비판하다, 비난하다 명 criticism 비판, 비평 참고 critic 비평가
Sensible people will not get angry when **criticized**.
현명한 사람은 비판받을 때 화내지 않을 것이다.

444 **cure** [kjúər]
명 치료(법) 동 치료하다 유 heal, treat 치료하다
I hope to find **cures** for fatal diseases such as cancer.
나는 암과 같은 치명적인 질병의 치료법을 찾고 싶다.

445 **discover** [diskʌ́vər]
동 발견하다, 깨닫다 명 discovery 발견
The farmer **discovered** a puppy in the backyard.
농부는 뒷마당에서 강아지 한 마리를 발견했다.

446 **dump** [dʌmp]
동 (쓰레기를) 버리다, (헐값에) 처분하다 명 쓰레기 (더미)
We need to reduce the amount of garbage we **dump**.
우리는 쓰레기 배출량을 줄여야 한다.

447 **efficient** [ifíʃənt]
형 능률적인, 효과적인, 유능한 명 efficiency 능률
The store put the money into energy-**efficient** lights.
그 가게는 고효율 전등을 구입하는데 돈을 지출했다.

448 **idle** [áidl]
형 게으른, 놀고 있는 동 빈둥거리다
The machine sits **idle** for months.
그 기계는 여러 달 동안 가동되지 않고 있다.

449 **instruction** [instrʌ́kʃən]
명 설명, 지시, 가르침 동 instruct 가르치다, 설명하다
He was acting on my **instructions**.
그는 나의 지시에 따라 행동하고 있었다.

450 **negative** [négətiv]

형 부정적인 반 positive 긍정적인

Try not to make **negative** comments about other cultures.
다른 문화에 대해 부정적인 말을 하지 않도록 노력하라.

451 **pardon** [pá:rdn]

명 용서, 사면 동 용서하다 유 forgive 용서하다

The group asked the president for a **pardon**.
그 집단은 대통령에게 사면을 요청했다.

452 **passionate** [pǽʃənit]

형 열성적인, 열정적인 명 passion 열성, 열정

Ted is **passionate** about guiding tourists.
Ted는 관광객을 안내하는 데 열성적이다.

453 **poverty** [pávərti]

명 가난 형 poor 가난한

More than half of the world's children suffer from **poverty**.
세계 어린이의 절반 이상이 가난에 시달리고 있다.

454 **proof** [pru:f]

명 증거 동 prove 증명하다 유 evidence

The document was **proof** that her story was true.
그 자료는 그녀의 이야기가 사실이라는 증거이다.

455 **pupil** [pjú:pəl]

명 (초 · 중등)학생; 눈동자

Pupils often misspell the word flash as flesh.
학생들은 자주 flash라는 단어를 flesh로 잘못 쓴다.

456 **responsible** [rispánsəbl]

형 책임지고(맡고) 있는, 신뢰할 수 있는 명 responsibility 책임

I'm **responsible** for organizing this event.
저는 이 행사 주최와 관련한 책임을 지고 있습니다.

457 **suicide** [sú:əsàid]

명 자살, 자결, 자해 동 자살하다

He committed **suicide** for the glory of Calais.
그는 칼레의 영광을 위해 목숨을 끊었다.

458 **uncomfortable** [ʌnkʌ́mfərtəbl]

형 불편한 유 inconvenient

Going on a backpacking trip sounds a little bit **uncomfortable**.
배낭여행을 가는 것은 약간 불편할 것 같다.

459 **show up**

나타나다 유 appear, arrive

A large crowd suddenly **showed up** at the city hall square.
많은 수의 군중이 시청 광장에 갑자기 나타났다.

460 **sign up for**

~을 신청(가입)하다 유 enroll in ~에 등록하다

I **signed up for** a French class for this semester.
나는 이번 학기에 프랑스어 수업을 신청했다.

23B Complete the Phrases 빈칸에 알맞은 말을 넣어 어구를 완성하세요.

1 to make a ________________ change (책임 있는 변화를 이룩하다)

2 to ________________ a swimming class (수영 강좌에 등록하다)

3 to ________________ for the appointment (약속 장소에 나타나다)

4 a garbage ________________ in the town (그 마을의 쓰레기장)

5 conditions of extreme ________________ (극도로 가난한 상태)

6 to be living ________________ of UFOs (UFO의 살아있는 증거)

7 to take the girl as my ________________ (그 소녀를 나의 제자로 받아들이다)

8 to make a ________________ speech (열정적인 연설을 하다)

23C Complete the Sentences [보기]에서 알맞은 단어를 골라 어법에 맞게 완성하세요.

[보기]

chairperson criticize idle negative poverty proof uncomfortable

1 The critics who had disliked Rodin started to ________________ the work.
로댕을 싫어했던 비평가들이 그 작품을 비난하기 시작했다.

2 I feel a little bit ________________ wearing this pink shirt.
이 분홍 셔츠를 입는 게 약간 불편하다.

3 The people were told not to write ________________ reviews about the hotel.
사람들은 그 호텔에 대해 부정적인 후기를 쓰지 말라는 얘기를 들었다.

4 The ________________ is elected by the committee from among its members.
의장은 회원들 중에서 위원회에 의해 선출된다.

5 For the world to believe the findings, the research team needed ________________.
발견한 내용을 세상 사람들이 믿게끔 하려면 연구팀은 증거가 필요했다.

6 Some people ignore the fact that the ________________ rate is high.
몇몇 사람들은 빈곤율이 높다는 사실을 무시한다.

7 She likes to be ________________ and watch DVDs all day at home.
그녀는 한가하게 쉬며 하루 종일 집에서 DVD 보는 것을 좋아한다.

23D Fill in the Blanks *빈칸에 공통으로 들어갈 단어를 문장에 맞게 고쳐 쓰세요.*

1 • His a_______________ essay provides a new insight into human voices.
그의 학술 논문은 인간의 목소리에 대한 새로운 통찰력을 제공한다.
• There are a_______________ conferences held in Helsinki.
헬싱키에서 몇몇 학회가 개최된다.

2 • She d_______________ a very old book, written in Chinese characters.
그녀는 아주 오래된 책을 발견했는데 한자로 쓰인 것이었다.
• The explorers d_______________ the documents in the desert.
탐험가들은 사막에서 그 문서들을 발견했다.

3 • Sick people wash themselves hoping to c_______________ their illnesses.
아픈 사람들이 병을 치료하기를 바라면서 몸을 씻는다.
• A common c_______________ for hiccups is gulping a glass of water.
딸꾹질에 대한 하나의 치료법은 물 한 잔을 꿀꺽 마시는 것이다.

4 • We should replace street lamps with energy e_______________ ones.
우리는 에너지 효율이 높은 가로등으로 교체해야 한다.
• It would be more e_______________ than trying to build the ship on earth.
그것은 육지에서 배를 만들려 시도하는 것보다 더 효율적일 것이다.

23E Choose Synonyms *문장의 밑줄 친 부분과 가장 유사한 뜻의 단어를 고르세요.*

1 The farmer had faith in gaining pardon from the king.
그 농부는 왕으로부터 사면 받으리라는 것을 굳게 믿었다.
① weight ② favor ③ trust ④ forgiveness

2 How was the seal different from other seals when it showed up again?
그 바다표범이 다시 나타났을 때 다른 바다표범들과의 차이점이 무엇이었는가?
① bragged ② changed ③ appeared ④ exhibited

3 The villagers were passionate defenders of their tradition.
그 마을 사람들은 전통을 지키는 데에 열성적이었다.
① envious ② intelligent ③ reluctant ④ enthusiastic

4 Did you sign up for that Thai conversation class you were talking about?
전에 말하던 태국어 회화 수업에 등록했는가?
① enroll in ② approve of ③ carry on ④ put off

23F Reading Passage 공부한 단어가 포함된 글을 잘 읽고 다음 문제를 풀어 보세요.

Tony was not very successful in **academics**. Rather, ⓐ he was the unruliest troublemaker in his town. I met Tony at a weekend leadership training. All the **pupils** at school had been invited to **sign up for** the training.

(A) He knew something about **poverty**, starvation, and hopelessness. The kids on the team were impressed with ⓑ his **passionate** concern and ideas. They elected Tony co-**chairperson** of the team. Teachers were **uncomfortable** with it, but the kids didn't care about ⓒ their responses. Tony was **responsible** for the food collecting drive and the student council followed Tony's **instruction**.

(B) At the training, ⓓ they talked about positive and **negative** things that had occurred at school. Kids in Tony's group welcomed his comments, since he didn't **criticize** but listened. Tony felt like a part of the group. Tony and other kids joined the Homeless Project team.

(C) Two weeks later, Tony and his friends collected a school record: 2,854 cans of food. Tony started **showing up** at school every day and answered questions from teachers. Tony is proof that ⓔ all birds can fly once the broken wings are **cured**.

* starvation 굶주림

1 주어진 글 다음에 이어질 글의 순서로 가장 적절한 것은?

① (A)-(C)-(B) ② (B)-(A)-(C) ③ (B)-(C)-(A)
④ (C)-(A)-(B) ⑤ (C)-(B)-(A)

2 위 글의 내용과 일치하는 것은?

① Tony는 주말 리더십 훈련에 불참했다.
② 아이들은 Tony의 열정적인 아이디어를 무시했다.
③ 선생님들은 Tony가 팀의 공동 의장이 된 것을 환영했다.
④ Tony와 친구들은 2천 개 이상의 식품 통조림을 모았다.
⑤ Tony는 출석일이 모자라서 결국 학교를 졸업하지 못했다.

English Only

3 Which of the underlined references(ⓐ~ⓔ) is NOT correct?

① he: Tony
② his: Tony's
③ their: other kids'
④ they: the kids at the training
⑤ all birds: all teens

서술형

4 Fill in the blanks to complete the answer. Use words from the passage.

How did the kids at the leadership training feel about Tony?
→ They were impressed with Tony's ___________ concern and ideas. They also felt he didn't judge or ___________ but tried to listen and understand.

Lesson 24

SUMMA CUM LAUDE

Word 500 461~480
Reading 25 24

24A Word List

중학교 3학년 필수단어를 예문과 함께 공부하세요.

461 **attract** [ətrǽkt]
동 마음을 끌다, 끌어 모으다 명 attraction 매력, 명소
Most of them are boring and **attract** no attention.
그것들 대부분은 지루하고 어떠한 관심도 끌지 못했다.

462 **bitter** [bítər]
형 (맛이) 쓴, 격렬한, 지독한 참고 sour (맛이) 신
Most chemicals in toothpaste taste **bitter**.
치약에 들어 있는 대부분의 화학 약품들은 쓴 맛이 난다.

463 **border** [bɔ́ːrdər]
명 국경, 경계 (지역) 동 (국경 · 경계를) 접하다
A man was caught crossing the **border**.
한 남자가 국경을 넘다가 체포되었다.

464 **boundary** [báundəri]
명 경계선, 한계선 유 borderline 국경선, 경계선
The river marks the **boundary** between my property and his.
이 강은 나와 그의 소유지 사이의 경계선을 표시한다.

465 **broadcast** [brɔ́ːdkæ̀st]
동 방송하다; 광고하다 명 방송 broadcast-broadcast-broadcast
The opening ceremonies will be **broadcast** on NBS.
개회식은 NBS에서 방송될 것이다.

466 **bunch** [bʌntʃ]
명 다발, 송이, 묶음
The customer ahead of me purchased the last **bunch** of grapes.
내 앞에 있는 손님이 마지막 남은 포도 한 송이를 샀다.

467 **compose** [kəmpóuz]
동 구성하다; 작곡하다 참고 be composed of ~로 구성되다
It inspired him to **compose** a song on the spot.
그것이 그에게 즉석에서 노래를 작곡하도록 영감을 불어넣었다.

468 **conquer** [káŋkər]
동 정복하다; 물리치다 명 conquest 정복
There is so much to learn and so much to **conquer** in the world.
세상에는 배워야 할 것이 무척 많고 물리쳐야 할 것도 많이 있다.

469 **cooperate** [kouápərèit]
동 협력[협동]하다(with) 명 cooperation 협력, 협동
Many animal species **cooperate** with each other.
많은 종의 동물들은 서로 협력한다.

470 **crash** [kræʃ]

명 사고; 붕괴 동 충돌하다, 부딪치다(=collide)

A boy miraculously survived an airplane **crash**.
한 소년이 비행기 추락 사고에서 기적적으로 살아남았다.

471 **crop** [krɑp]

명 (농)작물; 수확량

Corn is an important **crop** in temperate climates.
옥수수는 온대 기후에서 중요한 작물이다.

472 **dictation** [diktéiʃən]

명 받아쓰기, 구술 동 dictate 받아쓰게 하다, 구술하다; 명령하다

The best listening practice is **dictation**.
최고의 듣기 연습은 받아쓰기이다.

473 **eastern** [íːstərn]

형 동쪽의, 동쪽에 있는; 동양(식)의

They live in the **eastern** part of London.
그들은 런던의 동부 지역에 산다.

474 **mend** [mend]

동 수선하다, 고치다 유 repair

The service engineer will **mend** that leaking roof.
수리 기사가 물이 새는 지붕을 수리할 것이다.

475 **oar** [ɔːr]

명 (보트의) 노 유 paddle 노, 주걱

As soon as the **oar** broke, I knew we were in trouble.
노가 부러지자마자 나는 우리가 곤경에 처했음을 알았다.

476 **region** [ríːdʒən]

명 지역, 지방 형 regional 지역의, 지방의

There are several rivers in the **region**.
그 지역에는 강이 여러 개 있다.

477 **unfortunately** [ʌnfɔ́ːrtʃənitli]

부 불행하게도, 유감스럽게도

Unfortunately, he didn't make it to the final round.
불행하게도 그는 결승전에 진출하지 못했다.

478 **violent** [váiələnt]

형 폭력적인, 격렬한, 사나운 명 violence 폭력 유 fierce 사나운

There are too many **violent** scenes in the movie.
그 영화에는 폭력적인 장면이 너무 많다.

479 **play a part in**

(~에 있어) 역할을 하다, 일익을 담당하다 유 play a role in

Girls' education **plays a** large **part in** global development.
소녀들의 교육은 전 세계의 발전에 큰 역할을 한다.

480 **when it comes to**

~에 관해서라면, ~의 때가 되면

When it comes to playing tennis, he is second to none.
테니스 치는 것에 관해서라면 그는 누구에게도 뒤지지 않는다.

24B Complete the Phrases *빈칸에 알맞은 말을 넣어 어구를 완성하세요.*

1 ______________ and sweet taste (쓰고 단 맛)

2 the ______________ end of the Himalayas (히말라야 동쪽의 끝)

3 ______________ gardening (원예에 관해서라면)

4 a ______________ of roses (한 다발의 장미)

5 ______________ tourists (관광객을 끌어 모으다)

6 ______________ to the ground (땅과 충돌하다)

7 ______________ the fence (울타리를 고치다)

8 pull an ______________ (노를 젓다)

24C Complete the Sentences *[보기]에서 알맞은 단어를 골라 어법에 맞게 완성하세요.*

[보기]

broadcast unfortunately dictation border region play a part in bunch

1 The show will be ______________ live at 3 p.m. on Saturday, March 1.
그 쇼는 3월 1일 토요일 오후 3시에 생방송으로 중계될 것이다.

2 Dried roses hung in a ______________ on the bookshelf.
말린 장미 한 다발이 책장에 걸려 있었다.

3 A ______________ test will be given this Friday.
이번 주 금요일에 받아쓰기 시험이 있을 것이다.

4 He ______________ making the concert a success.
그는 콘서트를 성공적으로 만드는 데 제 역할을 했다.

5 ______________ he broke up with his girlfriend.
불행하게도 그는 자신의 여자 친구와 헤어졌다.

6 Tundra ______________ are like cold deserts.
툰드라 지역은 추운 사막과 같다.

7 This country shares ______________ with two other countries.
이 나라는 다른 두 나라와 국경을 맞대고 있다.

24D Fill in the Blanks *빈칸에 공통으로 들어갈 단어를 문장에 맞게 고쳐 쓰세요.*

1 • The Earth is c______________ of many different layers of rock.
지구는 서로 다른 여러 개의 암석층으로 이루어져 있다.
• Beethoven c______________ Symphony No. 5 between 1804 and 1808.
베토벤은 5번 교향곡을 1804년부터 1808년 사이에 작곡했다.

2 • She c______________ the mountain in 2013 at the age of 25.
그녀는 25살이 되던 해인 2013년에 그 산을 정복했다.
• He has c______________ his disability and emerged a winner.
그는 그의 장애를 극복하여 승리자로서의 모습을 드러냈다.

3 • The motor show a______________ about one thousand visitors.
그 모터쇼는 약 천 명의 관람객들을 끌어 모았다.
• The policy a______________ more foreign students to Korea.
그 정책은 더 많은 학생들을 한국으로 끌어 모았다.

4 • Many violent scenes are b______________ worldwide.
수많은 폭력적인 장면들이 전 세계로 방송되고 있다.
• I'd like to apply for the job at the b______________ company.
나는 그 방송국에 입사 지원하고 싶다.

24E Choose Synonyms *문장의 밑줄 친 부분과 가장 유사한 뜻의 단어를 고르세요.*

1 People around the man suddenly turned <u>violent</u>.
그 남자 주변에 있던 사람들이 갑자기 폭력적으로 변했다.
① ordinary ② creative ③ irritated ④ fierce

2 They pulled as hard as they could on the <u>oars</u>.
그들은 할 수 있는 한 세게 노를 저었다.
① wheel ② paddle ③ vehicle ④ device

3 This is considered to be one of the world's richest <u>regions</u>.
이곳은 세계에서 가장 부유한 지역 중에 하나라고 여겨진다.
① addition ② access ③ area ④ era

4 Fishermen were <u>mending</u> their nets.
어부들은 그들의 그물을 수리하고 있었다.
① fixing ② robbing ③ borrowing ④ purchasing

24F Reading Passage 공부한 단어가 포함된 글을 잘 읽고 다음 문제를 풀어 보세요.

The river has always been and continues to be a **boundary** between areas where people live or gather. In ancient times, rivers were natural boundaries. The people living in one village would plant **crops** on one side of a river, build living areas on that same side of the river, and generally have no use for the land on the other side of the river. Especially if the river was a wide one, crossing ⓐ it by rowing **oars**, **unfortunately**, was too much work. Except, of course, if you wanted to **conquer** your neighbors. Rivers have slowed down many conquerors in times past. Even in the "modernized" 20th Century, rivers have **played** major **parts in** protecting countries from attack and slowing down attacks by **violent** neighbors.

Rivers make natural boundaries. It's a lot easier to just say that the **eastern** boundary of the state of Missouri is the Mississippi River in many places than it is to get a **bunch** of surveyors and mark the boundary the hard way. Check out the map of the United States. Make sure ⓑ it includes rivers. You'll find that the eastern boundary of Nebraska is also a river, the Missouri River.

Rivers are boundaries for counties and cities, too. You can probably find some on the map of your place or other **regions**. And it's not just the United States. The Huang He River marks the eastern **border** of China's Shensi province. The Danube River helps form the border between Romania and Bulgaria. **When it comes to** boundaries, you ______________________.

1 위 글의 제목으로 가장 적절한 것은?

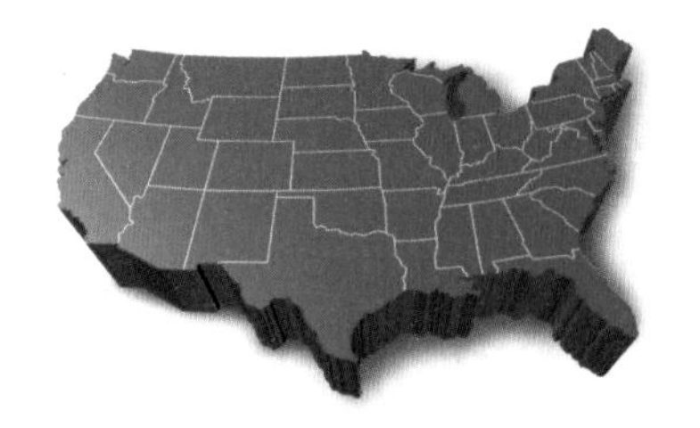

① The River as a Boundary
② Nature vs. Human Beings
③ The Wider River, the Better
④ The River as a Source of Life
⑤ Once a Neighbor, Always a Neighbor

2 위 글의 빈칸에 들어갈 말로 가장 적절한 것은?

① can't help creating one for yourself
② shouldn't think of a river as a boundary
③ wouldn't predict which represents which
④ don't get much more natural than a river
⑤ aren't sure of their various kinds of ones

English Only

3 According to the passage, which is NOT true?

① The river has been used as a natural boundary.
② In ancient times, people planted crops on both sides of a river.
③ In the 20th century, rivers protected countries from neighbors.
④ The Missouri River separates Nebraska from other regions.
⑤ There are nations separated from other nations by a river.

서술형

4 What do the underlined ⓐ and ⓑ refer to?

ⓐ ______________________________
ⓑ ______________________________

Lesson 25

Word 500 481~500
Reading 25 25

SUMMA CUM LAUDE

25A Word List

중학교 3학년 필수단어를 예문과 함께 공부하세요.

481 **approach** [əpróutʃ]
동 접근하다, 다가가다 명 접근(법)
I slowly **approached** the door and quietly pushed it open.
나는 천천히 다가가서 조용히 문을 밀어서 열었다.

482 **civilization** [sìvəlizéiʃən]
명 문명, 문명 세계(사회), 문명화 동 civilize 개화(교화)하다, 세련되게 하다
This modern **civilization** is making us slaves.
이런 현대 문명이 우리를 노예로 만들어가고 있다.

483 **compete** [kəmpí:t]
동 경쟁하다 명 competition 경쟁 형 competitive 경쟁의
No company can **compete** with us in terms of quality and price.
제품의 질과 가격 면에서 어떤 회사도 우리와 경쟁할 수 없다.

484 **concept** [kánsept]
명 개념, 발상, (상품 등의) 테마
The basic **concept** of this book is very simple.
이 책의 기본 개념은 매우 간단하다.

485 **crisis** [kráisis]
명 위기, 중대 국면 유 emergency 비상 사태
The world economy has experienced a financial **crisis**.
세계 경제가 재정 위기를 겪어왔다.

486 **defend** [difénd]
동 방어하다, 변호하다 명 방어, 변호
Additional troops were sent to **defend** the borders.
국경을 방어하기 위해서 추가 병력이 파견되었다.

487 **development** [divéləpmənt]
명 발달, 성장, 개발 동 develop 발달시키다
Music is very helpful for children's emotional **development**.
음악은 아이들의 정서 발달에 큰 도움이 된다.

488 **dominant** [dámənənt]
형 우세한, 지배적인 명 dominance 지배
Change is the **dominant** factor in society today.
변화는 오늘날의 사회에서 지배적인 요소이다.

489 **electronic** [ilèktránik]
형 전자 (공학)의, 전자에 의한 참고 electronics 전자 제품, 전자 공학
This person obviously doesn't like **electronic** music.
이 사람은 분명히 전자 음악을 좋아하지 않는다.

490 **emphasize** [émfəsàiz]

동 강조하다(=stress), 역설하다 명 emphasis 강조

Her writing **emphasized** the importance of creativity.
그녀의 글은 창조의 중요성을 강조했다.

491 **exhibition** [èksəbíʃən]

명 전시, 전시회 동 exhibit 전시하다

We were invited to a photo **exhibition**.
우리는 어느 사진 전시회에 초대 받았다.

492 **harsh** [hɑːrʃ]

형 가혹한, 맹렬한(=fierce) 부 harshly 가혹하게

His dismissal was **harsh** and unfair.
그의 해고는 가혹하고 불공평했다.

493 **majority** [mədʒɔ́ːrəti]

명 가장 많은 수, 다수 반 minority 소수

The **majority** of people surveyed felt uncomfortable.
설문에 응한 사람들의 대다수가 불편함을 느꼈다.

494 **optional** [ɑ́pʃənəl]

형 선택적인 명 option 선택 참고 elective 선거의, 선택 가능한

Many **optional** features are available on this car.
이 차에는 선택 가능한 기능이 많이 있습니다.

495 **pollution** [pəlúːʃən]

명 오염, 공해 동 pollute 오염시키다

There are many ways to take action to reduce air **pollution**.
대기 오염을 줄이기 위해서 조치를 취할 방법들은 많이 있다.

496 **professional** [prəféʃənəl]

형 직업적인, 전문적인 명 전문직 종사자

I came across a **professional** golfer at the airport.
나는 공항에서 우연히 한 프로 골프 선수를 만났다.

497 **standard** [stǽndərd]

명 수준, 기준 형 일반적인, 보통의 유 average 평균(의)

His overall performance was not up to **standard**.
전반적인 그의 실적은 기준에 미치지 못했다.

498 **transaction** [trænsǽkʃən]

명 거래, 매매 동 transact 거래하다 유 deal

All **transactions** between international customers are permitted.
국제 고객들 사이의 모든 거래가 허용된다.

499 **tremble** [trémbl]

동 (몸을) 떨다, 떨리다; 흔들리다 유 shake 흔들다

I **tremble** with excitement when I see him sing on the stage.
그가 무대 위에서 노래하는 것을 볼 때 나는 기뻐서 떨린다.

500 **widespread** [wàidspréd]

형 광범위한, 널리 퍼진 유 common, general 흔한, 일반적인

Computers have become **widespread** in all areas of life.
컴퓨터가 삶의 모든 영역에 널리 퍼져 있다.

25B Complete the Phrases

빈칸에 알맞은 말을 넣어 어구를 완성하세요.

1 the global economic ______________ (세계적인 경제 위기)

2 an ______________ course (선택 과목)

3 noise ______________ (소음 공해)

4 a ______________ value (지배적인 가치)

5 ______________ one's own country (자기 자신의 나라를 방어하다)

6 ancient ______________ (여러 고대 문명)

7 ______________ surroundings (가혹한 환경)

8 a cautious ______________ (조심스러운 접근법)

25C Complete the Sentences

[보기]에서 알맞은 단어를 골라 어법에 맞게 완성하세요.

[보기]

concept professional tremble development widespread standard

1 A ______________ athlete is a person who is paid to play a sport.
직업으로 활동하는 운동선수는 운동을 하면서 돈을 받는 사람이다.

2 Free public education became ______________ in the country.
무상 공교육이 그 나라에 널리 퍼지게 되었다.

3 Many woodlands are currently under threat from ______________.
현재 많은 삼림지대가 개발로 인한 위협을 받고 있다.

4 The restaurant offers a high ______________ of service.
그 식당은 높은 수준의 서비스를 제공한다.

5 The shadows grow long and the leaves ______________ in the breeze.
그림자는 길어지고 나뭇잎들은 산들바람에 흔들린다.

6 The Incan ______________ of time was different from that of most other cultures.
잉카의 시간 개념은 대부분의 다른 문화의 것과 달랐다.

25D Fill in the Blanks 빈칸에 공통으로 들어갈 단어를 문장에 맞게 고쳐 쓰세요.

1 • This kind of view became w________________ across the world.
이 같은 의견이 세계적으로 널리 퍼져 나갔다.

• Superstition was w________________ among all classes of society.
미신은 사회의 모든 계층 사이에 광범위하게 퍼져 있었다.

2 • I had to c________________ against 19 other people for the job.
나는 그 일자리를 위해 19명의 다른 사람들과 경쟁해야 했다.

• We need to c________________ in terms of quality.
우리는 품질적인 면에서 경쟁할 필요가 있다.

3 • Africa is going to face a food c________________.
아프리카는 식량 위기에 직면할 것이다.

• The current economic c________________ will affect everyone.
현재의 경제 위기는 모든 사람들에게 영향을 미칠 것이다.

4 • Farming is the d________________ industry in the Texas region.
농업은 텍사스 지역의 지배적인 산업이다.

• The company is d________________ in its market.
그 회사는 이 분야의 시장에서 우위를 차지하고 있다.

25E Choose Synonyms 문장의 밑줄 친 부분과 가장 유사한 뜻의 단어를 고르세요.

1 Earth science is one of the <u>optional</u> subjects.
지구 과학은 선택 과목 중의 하나이다.

① elective ② professional ③ creative ④ obvious

2 The book has received some <u>harsh</u> criticism over the past week.
그 책은 지난주 내내 혹독한 비평을 받았다.

① anxious ② ridiculous ③ fierce ④ soft

3 My school <u>emphasizes</u> the virtue of kindness.
우리 학교는 친절함의 미덕을 강조한다.

① exist ② rely ③ take ④ stress

4 He doesn't have the ability to <u>defend</u> himself against them.
그는 그들에 대항하여 자신을 방어할 능력을 갖고 있지 않다.

① deceive ② abandon ③ evaluate ④ protect

25F Reading Passage 공부한 단어가 포함된 글을 잘 읽고 다음 문제를 풀어 보세요.

According to the **professionals** familiar with money **development**, money in coin form has been around since about 600 B.C. When the Greek and Roman **civilizations** — the **dominant** economies and civilizations of the times — began accepting coins as money, most of the rest of the world followed suit. Coins are still accepted today but usually as percentages of paper money.

The first paper money was issued in China in the 13th century. The **concept** didn't become popular in the West until about 400 years later. The paper dollar appeared in the United States after the Revolutionary War and slowly became the national **standard** of value.

Most of the common forms of money today — including checks, money orders, and government bonds, just to name a few — are based on the dollar. A **majority** of people in the country (and even the world) accept it as a means of exchange. In historical terms, the dollar is a new form of money, but it is accepted almost everywhere in the world.

An even newer form of money is **electronic** money. With the **widespread** use of computers today, a great many **transactions** are electronic. Physical money remains just the same, and paper records are **optional**. The dollars and cents are represented by bits and bytes. The standard hasn't changed, just ____________________.

1 위 글의 제목으로 가장 적절한 것은?

① Uselessness of Coins
② What Money Can't Buy
③ Money Throughout History
④ Money: A Necessary Evil
⑤ The Convenience of Paper Money

2 위 글의 빈칸에 들어갈 말로 가장 적절한 것은?

① the means of supply
② the material of money
③ the types of consumers
④ the method of exchange
⑤ the demand of computers

English Only

3 Which one is closest in meaning to the underlined followed suit in the first paragraph?

① accepted coins as money
② created a new form of money
③ began to conquer other areas
④ refused to make paper money
⑤ preferred paper money to coins

서술형

4 According to the passage, how have the forms of money changed?

The first form of money was the ___________, which is still used. Then ___________ ___________ was first used in China in the 13th century. With the widespread of computers, the use of ___________ ___________ is common these days.

Speedy Check-up 5

Lesson별로 모르는 단어에 체크한 후, 그 갯수를 /20 안에 쓰고 학습성과를 점검해 보세요.
모르는 단어는 다시 찾아 학습하세요.

Lesson 21 /20

- ▢ attitude
- ▢ cast
- ▢ childhood
- ▢ compromise
- ▢ creative
- ▢ encourage
- ▢ greedy
- ▢ nod
- ▢ obstacle
- ▢ opinion
- ▢ overcome
- ▢ pretend
- ▢ profit
- ▢ satisfactory
- ▢ scratch
- ▢ setback
- ▢ shoot
- ▢ struggle
- ▢ wisdom
- ▢ had it rough

Lesson 22 /20

- ▢ adopt
- ▢ ancestor
- ▢ artificial
- ▢ coal
- ▢ commercial
- ▢ communicate
- ▢ electricity
- ▢ erase
- ▢ exchange
- ▢ foolish
- ▢ preserve
- ▢ refer
- ▢ rubber
- ▢ skyscraper
- ▢ steam
- ▢ string
- ▢ thought
- ▢ trial
- ▢ volunteer
- ▢ a large number of

Lesson 23 /20

- ▢ academic
- ▢ chairperson
- ▢ criticize
- ▢ cure
- ▢ discover
- ▢ dump
- ▢ efficient
- ▢ idle
- ▢ instruction
- ▢ negative
- ▢ pardon
- ▢ passionate
- ▢ poverty
- ▢ proof
- ▢ pupil
- ▢ responsible
- ▢ suicide
- ▢ uncomfortable
- ▢ show up
- ▢ sign up for

Lesson 24 /20

- ▢ attract
- ▢ bitter
- ▢ border
- ▢ boundary
- ▢ broadcast
- ▢ bunch
- ▢ compose
- ▢ conquer
- ▢ cooperate
- ▢ crash
- ▢ crop
- ▢ dictation
- ▢ eastern
- ▢ mend
- ▢ oar
- ▢ region
- ▢ unfortunately
- ▢ violent
- ▢ play a part in
- ▢ when it comes to

Lesson 25 /20

- ▢ approach
- ▢ civilization
- ▢ compete
- ▢ concept
- ▢ crisis
- ▢ defend
- ▢ development
- ▢ dominant
- ▢ electronic
- ▢ emphasize
- ▢ exhibition
- ▢ harsh
- ▢ majority
- ▢ optional
- ▢ pollution
- ▢ professional
- ▢ standard
- ▢ transaction
- ▢ tremble
- ▢ widespread

우편봉합엽서

보내는 사람

Stamp

받는 사람

이룸이앤비 Education & Books
www.erumenb.com

서울시 강남구 논현로 16길 4-3 이룸빌딩

(주)이룸이앤비 기획팀

135-963

숨마 주니어®

중학 영어교과서

WORD MANUAL ③

자르는 선

풀 칠 하 세 요

접는 선

성 명		남□ 여□	학교(학원) 학년
휴대전화		e-mail	

숨마 주니어® 중학 영어교과서 **WORD MANUAL ❸**

- 교재를 구입하게 된 동기는 무엇입니까?

□ 학교 교재 □ 학원 교재 □ 선생님의 추천 □ 친구 · 선배의 소개
□ 스스로 선택: (□디자인 □내용 □전체적으로) 좋아서 □ 기타 ____________

- 주로 언제 듣기 mp3파일을 활용하나요?

□ 예습하며 □ 진도 나가며 □ 복습하며 □ 통학시간 □ 기타 ____________

- 교재의 디자인 및 내용에 대한 의견을 들려주세요.

표지디자인:	□ 매우 좋다	□ 좋다	□ 보통이다	□ 좋지 않다
본문디자인:	□ 매우 좋다	□ 좋다	□ 보통이다	□ 좋지 않다
내용 구성:	□ 매우 좋다	□ 좋다	□ 보통이다	□ 좋지 않다

- 교재의 세부적인 내용에 대한 의견을 들려주세요.

[표제어] Part A	분 량	□ 많다	□ 적당하다	□ 조금 부족하다	□ 많이 부족하다
	난이도	□ 쉽다	□ 적당하다	□ 조금 어렵다	□ 많이 어렵다
[단어 확인 문제] Part B·C·D·E	분 량	□ 많다	□ 적당하다	□ 조금 부족하다	□ 많이 부족하다
	난이도	□ 쉽다	□ 적당하다	□ 조금 어렵다	□ 많이 어렵다
[독해지문] Part F	내 용	□ 매우 좋다	□ 좋다	□ 보통이다	□ 좋지 않다
	난이도	□ 쉽다	□ 적당하다	□ 조금 어렵다	□ 많이 어렵다
[워크북]	분 량	□ 많다	□ 적당하다	□ 조금 부족하다	□ 많이 부족하다
	난이도	□ 쉽다	□ 적당하다	□ 조금 어렵다	□ 많이 어렵다

- 이 책에 대해 느낀 점이나 바라는 점을 자유롭게 적어 주세요.

성의껏 작성해서 보내주신 엽서는 뽑아서 선물을 보내드립니다.

자르는 선

쎄듀 주니어®

중학 영어교과서

WORD MANUAL 3

Workbook & Answers

숨마 주니어®

중학 영어교과서

WORD MANUAL ③

Workbook

Answers

Lesson 1

Translation of Words | 영어는 한글로, 한글은 영어로 써 보세요.

1	timid	______	2	forbid	______
3	sight	______	4	prevent	______
5	overweight	______	6	strike	______
7	creature	______	8	awkward	______
9	deserve	______	10	depend on	______
11	소리치다	______	12	마치 ~인 것처럼	______
13	우화	______	14	열, 열병	______
15	항의하다	______	16	효과적인	______
17	갈등, 충돌	______	18	계산하다	______
19	좌절시키다	______	20	방법	______

Passage Dictation | 녹음된 내용을 들으며 글의 빈칸에 알맞은 단어를 쓰세요. 독해01

Here's one of Aesop's ______. Having dreamed that a ______, ______ old man saw his only son killed by a lion, he was afraid that the dream was a vision of what was actually going to happen.

(B) To ______ it from coming true, therefore, he built a very terrific hall raised high above the ground and kept his son there under guard. The hall was decorated with pictures of all sorts of ______, including a lion; but the ______ of them only made him more ______.

(A) One day he stood in front of the lion and ______: "Curse you! It is because of you and my father's dream that I must stay here like a woman. How can I pay you out?" And as he spoke he ______ his hand against the wall ______ he would knock out the lion's eye.

(C) A thin, sharp piece of stone went in under his nail. He felt severe pain and had a high ____________. Before long he died. So although it was but a painted picture, the lion had caused the boy's death, and the ____________ his father used, finally, was not ____________.

Lesson 2

Translation of Words | 영어는 한글로, 한글은 영어로 써 보세요.

1 replace	____________	2 injury	____________
3 strength	____________	4 worth	____________
5 abstract	____________	6 breathe	____________
7 cling	____________	8 expert	____________
9 cheerful	____________	10 accuse	____________
11 생산하다	____________	12 꽃이 피다	____________
13 회상하다	____________	14 정말, 확실히	____________
15 절망적인	____________	16 구매하다	____________
17 회복하다	____________	18 (화산이) 분출하다	____________
19 기적	____________	20 비상사태	____________

Passage Dictation | 녹음된 내용을 들으며 글의 빈칸에 알맞은 단어를 쓰세요. 독해02

On June 23, Jim Smith heard the ____________ screams of a woman whose son was ____________ onto the veranda. "It wasn't a normal scream, so I knew it was an ____________," said Jim. "It was a scream ____________ in the most urgent moment in one's life" He couldn't ignore the situation. He ran 30 meters and spread his arms wide, much like a goalkeeper ready to block a shot. At that moment, the boy's fingers slipped, and he fell right into Jim's ready arms, which lasted only 15 to

20 seconds. "It all happened so fast. It's a ___________. I couldn't really think, not even for a second," Jim ___________. True to his words, catching a 17kg child falling from 15 meters high is ___________ a miracle. "It would be the same as being hit by an object travelling at 70km per hour," an ___________ said. Although he was unable to move comfortably due to ___________ and had a bit of difficulty ___________ for a moment, Jim is ___________ in the hospital. The boy luckily suffered from just a nosebleed. The boy's parents came to the hospital and asked Jim what he wanted. But he didn't want any reward. He said saving a life was ___________ the risk.

Lesson 3

Translation of Words | 영어는 한글로, 한글은 영어로 써 보세요.

1	succeed	___________	2	whisper	___________
3	relate	___________	4	opportunity	___________
5	pursuit	___________	6	authority	___________
7	principle	___________	8	aim	___________
9	contrast	___________	10	possibility	___________
11	영구적인	___________	12	복도, 통로	___________
13	시작하다, 출시하다	___________	14	보장, 보장하다	___________
15	기꺼이 ~하다	___________	16	종교	___________
17	표면	___________	18	그러므로, 따라서	___________
19	품질	___________	20	주거지, 피신처	___________

Passage Dictation | 녹음된 내용을 들으며 글의 빈칸에 알맞은 단어를 쓰세요. 독해03

In a 12-year study at Babson College, Dr. Robert Miller, an ___________ on businessmen education, searched for the reasons for success or failure among the students who graduated from the business school. Some went on to build successful businesses, but most did not. He discovered that those who built successful businesses had a special __________. It was that they had the courage to __________ their businesses with no __________ of success. They ______________ risk failure in the pursuit of their dreams.

Professor Miller called this the "__________ __________." He said that when you launch toward your goal, however distant, you begin to move down a corridor of time. As you move down this corridor, other doors of __________ will open up on either side of you. But you would not have been able to see these other doors of opportunity if you were not already in motion down this psychological corridor toward your goal.

Most people who __________ in life achieve their success in an area completely different from the field in which they started off. But because they were in motion, they saw opportunities and __________ that they would not have been aware of if they had waited until everything was just right. And the reality is that everything will never be just right.

Lesson 4

Translation of Words | 영어는 한글로, 한글은 영어로 써 보세요.

1 demanding	__________	2 casually	__________
3 mature	__________	4 adapt	__________
5 fairly	__________	6 declare	__________
7 persuade	__________	8 dumb	__________
9 boast	__________	10 improve	__________
11 어려움, 장애	__________	12 수행하다, 지휘하다	__________
13 공격적인	__________	14 박수를 치다	__________

15 결과	______________	16 수사하다	______________
17 제조하다	______________	18 특징, 특유의	______________
19 대하다	______________	20 장비	______________

Passage Dictation | 녹음된 내용을 들으며 글의 빈칸에 알맞은 단어를 쓰세요. 독해04

Many parents seem to adopt the attitude "My child, right or wrong"— with terrible results. Being a parent means being ____________ enough to help a child ____________ to disappointment. Parents who can't accept when their child isn't No.1 send the message that when they are frustrated, they blame the source of frustration instead of looking for a way to cope.

A better message parents can show is to teach children that while they cannot always control the ____________ of every situation, they can control how they respond. Children must learn to behave more politely than they feel. By doing so, they will not get hurt and will be able to deal with ____________. Being polite is about more than simply saying "please" and "thank you." It's about not ____________ or calling someone names behind their back, about winning fairly and losing graciously, and ____________ everyone with respect.

Of course, all the training in the world won't ____________ a child to behave politely if his parents become ____________, ____________ and rude. That's why experts agree the best way for parents to ____________ a child's manners is to improve their own first. Parents need to be especially careful not to say something ____________ that they may be alarmed to hear later in the mouths of their children. If we aren't practicing good manners, how can we expect our children to do so?

Lesson 5

Translation of Words | 영어는 한글로, 한글은 영어로 써 보세요.

1	property	________	2	operation	________
3	portable	________	4	device	________
5	attempt	________	6	loose	________
7	phrase	________	8	memorize	________
9	practice	________	10	panic	________
11	구조, 구조물	________	12	즉시, 동시에	________
13	큰 덩어리	________	14	과외의	________
15	철자법	________	16	행성	________
17	직업	________	18	예약하다	________
19	~에 애쓰다	________	20	화학	________

Passage Dictation | 녹음된 내용을 들으며 글의 빈칸에 알맞은 단어를 쓰세요. 독해05

When you have many subjects or many things, it can help to break things into ____________. Let's say you have a test on 20 ____________ words. Instead of thinking about all of the words ____________, try breaking them down into five-word chunks and ____________ one or two different chunks each night.

Don't worry if you can't remember something on the first ____________. That's where the practice comes in. The more days you spend reviewing something, the more likely it is to stick in your brain. There are also tricks called secret ____________ that can help you remember things. When you're trying to ____________ a list of things, make up a ____________ that uses the first letter of each. For example, are you trying to learn the eight planets and their order from the sun? Think: My Very Excellent Mother Just Served Us Nachos to remember Mercury, Venus, Earth, Mars, Jupiter, Saturn, Uranus, and Neptune. Your teacher can give you ideas, too.

Another way to break it up is to study regularly instead of just the night before. You can always review your notes and read over the chapters you're working on. Or, if you're studying math, ____________, or biology, do some ____________ problems.

Lesson 6

Translation of Words | 영어는 한글로, 한글은 영어로 써 보세요.

1	ridiculous	____________	2	classify	____________
3	raw	____________	4	associate	____________
5	according to	____________	6	accompany	____________
7	whereas	____________	8	focus	____________
9	applause	____________	10	atmosphere	____________
11	지지하다	____________	12	참가자	____________
13	온도	____________	14	후손	____________
15	논평	____________	16	충실한	____________
17	망치다	____________	18	표현	____________
19	현실	____________	20	무시하다	____________

Passage Dictation | 녹음된 내용을 들으며 글의 빈칸에 알맞은 단어를 쓰세요. 독해06

Marcel Zeelenberg found a pattern in observations of ____________ on a Dutch ____________ television show. If you happened to be in the Netherlands in the mid-1990s, you might have watched an episode or two of *I Am Sorry*, in which ordinary people explained some ____________ things they had done to someone ____________ to them.

One guest regretted ignoring a friend during a difficult time, another regretted saying unpleasant things about a deceased friend at his funeral, still another felt bad about slapping a friend's face. After expressing their regret on television, these participants were then presented with the opportunity to apologize and give flowers to the person who had been hurt.

__________________ Zeelenberg, "This was usually followed by emotional scenes with lots of hugging, kisses, and tears ____________ by ____________ from the audience." Zeelenberg's team collected 82 ____________ of regret that appeared on 18 different episodes, then ____________ these into regrets of inaction and action. They discovered that the inaction regrets had been becoming three and a half times longer than the action regrets. In short, regrets of action ____________ on the short term, ____________ regrets of inaction focus on the long term.

Lesson 7

Translation of Words | 영어는 한글로, 한글은 영어로 써 보세요.

1	leak	__________	2	article	__________
3	politics	__________	4	wonder	__________
5	entire	__________	6	detail	__________
7	custom	__________	8	institute	__________
9	hopeless	__________	10	pill	__________
11	세균	__________	12	반영하다	__________
13	개인(의)	__________	14	특징	__________
15	재활용하다	__________	16	요소	__________
17	신문, 언론계	__________	18	묘사하다	__________
19	윤리적인	__________	20	적절한	__________

Passage Dictation | 녹음된 내용을 들으며 글의 빈칸에 알맞은 단어를 쓰세요. 독해07

Newspaper ___________ can never tell the ___________ truth: some ___________ of lying is inherent in all ___________ because it is impossible for one article to include all the ___________ of the story. Journalists may also manipulate the order in which they present information to achieve more dramatic or other effects in their writing. Choosing details and the order to ___________ them is considered proper and ethical behavior for journalists. Editors can even ___________ their paper's political bias when writing opinion pieces about elections and ___________.

In book publishing, many companies do not always examine carefully the information authors write. A best-selling book can make a lot of money, so some authors find it tempting to make up lies. In one famous case, a writer invented a completely fictitious history about himself. The writing seemed credible, so most ___________ believed his story. However, the writer later was unable to make a record of the facts in the books, and he was revealed as a fake. Although the writer's tale was not ___________, many people still found it meaningful. Even these readers agree that they would rather not be left in the dark, ___________ whether or not a story is true. They would rather be aware of any major alteration of facts that made a good story possible.

Lesson 8

Translation of Words | 영어는 한글로, 한글은 영어로 써 보세요.

1 merit ___________ 2 brief ___________

3 aspect ___________ 4 independent ___________

5 obtain ___________ 6 seldom ___________

7	conform	______________	8	disaster	______________
9	confident	______________	10	comfort	______________
11	짜증나게 하다	______________	12	격리하다	______________
13	구별하다	______________	14	영향(을 미치다)	______________
15	껴안다	______________	16	금융의	______________
17	희생(하다)	______________	18	문서	______________
19	방해하다	______________	20	행동, 태도	______________

Passage Dictation | 녹음된 내용을 들으며 글의 빈칸에 알맞은 단어를 쓰세요. 독해08

We often look to others for cues on how we should behave. Most of us are followers, not leaders, traveling along the beaten path with ____________ and ease, ____________ striking out in our own direction. We prefer to let others set the standard and then fall into line, careful not to make waves. TV comedies use laugh tracks for this very reason. Will you think something is funnier if other people are laughing? A lot of people are betting you will.

This response is present in many other ____________ of your life. When you allow your ____________ to be ____________ by the behavior of others, you ____________ your own desires and needs to be ____________. ____________ and ____________ people are less likely to be swayed by the majority if they feel it's not in their best interest. They know what they want and do not care if they stand alone. But you don't want to stick out or gain attention as an independent thinker. For you, this label is ____________. You would rather ____________ to become part of the group.

It's for this reason that you often second-guess your own judgment based on the behavior of others. On the highway, if you see a lot of traffic going in the opposite direction, you wonder if you are going the wrong way. You are the one who asks everyone else what they are ordering at the restaurant. You want to make sure that you ____________ something that's "okay."

Lesson 9

Translation of Words | 영어는 한글로, 한글은 영어로 써 보세요.

1	represent	2	anywhere
3	intersection	4	regard
5	unusual	6	holy
7	symbolize	8	unite
9	exist	10	bloom
11	고정하다	12	관련시키다
13	뜨다, 띄우다	14	논평, 말하다
15	분명한	16	깨닫다, 실현하다
17	행운을 빌다	18	주먹
19	뿌리	20	민주주의

Passage Dictation | 녹음된 내용을 들으며 글의 빈칸에 알맞은 단어를 쓰세요. 독해09

If you tell a friend, "______________________", you're practicing a custom that required the intersecting and __________ of index fingers. It differed from the one that we know today, but symbolizes the same thing. The gesture is __________ in the belief that a cross __________ the __________ of two people; and that its point of __________ marked the place __________ spirits __________. So it __________ two people: one a wisher, and the other a supporter. A wish made on a cross was __________ as something anchored at the cross's intersection until that desire was __________. It was __________ in old books that the superstition was popular among many early European cultures. In crossing fingers for good luck, the index finger of a well wisher was placed over the index finger of the person expressing the wish. It is __________ that the ancient custom of the "crossed fingers" of friends was simplified to a wisher crossing his own fingers and finally to today's expression "I'll keep my fingers crossed."

Lesson 10

Translation of Words | 영어는 한글로, 한글은 영어로 써 보세요.

1	particle	____________	2	grip	____________
3	dim	____________	4	appear	____________
5	spoil	____________	6	rescue	____________
7	ethnic	____________	8	resource	____________
9	spill	____________	10	rainfall	____________
11	가뭄, 결핍	____________	12	굶주리다	____________
13	~와 관련 있다	____________	14	해결책	____________
15	도약하다	____________	16	제안하다	____________
17	익사하다	____________	18	높이	____________
19	해저의	____________	20	목적	____________

Passage Dictation | 녹음된 내용을 들으며 글의 빈칸에 알맞은 단어를 쓰세요. 독해10

The planet is getting hotter as a result of global warming. Experts warn that when the polar ice caps melt down, water will ____________ over and eventually ____________ villages in the lowlands and islands. However, some scientists are worried about something that is the complete opposite: global dimming. Global dimming ____________________ solid particles such as ash and soot that pollute the air and reduce the amount of sunlight reaching the planet's surface.

It ____________ that global dimming is the ____________ to global warming, but it does harm to the planet as well. It has a cooling effect on the northern hemisphere, reducing ground and ocean temperatures and thus reducing ____________. Experts ____________ that this could have had a significant effect on Africa. They believe that the global dimming contributed to the ____________ that ____________ the continent during the 1980s and made people ____________ to death.

Lesson 11

Translation of Words | 영어는 한글로, 한글은 영어로 써 보세요.

1	useless	____________	2	combine	____________
3	intelligent	____________	4	digital	____________
5	sheet	____________	6	aptitude	____________
7	vital	____________	8	turn out	____________
9	glue	____________	10	ensure	____________
11	안전	____________	12	허락하다	____________
13	거절하다	____________	14	규칙	____________
15	알아보다	____________	16	논리적인	____________
17	파도(타기를 하다)	____________	18	예측하다	____________
19	여권	____________	20	(가격이) 알맞은	____________

Passage Dictation | 녹음된 내용을 들으며 글의 빈칸에 알맞은 단어를 쓰세요. 독해11

In a sense, the ____________ revolution in telecommunications has already started. The ____________ technology industry is booming. Moore's Law, a rule that states microprocessor power doubles every 18 months, continues to hold true. In the same way Gilder's Law — available bandwidth will triple every 12 months — makes the Internet ____________. The Internet connection has become a ____________ part of both work and personal life. Moreover, we can easily ____________ that the value of the electronic device increases as it connects to the Internet. Take the doorbell, for example. When someone rings it and no one's at home, it turns out to be a ____________ device. But if you ____________ the doorbell and the cell phone, you can answer the door on the other side of the town. You recognize the 'ringer' via the video camera and talk to him. You can then decide whether to ____________ him to enter the house or not. The new doorbell can ____________ a higher level of ____________ for you!

Lesson 12

Translation of Words | 영어는 한글로, 한글은 영어로 써 보세요.

1	otherwise	____________	2	hibernate	____________
3	shadow	____________	4	principal	____________
5	endanger	____________	6	resemble	____________
7	consult	____________	8	translate	____________
9	exposure	____________	10	rob	____________
11	요리법	____________	12	이익, 장점	____________
13	기어가다, 서행	____________	14	전설	____________
15	이상적인	____________	16	결정하다	____________
17	매력	____________	18	기념	____________
19	가까운, 임박한	____________	20	재미, 오락	____________

Passage Dictation | 녹음된 내용을 들으며 글의 빈칸에 알맞은 단어를 쓰세요. 독해12

Punxsutawney, Pennsylvania, is the home of Punxsutawney Phil, the most famous of the furry weather forecasters who walk slowly forth from their holes every February 2 to predict how long winter will stay. In early February, this tiny town ____________ a large city. And on February 2, named Groundhog Day, leaders of the community gather on Gobbler's Knob to ____________ with Phil, who ____________ out of his hole and either sees his ____________ or doesn't. As the tradition goes, if Phil sees his shadow, that means that winter is still hanging around, for another six weeks; if Phil doesn't see his shadow, the ____________ says, then spring is ________________.

No one is sure just when this tradition began. It is first mentioned in the 18th Century, possibly connected with the ____________ of Candlemas, which occurred halfway between the first day of winter and the first day of spring. And although the dates are not the same, the belief that the weather on Candlemas ____________ how soon spring would come was ____________ to the groundhog, or woodchuck, who was a ____________ animal who usually chose early February to end his hibernation. Nowadays, however, it doesn't matter whether Phil is even right. It's all an excuse to get together and celebrate a "holiday" and ____________ for the small, ____________ ordinary town of Punxsutawney.

Lesson 13

Translation of Words | 영어는 한글로, 한글은 영어로 써 보세요.

1	clone	____________	2	organ	____________
3	lump	____________	4	disabled	____________
5	refresh	____________	6	damage	____________
7	backbone	____________	8	react	____________
9	emotion	____________	10	destination	____________
11	액체	____________	12	고장 나다	____________
13	산(성의)	____________	14	영양소	____________
15	녹다, 사라지다	____________	16	필요한	____________
17	위, 복부	____________	18	일생의	____________
19	비눗방울	____________	20	삼키다	____________

Passage Dictation | 녹음된 내용을 들으며 글의 빈칸에 알맞은 단어를 쓰세요. 독해13

Keep a piece of bread in your mouth for a few minutes and after a short while you'll notice a sweet taste. That is the beginning of digestion, as enzymes in your saliva begin to ____________ the food. The next step is when you ____________ the food. In the ____________, a pool of ____________, enzymes, and other fluids

__________ the food __________ further. That acid would be strong enough to dissolve iron nails. Luckily, your stomach has a special lining that keeps the chemicals from __________ it. The food is in the __________ form now and is pushed into the 5m coiled-up small intestine. When the food arrives, the small intestine __________ by pouring more digestive juices before at last everything is pushed out of the small intestine. By now the body has absorbed the __________ __________ to keep it fit. The next __________ is the large intestine. There, any remaining water is sucked out of the food and it goes down as a __________ of waste. Air __________ in the food leak out of your body. It's time for you to go to the bathroom!

Lesson 14

Translation of Words | 영어는 한글로, 한글은 영어로 써 보세요.

1	progress	__________	2	charity	__________
3	significant	__________	4	specifically	__________
5	refuse	__________	6	reveal	__________
7	unselfish	__________	8	contact	__________
9	harmful	__________	10	connection	__________
11	유사성	__________	12	(사회적) 유산	__________
13	관계	__________	14	복잡한, 복합 건물	__________
15	증거	__________	16	기부	__________
17	보상, 보답하다	__________	18	비공식의	__________
19	저지르다, 헌신하다	__________	20	영향을 미치다	__________

Passage Dictation | 녹음된 내용을 들으며 글의 빈칸에 알맞은 단어를 쓰세요. 독해14

Bill Harbaugh and his team at the University of Oregon looked ____________ at the ____________ between the brain and economic decisions. In one of their experiments to ____________ the seemingly ____________ ____________, the researchers tried seeing if people's ____________ to ____________ were ____________ by neurons. Nineteen women were given $100 to play a charity game on the computer. They could choose to donate or not to a charity and each decision led to other situations where they could gain or lose money. At the end of the game, the subjects were able to keep all the money that was left in their accounts.

As the subjects played the game, the scientists scanned their brains. They looked at the brain's "pleasure center," which controls how good people feel. When most subjects donated money to a charity, their pleasure centers lit up on the brain scan. Some even lit up when they were taxed on their donations. Both results suggest that the brain's pleasure center is ____________ for ____________ acts. In addition, the more people donated, the more their pleasure centers lit up. For some, the pleasure center lit up more when the computer gave the charity extra money than when they received extra money to keep for themselves. The scientists point out that this was the first neural ____________ for pure altruism, meaning that altruism may indeed have a biological connection.

Lesson 15

Translation of Words | 영어는 한글로, 한글은 영어로 써 보세요.

1 a series of ____________
2 technology ____________
3 viewpoint ____________
4 sunset ____________
5 experiment ____________
6 material ____________

7	concentrate	______________	8	consist	______________
9	indicate	______________	10	make sense	______________
11	지진	______________	12	연장하다	______________
13	조화, 화음	______________	14	풍경	______________
15	수평선	______________	16	온도, 정도	______________
17	길, 노선	______________	18	예보(하다)	______________
19	일시적인	______________	20	논쟁하다	______________

Passage Dictation | 녹음된 내용을 들으며 글의 빈칸에 알맞은 단어를 쓰세요. 독해15

There is a theory that our sun is a part of a Binary Solar system that ____________ of two suns and their planets. If we had two suns, the ____________ would be very different and we would see a ____________ twice a day! Well, our solar system actually orbits around this other solar system, so we can see only one sun that rises on the ____________. The orbit, or the ____________ that the other solar system moves is bound to our own solar system and they meet each other every 25,920 years. So we can ____________ the next "encounter" with the second sun. Our ____________ can prove whether our sun has a companion. Through ________________________, NASA has gathered evidence of the other sun, but it hasn't been released because of the ____________ it could create. The other sun is really far and from our ____________, it's only a small brown star. To a certain ____________, it makes sense. It is known that about 80% of the stars in the galaxy are binary stars, and they are all in a perfect ____________.

Lesson 16

Translation of Words | 영어는 한글로, 한글은 영어로 써 보세요.

1 wildlife ______________
2 invasion ______________
3 cruel ______________
4 to death ______________
5 mankind ______________
6 blame ______________
7 suffer ______________
8 smooth ______________
9 physical ______________
10 bark ______________
11 포유동물 ______________
12 감염, 전염병 ______________
13 ~에 민감한 ______________
14 증가하다 ______________
15 끔찍한, 지독한 ______________
16 손바닥 ______________
17 펼치다 ______________
18 위협하다 ______________
19 하품하다 ______________
20 돌아다니다 ______________

Passage Dictation | 녹음된 내용을 들으며 글의 빈칸에 알맞은 단어를 쓰세요. 독해16

Marmots are members of the squirrel family, and they are about the size of a cat. Having large, round eyes and a small mouth and nose, they look cute and innocent. But they can be an ____________ enemy of ____________. A kind of marmot found on the Mongolian grasslands is genetically ____________________ a lung ____________ caused by the Yersinia pestis, commonly known as bubonic plague. The disease ____________ humans and makes them cough ____________________. In ____________, marmots spread it around by coughing on their neighbors, infecting fleas, rats, and humans. The bacteria are then transferred to the other creatures. The sick marmots ____________ the area, infecting others. The "marmot invasions" are blamed for all the great plagues that swept through Eastern Asia to Europe. When marmots and humans ____________ from the plague, they have a high fever and the lymph glands ____________ in size and become black. Mongolians enjoy marmot meat, but they will never eat a marmot's armpits because "they contain the soul of a dead hunter."

Lesson 17

Translation of Words | 영어는 한글로, 한글은 영어로 써 보세요.

1	compare	____________	2	pitcher	____________
3	scout	____________	4	appreciate	____________
5	defeat	____________	6	breeze	____________
7	accurate	____________	8	judge	____________
9	keep track of	____________	10	obey	____________
11	복잡한	____________	12	운동선수	____________
13	통계 (자료)	____________	14	~을 기반으로	____________
15	아픈, 슬픈	____________	16	기여하다	____________
17	휴양	____________	18	지식	____________
19	나누다	____________	20	실행, 공연	____________

Passage Dictation | 녹음된 내용을 들으며 글의 빈칸에 알맞은 단어를 쓰세요. 독해17

____________ are very important to baseball, perhaps more than any other sport. Since the game of baseball has a very structured flow to it, it's easy to predict the results of games. Experts say that an ____________ calculation of probabilities is possible. You may feel it's complicated, but once you learn to use the ____________, it is a ____________ to ____________________ the statistics. Traditionally, statistics like batting average for batters (the number of hits ____________ by the number of at bats) and earned run average (the number of runs given up by a ____________ per nine innings) are considered important.

These statistics are designed to be a better evaluation of a player's field ____________. Team managers and coaches ____________ how each player ____________ to his team ____________________ the statistics. Baseball scouts study player statistics in order to ____________ the players that have different abilities. Statistics are used to set a strategy to ____________ the rival teams. For example, managers often use statistics to base their decisions during the game, such as choosing who to put in the lineup, or which relief pitcher to bring in.

Lesson 18

Translation of Words | 영어는 한글로, 한글은 영어로 써 보세요.

1	flour	______	2	odd	______
3	trousers	______	4	keep A from -ing	______
5	mention	______	6	identify	______
7	revolution	______	8	honor	______
9	rinse	______	10	amount	______
11	성취	______	12	관중	______
13	유행하다	______	14	학설	______
15	장식하다	______	16	사용 가능한	______
17	바느질하다	______	18	재료	______
19	기능	______	20	전환하다	______

Passage Dictation | 녹음된 내용을 들으며 글의 빈칸에 알맞은 단어를 쓰세요. 독해18

What we wear ______ us. For example, salespeople wear a suit and a tie. Baseball players wear a cap. Then, what about cooks? All kinds of hats are ______, in ______, but they usually wear either ugly hair nets or ______ white caps with long tops. Can there possibly be a logical function for the shape of the chef's caps?

As early as the Romans, master chefs were rewarded for their ______ by receiving special headware. For them, laurel-______ caps were the ______.

In France up until the seventeenth century, chefs were awarded different colored caps depending on their ranks. During the early eighteenth century, Talleyrand's chef required his entire staff to wear white hats. He ____________ in his cookbook that the hat was designed to ____________ the cook's hair ____________ entering food while mixing ____________, such as ____________ and butter. But this original cap was flat. The high hat gradually ____________ on because it could provide some ventilation for the head, as chefs frequently work under extremely hot conditions. The large ____________ of heat produced by the cook's head could go up and then out of the hat, cooling the head.

Lesson 19

Translation of Words | 영어는 한글로, 한글은 영어로 써 보세요.

1	capable	________	2	southern	________
3	species	________	4	worldwide	________
5	motion	________	6	protect	________
7	transportation	________	8	surround	________
9	traffic	________	10	zone	________
11	유전자	________	12	인구	________
13	공격(하다)	________	14	서식지	________
15	고체의	________	16	소유하다	________
17	환경	________	18	대조적으로	________
19	조직, 단체	________	20	대륙, 육지	________

Passage Dictation | 녹음된 내용을 들으며 글의 빈칸에 알맞은 단어를 쓰세요. 독해19

Birds are ___________ of both walking and flying. But there are more birds that fly than flightless birds on this planet. Whether a ___________ of bird chooses to fly or walk depends on its ___________. Flying requires more energy than walking. Therefore, a bird without fear of ___________ by predators in its native habitat will eventually be flightless. Australia, a small ___________ far from the other continents, has many flightless birds. And many other flightless birds have been reported on the islands in the Pacific and the Indian Ocean. There, nature "chose" the ___________ that are better for walking. Usually, where a land is ___________ by water and the ___________ of its predators decreases, birds developed the ability to walk. In fact, 'walking' is not a proper expression to describe the ___________ of birds. More birds are hoppers than walkers. ___________, birds that walk or run like an ostrich or flamingo ___________ long legs and live in wide open spaces. In contrast, most tree-living birds are hoppers, because it is easier to move from branch to branch by hopping than by walking or flying.

Lesson 20

Translation of Words | 영어는 한글로, 한글은 영어로 써 보세요.

1	primary	___________
2	courage	___________
3	conductor	___________
4	affair	___________
5	immigrant	___________
6	disguise	___________
7	impress	___________
8	agent	___________
9	confuse	___________
10	illusion	___________
11	이익	___________
12	초래하다	___________
13	설립하다	___________
14	우정	___________

15 희미한, 약한 ______________

16 황제 ______________

17 군대의 ______________

18 고용하다 ______________

19 탐정 ______________

20 정부 ______________

Passage Dictation | 녹음된 내용을 들으며 글의 빈칸에 알맞은 단어를 쓰세요. 독해20

Spies are frequently used in the world of international __________. For example, Chevalier D'Eon, a French __________ __________ by King Louis XV in 1756, arranged a secret treaty with the Empress of Russia for the __________ of his country. As no foreign man could have the opportunity to meet the empress, D'Eon had the __________ to disguise himself as a woman and secure the meeting and negotiate the treaty.

The French Emperor Napoleon, apart from being a great military tactician was also a master in the art of espionage, as he proved during the war against Austria. In 1804 he sent his top spy, Karl Schulmeister, to Vienna where Schulmeister told the story that he had been expelled from France. He __________ a __________ with the Austrian army chief, Marshall Mack. He was so __________ with Schulmeister's knowledge of French military matters he made him a __________ official — Chief of Intelligence for the Austrians. He didn't have a hint of suspicion on Schulmeister. In this position, Schulmeister was able to __________ Mack with false __________ of the strength of Napoleon's army, eventually ________________ the defeat of the Austrian army.

Lesson 21

Translation of Words | 영어는 한글로, 한글은 영어로 써 보세요.

1	cast ____________	2	wisdom ____________
3	setback ____________	4	satisfactory ____________
5	struggle ____________	6	shoot ____________
7	opinion ____________	8	creative ____________
9	scratch ____________	10	overcome ____________
11	타협, 양보하다 ____________	12	격려하다 ____________
13	가장하다 ____________	14	끄덕이다 ____________
15	탐욕스러운 ____________	16	고생하다 ____________
17	이익 ____________	18	어린 시절 ____________
19	장애물 ____________	20	태도, 마음가짐 ____________

Passage Dictation | 녹음된 내용을 들으며 글의 빈칸에 알맞은 단어를 쓰세요. 독해21

Sylvester Stallone ____________ in his ____________. He didn't have it much better as an adult. Not able to earn a steady income, and having to sell his dog for $25.00 to help turn on his electricity, he was faced with many ____________. But he didn't lose faith in himself and ____________ through the obstacles. It was only 2 weeks after selling his dog that he wrote the Rocky script in nearly 20 hours straight from ____________. He sent it to many studios. Finally, being rejected over 1,500 times, Stallone was given a ____________ by United Artists for $125,000, but only if Stallone would not star in it. They thought he was too ____________. But Stallone would not accept unless he starred in it. Finally, they ____________. The ____________ director called him: He said they would allow him to play the role of Rocky, but would only pay him $35,000 and a percentage of the ____________. He accepted and the ____________ started. Rocky cost $1,000,000 to make, but it grossed over $200,000,000! The Rocky series earned over a billion dollars. Success comes after ____________. What matters is your ____________.

Lesson 22

Translation of Words | 영어는 한글로, 한글은 영어로 써 보세요.

1	skyscraper ______	2	trial ______
3	communicate ______	4	refer ______
5	electricity ______	6	steam ______
7	thought ______	8	erase ______
9	preserve ______	10	string ______
11	자원하다 ______	12	상업적인 ______
13	석탄 ______	14	채택하다 ______
15	교환(하다) ______	16	수많은 ______
17	인조의 ______	18	조상 ______
19	고무 ______	20	어리석은 ______

Passage Dictation | 녹음된 내용을 들으며 글의 빈칸에 알맞은 단어를 쓰세요. 독해22

The enigma machine ______ to a portable device run by ______ for ______ secret messages. It encoded the message into a ______ of letters and then decoded at the other end of the line. An ______ of the computer, it resembled a typewriter keyboard.

Its ______ use was not recorded, but it was adopted by the German army in World War II. The Germans were ______ enough to believe that the Allies would never be able to break the machine's codes. But it was very difficult to ______ with each other: Each day's settings for a machine had to be sent between encoder and decoder. After a day, the settings would be ______ and the records would not be ______. But these settings were often captured by the Allies. Even more, the codes, as well as the machine were stolen and cracked, leaking important information. One of the machines was intercepted in Poland and sent to Britain. With the help of Polish mathematicians who ____________ to break the codes, experts in the UK succeeded in breaking the codes of a large number of intercepted Nazi messages and gained vital military intelligence from them.

Lesson 23

Translation of Words | 영어는 한글로, 한글은 영어로 써 보세요.

1 chairperson	____________	2 poverty	____________
3 dump	____________	4 instruction	____________
5 suicide	____________	6 idle	____________
7 pardon	____________	8 uncomfortable	____________
9 pupil	____________	10 cure	____________
11 비판하다	____________	12 열성적인	____________
13 ~을 신청하다	____________	14 부정적인	____________
15 능률적인	____________	16 증거	____________
17 나타나다	____________	18 발견하다	____________
19 책임지고 있는	____________	20 학업의, 학교의	____________

Passage Dictation | 녹음된 내용을 들으며 글의 빈칸에 알맞은 단어를 쓰세요. 독해23

Tony was not very successful in ____________. Rather, he was the unruliest troublemaker in his town. I met Tony at a weekend leadership training. All the ____________ at school had been invited to ________________ the training.

(B) At the training, they talked about positive and ____________ things that had occurred at school. Kids in Tony's group welcomed his comments, since he didn't ____________ but listened. Tony felt like a part of the group. Tony and other kids joined the Homeless Project team.

(A) He knew something about ____________, starvation, and hopelessness. The kids on the team were impressed with his ____________ concern and ideas. They elected Tony co-____________ of the team. Teachers were ____________ with it, but the kids didn't care about their responses. Tony was ____________ for the food collecting drive and the student council followed Tony's ____________.

(C) Two weeks later, Tony and his friends collected a school record: 2,854 cans of food. Tony started ____________________ at school every day and answered questions from teachers. Tony is proof that all birds can fly once the broken wings are ____________.

Lesson 24

Translation of Words | 영어는 한글로, 한글은 영어로 써 보세요.

1	border	____________	2	bunch	____________
3	unfortunately	____________	4	cooperate	____________
5	eastern	____________	6	crash	____________
7	boundary	____________	8	bitter	____________
9	attract	____________	10	broadcast	____________
11	(농)작물	____________	12	받아쓰기	____________
13	고치다	____________	14	지역	____________
15	폭력적인	____________	16	구성하다	____________
17	(~에서) 역할을 하다	____________	18	정복하다	____________
19	~에 관해서라면	____________	20	(보트의) 노	____________

Passage Dictation | 녹음된 내용을 들으며 글의 빈칸에 알맞은 단어를 쓰세요. 독해24

The river has always been and continues to be a ___________ between areas where people live or gather. In ancient times, rivers were natural boundaries. The people living in one village would plant ___________ on one side of a river, build living areas on that same side of the river, and generally have no use for the land on the other side of the river. Especially if the river was a wide one, crossing it by rowing ___________, ___________, was too much work. Except, of course, if you wanted to ___________ your neighbors. Rivers have slowed down many conquerors in times past. Even in the "modernized" 20th Century, rivers have ___________ major ________________ protecting countries from attack and slowing down attacks by ___________ neighbors.

Rivers make natural boundaries. It's a lot easier to just say that the ___________ boundary of the state of Missouri is the Mississippi River in many places than it is to get a ___________ of surveyors and mark the boundary the hard way. Check out the map of the United States. Make sure it includes rivers. You'll find that the eastern boundary of Nebraska is also a river, the Missouri River.

Rivers are boundaries for counties and cities, too. You can probably find some on the map of your place or other ___________. And it's not just the United States. The Huang He River marks the eastern ___________ of China's Shensi province. The Danube River helps form the border between Romania and Bulgaria. _____________ _____________ boundaries, you don't get much more natural than a river.

Lesson 25

Translation of Words | 영어는 한글로, 한글은 영어로 써 보세요.

1 widespread ________________ 2 civilization ________________

3 optional ________________ 4 standard ________________

5	transaction	____________	6	crisis	____________
7	pollution	____________	8	professional	____________
9	defend	____________	10	majority	____________
11	전시회	____________	12	개발	____________
13	우세한	____________	14	전자(공학)의	____________
15	가혹한	____________	16	개념	____________
17	경쟁하다	____________	18	강조하다	____________
19	접근하다	____________	20	(몸을) 떨다	____________

Passage Dictation | 녹음된 내용을 들으며 글의 빈칸에 알맞은 단어를 쓰세요. 독해25

According to the ____________ familiar with money ____________, money in coin form has been around since about 600 B.C. When the Greek and Roman ____________ — the ____________ economies and civilizations of the times — began accepting coins as money, most of the rest of the world followed suit. Coins are still accepted today but usually as percentages of paper money.

The first paper money was issued in China in the 13th century. The ____________ didn't become popular in the West until about 400 years later. The paper dollar appeared in the United States after the Revolutionary War and slowly became the national ____________ of value.

Most of the common forms of money today — including checks, money orders, and government bonds, just to name a few — are based on the dollar. A ____________ of people in the country (and even the world) accept it as a means of exchange. In historical terms, the dollar is a new form of money, but it is accepted almost everywhere in the world.

An even newer form of money is ____________ money. With the ____________ use of computers today, a great many ____________ are electronic. Physical money remains just the same, and paper records are ____________. The dollars and cents are represented by bits and bytes. The standard hasn't changed, just the method of exchange.

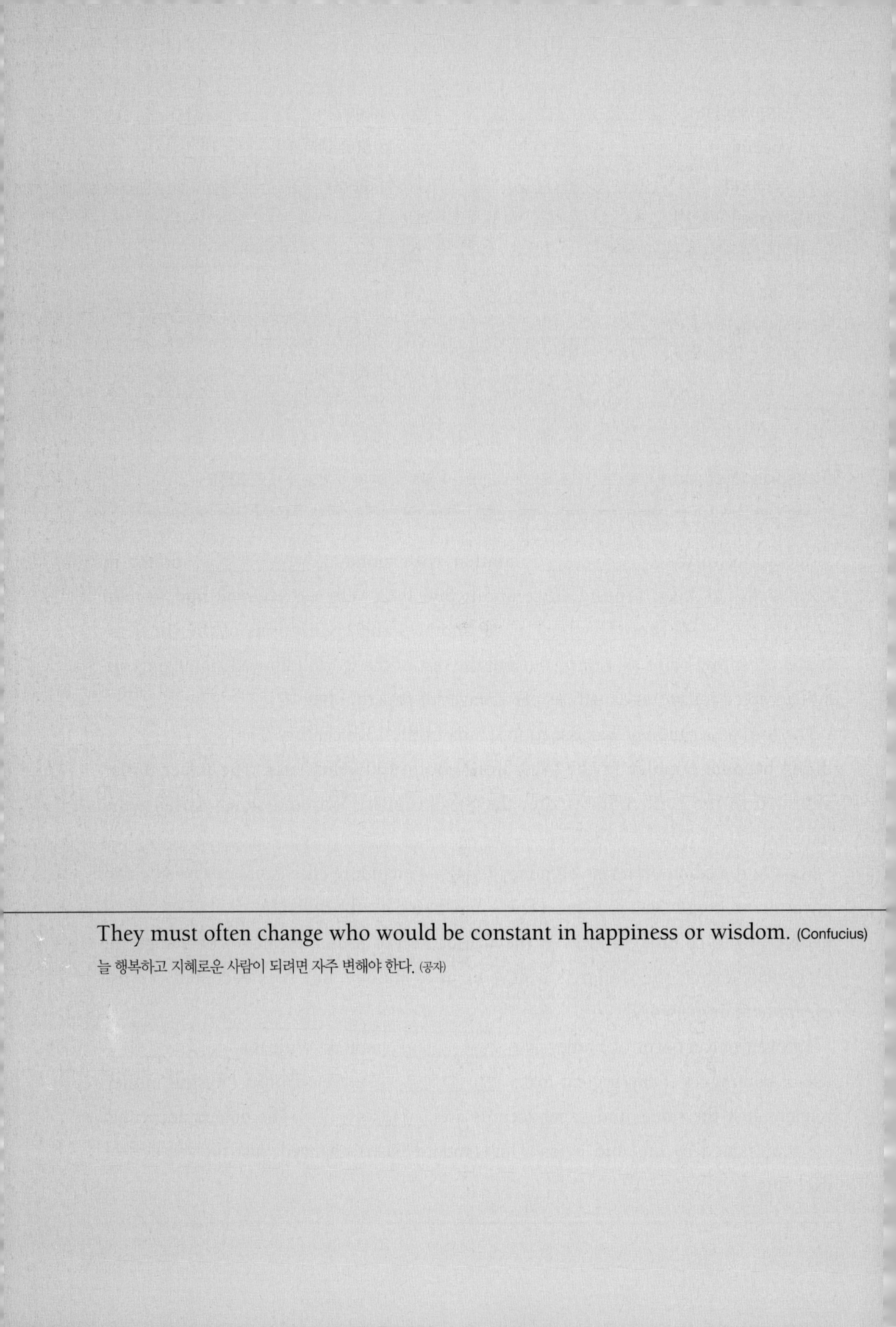

They must often change who would be constant in happiness or wisdom. (Confucius)

늘 행복하고 지혜로운 사람이 되려면 자주 변해야 한다. (공자)

정답 [Workbook]

Workbook Answers

Lesson 1

Ⓣ 1 소심한, 용기가 없는 2 금지하다 3 시력, 시야 4 막다, 방해하다 5 과체중의, 비만의 6 세게 치다, 공격하다 7 생물, 생명체 8 어색한, 서투른 9 ~을 받을 만하다, ~의 자격이 있다 10 의존하다, ~에 달려 있다 11 yell 12 as though 13 fable 14 fever 15 protest 16 effective 17 conflict 18 calculate 19 frustrate 20 method

Ⓟ fables / timid / overweight / prevent / creatures / sight / frustrated / yelled / struck / as though / fever / method / effective

Lesson 2

Ⓣ 1 대신하다, 교체하다 2 부상, 상처 3 힘, 강점 4 ~의 가치가 있는 5 추상적인, 관념적인 6 호흡하다 7 달라붙다 8 전문가 9 발랄한, 쾌활한 10 고발하다, 비난하다 11 produce 12 blossom 13 recall 14 indeed 15 desperate 16 purchase 17 recover 18 erupt 19 miracle 20 emergency

Ⓟ desperate / clinging / emergency / produced / miracle / recalled / indeed / expert / injuries / breathing / recovering / worth

Lesson 3

Ⓣ 1 성공하다 2 속삭이다 3 관련시키다 4 기회 5 추격, 추적, 추구하다 6 권위, 권한 7 원리, 원칙 8 목표(하다) 9 차이, 대조하다 10 가능성, 가능한 일 11 permanent 12 corridor 13 launch 14 guarantee 15 be willing to 16 religion 17 surface 18 therefore 19 quality 20 shelter

Ⓟ authority / quality / launch / guarantees / were willing to / corridor / principle / opportunity / succeed / possibilities

Lesson 4

Ⓣ 1 힘든, 요구가 많은 2 아무 생각 없이, 무심코 3 성숙한, 잘 익은 4 맞추다, 적응하다 5 상당히 6 선언하다 7 설득하다 8 벙어리의 9 뽐내다 10 개선하다 11 difficulty 12 conduct 13 aggressive 14 clap 15 outcome 16 investigate 17 manufacture 18 characteristic 19 treat 20 equipment

Ⓟ mature / adapt / outcome / difficulties / boasting / treating / persuade / aggressive / demanding / improve / casually

Lesson 5

T 1 재산 2 수술, 가동 3 휴대용의 4 장치 5 시도(하다) 6 느슨한 7 어구, 구절 8 암기하다 9 연습(하다) 10 공황 상태(에 빠지다) 11 structure 12 at once 13 chunk 14 extracurricular 15 spelling 16 planet 17 occupation 18 reserve 19 work on 20 chemistry

P chunks / spelling / at once / working on / attempt / devices / memorize / phrase / chemistry / practice

Lesson 6

T 1 터무니없는 2 분류하다 3 날것의 4 관련지어 생각하다, 연관 5 ~에 따르면 6 동행하다 7 반면에 8 집중하다 9 박수 10 대기, 분위기 11 support 12 participant 13 temperature 14 descendant 15 comment 16 faithful 17 ruin 18 expression 19 reality 20 ignore

P participants / reality / ridiculous / faithful / According to / accompanied / applause / expressions / classified / focus / whereas

Lesson 7

T 1 새다 2 글, 기사 3 정치(학) 4 궁금해 하다 5 전체의, 완전한 6 세부 사항 7 관습 8 기관, 협회 9 절망적인 10 알약 11 germ 12 reflect 13 individual 14 feature 15 recycle 16 element 17 journalism 18 describe 19 ethical 20 appropriate

P articles / entire / element / journalism / details / describe / reflect / politics / individuals / appropriate / wondering

Lesson 8

T 1 가치 2 간단한 3 측면, 면 4 독립적인 5 얻다 6 드물게, 좀처럼 ~ 않는 7 순응하다 8 재난 9 자신감 있는 10 안락 11 annoy 12 isolate 13 distinguish 14 influence 15 embrace 16 financial 17 sacrifice 18 document 19 interrupt 20 behavior

P comfort / seldom / aspects / behavior / influenced / sacrifice / embraced / Independent / confident / isolating / conform / obtain

Lesson 9

T 1 나타내다 2 어디든지 3 교차 지점 4 여기다, 관심 5 특이한 6 신성한 7 상징하다 8 연합하다 9 존재하다 10 꽃이 피다 11 fasten 12 involve 13 float 14 remark 15 obvious 16 realize 17 keep one's fingers crossed 18 fist 19 root 20 democracy

P Keep your fingers crossed / fastening / rooted / represents / uniting / intersection / holy / exist / involved / regarded / realized / remarked / obvious

Lesson 10

T 1 입자, 작은 조각 2 움켜쥠 3 어둑한 4 나타나다 5 망치다 6 구조하다 7 민족의 8 자원, 수단 9 쏟아지다 10 강우, 강수량 11 drought 12 starve 13 be concerned with 14 solution 15 leap 16 propose 17 drown 18 height 19 underwater 20 purpose

P spill / drown / is concerned with / appears / solution / rainfall / propose / droughts / gripped / starve

Lesson 11

T 1 쓸모없는 2 결합시키다 3 지적인 4 디지털 방식의 5 시트, 얇은 판 6 소질 7 필수적인 8 ~인 것으로 밝혀지다 9 접착제, 붙이다 10 책임지다, 보장하다 11 security 12 permit 13 reject 14 rule 15 recognize 16 logical 17 surf 18 predict 19 passport 20 affordable

P digital / intelligent / affordable / vital / predict / useless / combine / permit / ensure / security

Lesson 12

T 1 그렇지 않으면 2 동면하다 3 그림자 4 주요한, 교장 5 위험에 빠뜨리다 6 닮다 7 상담하다 8 번역하다 9 노출 10 강탈하다 11 recipe 12 advantage 13 crawl 14 legend 15 ideal 16 determine 17 charm 18 celebration 19 just around the corner 20 amusement

P resembles / consult / crawls / shadow / legend / just around the corner / celebration / determined / translated / hibernating / exposure / otherwise

Lesson 13

Ⓣ 1 복제(하다) 2 (신체) 기관 3 덩어리 4 장애를 가진 5 재충전하다 6 손상, 손상을 입히다 7 척추 8 반응하다 9 감정 10 목적지 11 liquid 12 break down 13 acid 14 nutrient 15 dissolve 16 necessary 17 stomach 18 lifelong 19 bubble 20 swallow

Ⓟ dissolve / swallow / stomach / acid / break / down / damaging / liquid / reacts / necessary / nutrients / destination / lump / bubbles

Lesson 14

Ⓣ 1 진행, 발전하다 2 자선(단체) 3 의미 있는 4 분명히 5 거절하다 6 밝히다 7 사심이 없는 8 연락(하다) 9 해로운 10 연결 11 similarity 12 heritage 13 relationship 14 complex 15 evidence 16 donation 17 reward 18 informal 19 commit 20 affect

Ⓟ specifically / connection / reveal / complex / relationship / donations / charity / affected / rewarded / unselfish / evidence

Lesson 15

Ⓣ 1 계속되는 2 기술 3 관점 4 일몰 5 실험(하다) 6 재료 7 집중하다 8 이루어져 있다 9 나타내다 10 타당하다 11 earthquake 12 extend 13 harmony 14 landscape 15 horizon 16 degree 17 route 18 forecast 19 temporary 20 dispute

Ⓟ consists / landscape / sunset / horizon / route / forecast / technology / a series of experiments / disputes / viewpoint / degree / harmony

Lesson 16

Ⓣ 1 야생 동물 2 침입 3 잔인한 4 죽도록 5 인류 6 비난하다 7 겪다 8 매끄러운 9 육체의 10 짖다, 소리를 지르다 11 mammal 12 infection 13 be susceptible to 14 increase 15 awful 16 palm 17 spread 18 threaten 19 yawn 20 wander

Ⓟ awful / mankind / susceptible to / infection / threatens / to death / wildlife / wander / suffer / increase

Lesson 17

T 1 비교하다 2 투수, 주전자 3 정찰하다, 발굴하다 4 진가를 알아보다, 고마워하다 5 이기다, 무산시키다 6 산들바람, 쉬운 일 7 정확한 8 판사, 판결을 내리다 9 ~에 대해 파악하고 있다 10 복종하다 11 complicated 12 athlete 13 statistics 14 on the basis of 15 sore 16 contribute 17 recreation 18 knowledge 19 divide 20 performance

P Statistics / accurate / knowledge / breeze / keep track of / divided / pitcher / performance / appreciate / contributed / on the basis of / compare / defeat

Lesson 18

T 1 밀가루 2 이상한, 특이한 3 바지 4 A가 ~하지 못하게 하다 5 말하다 6 (신원을) 확인하다 7 혁명 8 명예 9 헹구기, 헹구다 10 양, 총계 11 achievement 12 spectator 13 catch on 14 theory 15 decorate 16 available 17 sew 18 ingredient 19 function 20 convert

P identifies / available / theory / odd / achievements / decorated / honor / mentioned / keep / from / ingredients / flour / caught / amount

Lesson 19

T 1 ~할 수 있는, 유능한 2 남쪽의 3 종, 종류 4 세계적인 5 운동, 동작 6 보호하다 7 운송, 교통 수단 8 둘러싸다 9 교통 10 지역 11 gene 12 population 13 attack 14 habitat 15 solid 16 possess 17 environment 18 in contrast 19 organization 20 continent

P capable / species / environment / attack / continent / genes / surrounded / population / motion / Worldwide / possess

Lesson 20

T 1 주요한 2 용기 3 지휘자, 전도체 4 업무, 사건 5 이민자 6 변장하다 7 감명을 주다 8 대리인, 기관 9 혼동시키다 10 환상, 오해 11 benefit 12 bring about 13 establish 14 friendship 15 faint 16 emperor 17 military 18 employ 19 detective 20 government

P affairs / agent / employed / benefit / courage / established / friendship / impressed / government / confuse / illusion / bring about

Lesson 21

Ⓣ 1 던지다, 배역을 정하다 2 지혜 3 좌절 4 만족스러운 5 투쟁하다 6 쏘다, 촬영하다 7 의견 8 창조적인 9 긁다 10 극복하다 11 compromise 12 encourage 13 pretend 14 nod 15 greedy 16 had it rough 17 profit 18 childhood 19 obstacle 20 attitude

Ⓟ had it rough / childhood / obstacles / struggled / scratch / nod / greedy / compromised / casting / profits / shooting / setbacks / attitude

Lesson 22

Ⓣ 1 고층 건물 2 재판, 시도 3 의사소통하다 4 문의하다, 나타내다 5 전기 6 증기(로 찌다) 7 생각, 사상 8 지우다 9 보존하다 10 끈(에 묶다) 11 volunteer 12 commercial 13 coal 14 adopt 15 exchange 16 a large number of 17 artificial 18 ancestor 19 rubber 20 foolish

Ⓟ refers / electricity / exchanging / string / ancestor / commercial / foolish / communicate / erased / preserved / volunteered

Lesson 23

Ⓣ 1 의장 2 가난 3 (쓰레기를) 버리다 4 설명 5 자살(하다) 6 게으른, 빈둥거리다 7 용서(하다) 8 불편한 9 학생, 눈동자 10 치료(하다) 11 criticize 12 passionate 13 sign up for 14 negative 15 efficient 16 proof 17 show up 18 discover 19 responsible 20 academic

Ⓟ academics / pupils / sing up for / negative / criticize / poverty / passionate / chairperson / uncomfortable / responsible / instruction / showing up / cured

Lesson 24

Ⓣ 1 국경 2 다발 3 불행하게도 4 협력하다 5 동쪽의 6 사고 7 경계선 8 맛이 쓴 9 마음을 끌다 10 방송하다 11 crop 12 dictation 13 mend 14 region 15 violent 16 compose 17 play a part in 18 conquer 19 when it comes to 20 oar

Ⓟ boundary / crops / oars / unfortunately / conquer / played / parts in / violent / eastern / bunch / regions / border / When it comes to

Lesson 25

T 1 광범위한, 널리 퍼진 2 문명 3 선택적인 4 수준, 기준 5 거래 6 위기 7 공해
8 직업적인 9 방어하다 10 다수 11 exhibition 12 development 13 dominant
14 electronic 15 harsh 16 concept 17 compete 18 emphasize 19 approach
20 tremble

P professionals / development / civilizations / dominant / concept / standard / majority / electronic / widespread / transactions / optional

Middle School English
WORD MANUAL

Answer Key

Lesson 1

1B 1 fable 2 method 3 effective 4 sight 5 deserve 6 awkward 7 overweight 8 creature

1C 1 as though 2 yelled 3 fever 4 depend on 5 protest 6 timid 7 conflicts

1D 1 protest 2 deserves 3 effective 4 conflict

1E 1 ③ 2 ② 3 ③ 4 ②

1F 전문 해석 여기에 이솝 우화 중 하나의 이야기가 있다. 소심하고 뚱뚱한 노인이 자신의 외동아들이 사자에게 물려 죽는 꿈을 꾼 후에, 그 꿈이 실제로 일어날 일의 예지몽일까봐 두려운 마음이 들었다. (B) 그래서 그것이 사실이 되는 것을 막기 위해, 그는 땅 위에 높이 솟은 매우 멋진 건물을 지어 자신의 아들을 거기에 두고 경호를 받게 하였다. 건물은 사자를 포함해 온갖 종류의 동물 그림으로 장식되었다. 하지만 그의 아들은 그 그림을 보고 더욱 좌절스러울 뿐이었다. (A) 하루는 그가 사자 앞에 서서 소리쳤다. "널 저주한다! 내가 여자처럼 여기에 있어야 하는 것이 바로 너와 내 아버지의 꿈 때문이야. 내가 어떻게 너에게 갚아줄 수 있을까?" 그리고 그는 말하면서 사자의 눈을 나가떨어지게 할 것처럼 자신의 손으로 벽을 쳤다. (C) 가느다랗고 날카로운 돌 조각이 그의 손톱 밑에 박혔다. 그는 심한 통증을 느끼고 고열이 났다. 머지않아 그는 죽었다. 그러므로 그것이 단지 그림이라고 하더라도, 사자는 소년의 죽음을 야기했고 그의 아버지가 사용한 방법은 결국 효과가 없었다.

1 ② 아들의 죽음을 막기 위해 높은 곳에 건물을 짓고 그곳에 아들을 가두는 (B)가 주어진 문장 뒤에 이어지고, 다음으로 그 사자를 저주하며 주먹을 휘두르는 (A)가 오며 마지막으로, 아들의 손톱 밑에 돌조각이 박혀 죽게 된다는 내용의 (C)가 오는 것이 적절하다.

2 ④ 아들이 사자에게 물려 죽는 꿈을 꾼 후 두려워서 자신만의 방법으로 대처했다는 내용이므로 빈칸에 들어갈 말로는 therefore(그래서)가 적절하다.

3 ② 노인의 아들은 자신이 처한 상황을 사자의 탓으로 돌렸다.

4 raised high above 그 노인은 그의 아들을 땅 위로 높게 있는 큰 방에 머물게 하였다.

Lesson 2

2B 1 expert 2 abstract 3 desperate 4 miracle 5 accuse 6 worth 7 strength 8 blossom

2C 1 recall 2 indeed 3 emergency 4 replaced 5 abstract 6 breathing 7 erupted

2D 1 desperate 2 produces 3 recover 4 worth

2E 1 ② 2 ④ 3 ② 4 ①

2F 전문 해석 6월 23일, Jim Smith는 어떤 여자의 아들이 베란다에 매달려 있는 상황에서 그녀의 절망적인 외침을 들었다. "그것은 일반적인 외침이 아니었고요 그래서 저는 비상 상황이라는 걸 알아챘어요."라고 Jim은 말했다.

"그것은 한 사람의 인생에서 가장 긴박한 순간에 내질러지는 외침이었어요." 그는 그 상황을 무시할 수 없었다. 그는 30미터를 달려 슛을 막을 준비를 하는 골키퍼처럼 자신의 팔을 넓게 벌렸다. 그 순간, 그 소년의 손가락이 미끄러졌고, 그는 기다라고 있던 Jim의 팔로 곧장 떨어졌는데, 그것은 15~20초밖에 걸리지 않았다. "모든 게 순식간에 일어났어요. 그것은 기적이에요. 저는 단 한순간도, 정말 아무 생각도 들지 않았어요."라고 Jim은 회상했다. 그의 말이 사실인 것처럼 15미터 높이에서 떨어지는 17킬로그램의 아이를 받는 것은 정말로 기적이다. "그건 시속 70킬로미터로 이동하는 물체에 부딪히는 것과 똑같은 겁니다."라고 한 전문가가 말했다. 부상 때문에 원활하게 움직일 수 없고 잠시 동안 숨 쉬는 게 약간 어려웠지만, Jim은 병원에서 회복 중이다. 그 소년은 운 좋게도 코피가 나는 정도만 부상을 당했다. 그 소년의 부모가 병원에 와서 Jim에게 원하는 것을 물었다. 그러나 그는 어떤 보상도 원하지 않았다. 생명을 구하는 것은 위험을 무릅쓸 가치가 있다고 그가 말했다.

1 ⑤ 15미터 높이에서 떨어진 한 소년을 구한 사람의 이야기이므로, 이 글의 제목으로는 ⑤ '추락하다가 한 남자에 의해 기적적으로 구조된 소년'이 적절하다.

2 ② 문맥상 소년이 팔을 벌리고 있던 남자의 품속에 떨어지는 순간을 묘사하고 있으므로, 주어진 문장은 남자가 소년을 구하기 위해 골키퍼처럼 팔을 넓게 벌렸다는 내용 다음에 오는 것에 적절하다.

3 ④ Jim은 아이를 구하는 과정에서 부상을 당해 병원에 입원해 있다고 했다.

4 한 아이가 베란다에 매달려 있는 상황

Lesson 3

3B 1 religion 2 permanent 3 pursuit 4 opportunity 5 contrast 6 quality 7 willing 8 related

3C 1 possibility 2 whispered 3 corridor 4 surfaces 5 aim 6 quality 7 principle

3D 1 succeed 2 shelter 3 authority 4 contrast

3E 1 ④ 2 ④ 3 ② 4 ①

3F [전문 해석] Babson 대학의 12년간에 걸친 연구에서, 경영 실무 교육의 권위자 Robert Miller 박사는 경영 대학원을 졸업한 학생들 사이에서 성공이나 실패의 이유를 조사했다. 몇몇은 계속해서 성공적인 사업을 해나갔지만 대부분은 그러지 못했다. 그는 성공적인 사업을 한 사람들에게는 특별한 자질이 있다는 것을 발견했다. 그것은 그들이 성공에 대한 어떤 보장도 없이 사업을 시작할 용기를 가지고 있었다는 것이었다. 그들은 자신의 꿈을 추구하는 데 있어 기꺼이 실패의 위험을 감수했다.

Miller 교수는 이것을 '복도의 원칙'이라고 불렀다. 아무리 거리가 멀다고 해도 여러분이 자신의 목표를 향해 출발할 때, 여러분은 시간의 복도를 이동해가기 시작한다고 그는 말했다. 여러분이 이 복도를 이동해가면서 여러분의 양쪽 어디서든 다른 기회의 문들이 열릴 것이다. 그러나 만약 아직 여러분이 목표를 향해 이 심리학적인 복도를 나아가고 있지 않았다면 다른 기회의 문을 볼 수 없었을 것이다.

삶에서 성공하는 대부분의 사람들은 그들이 시작했던 분야와는 완전히 다른 영역에서 자신의 성공을 성취한다. 그러나 그들은 움직이고 있었기 때문에 모든 것이 좋아질 때까지 기다렸다면 알지 못했을 기회와 가능성을 봤다. 그리고 현실에서는 모든 것이 완벽한 순간이란 없는 것이다.

1 ③ 성공의 비밀은 실패의 위험을 감수하는 것에 있다는 것이 이 연구의 결과이다.

2 ⑤ 성공에 대한 어떤 보장도 없이 기꺼이 실패의 위험을 감수하기 위해 필요한 것은 courage(용기)이다.

3 ③ Miller 박사의 연구에 따르면, 사람들이 성공하지 못하는 이유는 실패의 위험을 무릅쓰지 않기 때문이다.

4 move down toward our goal 기회의 문이 당신에게 열리길 바란다면 당신은 무엇을 해야 하는가? → 우리는 목표를 향해 나아가야 한다.

Lesson 4

4B 1 demanding 2 mature 3 clap 4 conduct 5 difficulties 6 improve 7 adapt 8 declare

4C 1 fairly 2 characteristics 3 adapted 4 casually 5 dumb 6 aggressive 7 equipment

4D 1 adapt 2 treat 3 conduct 4 demanding

4E 1 ③ 2 ① 3 ④ 4 ③

4F 전문 해석 많은 부모들은 '옳건 그르건 내 자식이 최고'라는 태도를 취하는 것 같은데 그건 끔찍한 결과를 가져온다. 부모가 된다는 것은 한 아이가 실망에 적응하는 것을 도울 만큼 충분히 성숙한 것을 의미한다. 자신의 아이가 최고가 아니라는 것을 받아들일 수 없는 부모들은 좌절감을 느낄 때, 대처할 방법을 찾는 대신 좌절을 일으킨 원인에 대해 비난하는 메시지를 전달한다.

부모들이 보여줄 수 있는 더 좋은 메시지는 아이들이 항상 모든 상황에서의 결과를 통제할 수는 없을지라도, 그들이 결과에 반응하는 태도는 통제할 수 있다는 것을 가르치는 것이다. 아이들은 자신이 느끼는 것보다 더욱 공손하게 행동하는 법을 배워야 한다. 그렇게 함으로써 그들은 상처를 받지 않고 어려움을 극복할 수 있게 될 것이다. 공손하다는 것은 단지 '해주세요'나 '감사합니다'라고 말하는 것 이상의 것에 관한 것이다. 그것은 과시하거나 등 뒤에서 누군가를 욕하지 않는 것이며, 공정하게 이기고 우아하게 패배를 인정하는 것이며, 모든 사람들을 존중하는 것에 관한 것이다.

물론, 부모들이 공격적이고 요구가 많고 무례하게 변하게 된다면 훈련을 아무리 한다고 해도 아이가 공손하게 행동하도록 설득하지(가르치지) 못할 것이다. 그것이 바로 전문가들이 아이를 예의바르게 만드는 최고의 방법은 부모들이 먼저 예의바른 모습을 보이는 것이라는 데 동의하는 이유이다. 부모들은 나중에 자기 아이들이 말하는 것을 듣고서 깜짝 놀랄 수도 있는 말을 생각 없이 하지 않는 데 특별히 주의할 필요가 있다. 우리가 예의바른 행동을 실천하지 않는다면, 어떻게 우리가 아이들이 그렇게 하는 것을 기대할 수 있겠는가?

1 ⑤ 아이를 공손하게 키우려면 부모가 먼저 모범을 보여야 한다는 내용이므로, 이 글의 제목으로는 '공손한 아이를 키우려면 모범을 보여라.'가 가장 적절하다.

2 ④ 결과는 통제할 수 없지만 어떤 일에 대한 대처나 반응은 통제할 수 있다는 내용이므로 빈칸에 들어갈 말로는 '그들이 어떻게 반응하는지를 통제한다'가 가장 적절하다.

3 ⑤ 생각 없이 어떤 말을 하는 것은 좋은 예절에 해당하지 않는다.

4 아이가 실망에 적응하는 것을 도울 만큼 충분히 성숙한 것을 의미한다.

Lesson 5

5B 1 phrase 2 extracurricular 3 planet 4 structure 5 spelling 6 attempt
7 portable 8 chunk

5C 1 devices 2 chemistry 3 Panic 4 loose 5 work on 6 occupations
7 planet

5D 1 structure 2 operation 3 reserve 4 phrases

5E 1 ③ 2 ④ 3 ② 4 ①

5F 전문 해석 (공부해야 할) 과목이나 내용이 많을 때, 그것들을 여러 개의 덩어리로 분리하는 것이 도움이 될 수 있다. 20개의 철자 시험을 본다고 해보자. 한꺼번에 그 모든 단어들을 생각하는 것 보다는 그것들을 5개의 덩어리로 분리해서 매일 밤 하나나 두 개씩 공부를 해보자.
첫 번째 시도에서 외울 수 없는 단어가 있다고 해도 걱정하지 마라. 거기서 연습이 시작된다. 여러분이 더 많은 날 동안 복습하는데 시간을 쓸수록 그것이 여러분의 머리에 남을 가능성은 더 높아진다. 또한 여러분이 어떤 것들을 암기하는 것을 도울 수 있는 비밀 도구라고 불리는 기법이 있다. 한 목록의 것들을 암기하려고 할 때, 각각의 첫 글자를 이용해 어구를 만들어라. 예를 들어, 태양에서부터 8개의 행성의 순서를 외우려고 노력하고 있는가? 수성, 금성, 지구, 화성, 목성, 토성, 천왕성, 해왕성을 기억하기 위해서, '매우 훌륭한 나의 엄마는 방금 우리에게 나초를 제공했다.'를 생각하라. (참고: 수금지화목토천해명) 선생님이 또한 여러분에게 좋은 방법을 알려줄 수 있다.
분리할 수 있는 또 다른 방법은 벼락치기 하는 대신 규칙적으로 공부하는 것이다. 여러분은 항상 여러분이 한 노트 필기를 복습하고 공부하는 있는 단원을 읽을 수 있다. 또는, 수학, 화학, 또는 생물을 공부하고 있다면 몇 가지 연습 문제를 풀어라.

1 ② 공부 방법 중의 하나로 한꺼번에 하려고 하지 말고 나눠서 하는 방법에 대해 말하고 있다.
2 ③ 연상 암기법에 관해 구체적으로 설명하고 있는 문장 앞인 ⓒ에 와서 암기법의 예를 보여주는 두 문장이 자연스럽게 이어지는 것이 적절하다.
3 ② '질문하는 것'은 본문에서 언급된 공부 방법이 아니다.
4 make up a phrase 그 방법은 각 단어의 머리글자를 이용해 어구를 만드는 것이다.

Lesson 6

6B 1 raw 2 faithful 3 reality 4 expression 5 descendant 6 comment
7 temperature 8 focus

6C 1 reality 2 associate 3 comments 4 expression(s) 5 classified 6 According to
7 ignored

6D 1 supported 2 associate 3 accompanied 4 atmosphere

6E 1 ② 2 ① 3 ④ 4 ②

6F 전문 해석 Marcel Zeelenberg는 네덜란드의 리얼리티 텔레비전 쇼의 참가자들을 관찰한 결과 어떤 유형을 발견

했다. 만약 여러분이 혹시라도 1990년대 중반 네덜란드에 있었다면, 일반인이 자신에게 충실했던 사람에게 했던 어리석은 몇 가지 일을 해명하는 'I Am Sorry'의 에피소드 한두 편은 시청했을지도 모른다.
한 출연자는 어려운 시절에 친구를 무시했던 것을 후회했고, 다른 출연자는 장례식장에서 죽은 친구에 관해 좋지 않은 말을 했던 것을 후회했고, 또 다른 출연자는 친구의 얼굴을 손바닥으로 친 것에 관해 기분이 좋지 않았다. 텔레비전에서 후회를 표현한 후에는 이 참가자들에게는 상처 받은 사람에게 사과하고 꽃을 전달하는 기회가 주어졌다. Zeelenberg에 따르면, "이 다음에는 보통 감정을 자극하는 장면이 뒤따르는데, 방청객들이 치는 박수 갈채와 함께 안고, 키스하고, 눈물을 흘리는 장면이 많았다." Zeelenberg의 팀은 18개의 다른 에피소드에 나타난 후회의 82가지의 표현을 모아서 이것들을 행한 것과 행하지 않은 것의 후회로 분류했다. 행하지 않은 것의 후회가 행한 것의 후회보다 세 배 반 이상 더 길었다. 요약하면, 행한 것의 후회는 단기 관점에 초점을 맞추는 반면에, 행하지 않은 것에 대한 후회는 장기 관점에 초점을 맞춘다.

1 ⑤ 행하지 않은 것의 후회가 행한 것의 후회보다 세 배 반 이상 길었다는 내용으로 보아 ⑤는 글의 내용과 일치하지 않는다.

2 ② 빈칸 뒤에는 글 전체의 내용을 요약하면서 행동해서 한 후회와 행동하지 못해서 한 후회를 비교하고 있으므로 요약의 연결사인 ②가 적절하다.

3 ① 이것은 과거에 잘못한 일에 대해 사과하는 프로그램이므로 친구를 위해 숙제를 해준 사람은 출연할 가능성이 적다고 볼 수 있다.

4 explain / apologize 그들은 과거의 잘못에 대해 설명하고 그들이 한 행동에 대해서 사과한다.

Lesson 7

7B 1 article 2 politics 3 reflect 4 details 5 hopeless 6 pill 7 recycle 8 element

7C 1 politics 2 appropriate 3 pills 4 journalism 5 entire 6 germs 7 ethical

7D 1 wonder 2 article 3 leaked 4 reflected

7E 1 ② 2 ③ 3 ③ 4 ②

7F 전문 해석 신문 기사는 결코 모든 진실을 밝혀줄 수는 없다. 다시 말해, 기사 하나에 사건의 모든 세부사항을 담는 것은 불가능하기 때문에 거짓이라는 약간의 요소가 기사 작성에 내재되어 있다. 기자들은 또한 자신의 기사에서 더욱 극적이거나 다른 효과를 나타내기 위해 정보를 제시하는 순서를 조작할 수도 있다. 세부 사항들과 그것들을 서술하기 위한 순서를 선택하는 것은 기자들에게 정당하고 윤리적인 행위라고 여겨진다. 기자들은 선거와 정치에 관한 견해를 작성할 때 자신이 속한 신문사의 정치적인 성향을 반영할 수도 있다.
도서 출판에 있어서는 많은 회사들이 저자가 쓰는 내용을 항상 세심하게 검토하는 것은 아니다. 베스트셀러는 많은 돈을 벌어들일 수 있어서 거짓을 지어내는 것에 현혹당하는 저자들이 몇몇 있다. 널리 알려진 하나의 사건에서, 한 작가는 자기 자신에 관한 완전히 허구적인 역사를 만들어냈다. 그 글은 신빙성이 있어서 대부분의 독자들은 그의 이야기를 믿었다. 그러나 나중에 그 작가는 책에서 언급한 사실들에 관한 증거를 제시할 수 없었고 그 결과 그는 사기꾼으로 밝혀졌다. 그 작가가 쓴 이야기는 부적절했지만 많은 사람들은 여전히 그것에 의미가 있다고 생각했다. 이런 독자들조차도 아무것도 모른 채 있는 것은 피하고 싶어 하지만 그 이야기가 사실인지 아닌지를 궁금해 하고 있다. 그들은 훌륭한 이야기를 가능케 하는 실상의 주요한 변형 내용에 대해 조금은 알고 있을 것이다.

1 ② 신문이나 글에서 거짓말은 불가피한 것이라는 내용이므로, 이 글의 제목으로는 '거짓말은 언론에서 불가피한 것이다.' 가 가장 적절하다.

2 ② 꾸며낸 이야기가 가져온 파장에 대한 내용 앞인 ⓑ가 적절하다.

3 ⑤ make up은 invent(만들어내다)의 뜻으로 쓰였다.
① 보충하다 ② 화해하다 ③ 차지하다 ④ 화장하다

4 fake / meaningful 독자들은 꾸며낸 이야기에 대해 어떻게 생각하는가? → 그 이야기가 거짓이라 할지라도 의미있는 것이라고 판단한다.

Lesson 8

8B 1 brief 2 financial 3 aspect 4 independent 5 disaster 6 sacrifice 7 comfort 8 behavior

8C 1 document(s) 2 confident 3 seldom 4 obtain 5 distinguish 6 annoy 7 conform

8D 1 document 2 interrupted 3 comfort 4 sacrifice

8E 1 ② 2 ③ 3 ① 4 ③

8F 전문 해석 보통 우리는 어떻게 행동해야 하는가에 관한 신호를 다른 사람에게서 찾는다. 우리 중 대부분은 지도자가 아니라 추종자로서, 편안함과 안락함으로 다져진 길을 따라 이동하면서 좀처럼 우리 자신의 방향으로 독립하지 않는다. 우리는 풍파를 일으키지 않으려 주의하면서, 다른 사람들이 기준을 세우는 것을 허용하고 그 다음 그 기준에 맞춰 서는 것을 더 선호한다. TV 코미디 프로그램에서는 바로 이런 이유 때문에 녹음된 관객의 웃음소리를 이용한다. 여러분은 다른 사람들이 웃는 경우 그것이 더 웃기다고 생각할까? 많은 사람들은 여러분이 그럴 거라고 확신하고 있다.

여러분의 삶의 다른 많은 측면에 이런 반응이 부재(→존재)한다. 여러분의 행동이 다른 사람들의 행동에 영향을 받도록 할 때, 여러분은 무난하게 보이기 위해 여러분 자신의 욕망과 욕구를 희생한다. 독립적이고 자신감 있는 사람들은 자신에게 절대적인 흥미를 끌지 않는다고 느낄 때는 다수에 의해 흔들릴 가능성이 더 적다. 그들은 자신이 원하는 것을 알고 있으며, 혼자 남더라도 개의치 않는다. 그러나 여러분은 독립적으로 생각하는 사람으로서 눈에 띄거나 주목을 받고 싶어 하지 않는다. 여러분에게 이런 딱지는 (여러분을) 고립시키는 것이다. 여러분은 차라리 집단의 일부분이 되는 것에 순응할 것이다.

여러분이 흔히 다른 사람들의 행동에 근거해서 여러분 자신의 판단을 재고하는 것은 바로 이 때문이다. 고속도로에서 많은 차량이 다른 방향으로 가고 있는 것을 본다면 여러분은 자신이 틀린 방향으로 가고 있는 게 아닌가를 의아해한다. 여러분은 레스토랑에서 다른 모든 사람들에게 무엇을 주문했는지를 묻는 사람이다. 여러분은 '적당히 괜찮은' 것을 얻고 싶어한다.

1 ③ 인간은 다른 사람들로부터 자신이 어떻게 행동해야 하는가에 관한 신호를 찾는다고 했으므로 이 글의 요지로는 '인간은 다른 사람들을 따르는 경향이 있다.' 가 적절하다.

2 ③ 코미디 프로그램을 보며 녹음된 관객의 웃음소리를 듣고 따라 웃는 이러한 반응이 삶의 많은 다른 측면에도

존재한다는 의미의 문장이므로 absent는 present로 고쳐 써야 한다.

3 ⑤ 'make waves'는 말 그대로 '풍파를 일으킨다'는 뜻으로 '문제를 일으킨다'는 뜻으로 이해할 수 있다.

4 the behavior of others

Lesson 9

9B 1 root 2 regard 3 symbolize 4 float 5 democracy 6 unite 7 fasten 8 bloom

9C 1 unite 2 unusual 3 bloom 4 democracy 5 fist 6 obvious 7 remarks

9D 1 involved 2 (R)root 3 anywhere 4 exist

9E 1 ③ 2 ③ 3 ④ 4 ②

9F 전문 해석 친구에게 "손가락을 꼬아 두어."라고 말한다면 여러분은 검지를 교차시키고 고정시키는 동작의 관습을 행하는 것이다. 그것은 우리가 오늘날 아는 것과 다르지만 같은 것을 상징한다. 그 몸짓은 십자가 두 사람의 결합을 나타내며 그 교차점은 성령이 있는 곳을 표시한다는 믿음에 뿌리를 두고 있다. 그래서 그것은 소원을 비는 사람과 다른 지지자, 두 명의 사람을 연관시킨다. 십자가를 두고 한 기원은 그 바람이 이루어지기 전까지 십자가의 교차점에 단단히 묶인 것으로 간주되었다. 많은 초기 유럽 문화권에서 이 미신이 일반적이었다는 것이 고서(古書)에 언급되고 있다. 행운을 빌며 손가락을 교차시킬 때 소원을 비는 사람의 검지가 소원을 표현하는 사람의 검지 위에 놓였다. 친구들이 "손가락을 교차시키는" 고대의 관습이 소원을 비는 사람이 자신의 손가락을 교차시키는 것으로 단순화되었고 결국 오늘날의 "행운을 빌어 줄게."라는 표현이 되었다는 점은 명백하다.

1 ④ 행운을 비는 몸짓이 손가락을 서로 겹쳐 놓던 것에서 손가락을 스스로 꼬아서 행운을 비는 것으로 단순화되어 변화한 것에 대한 글이므로, 제목으로는 ④ '소원을 비는 몸짓의 변화'가 가장 적절하다.
① 손으로 행운을 비는 다양한 방법 ② 손가락 겹치기: 다른 의미들 ③ 손가락과 불운에 대한 미신 ⑤ 소원을 이루려면 지지자가 필요하다

2 ③ 빈칸 다음에 과거와 현재의 몸짓이 달라도 의미가 같다는 것을 설명하고 있으므로 빈칸에 들어갈 말로는 ③ '같은 것을 상징한다'가 가장 적절하다.
① 널리 행해지지 않았다 ② 심각하게 여겨졌다 ④ 종교적인 믿음에 영향을 주었다 ⑤ 유럽 국가들에 퍼졌다

3 ② 십자가의 겹치는 부분은 소원이 고정되는 곳을 상징했으므로 정답으로는 ② '소원이 묶인 곳'이 적절하다.
① 우정이 존재하는 곳 ③ 사람의 정신이 존재하는 곳 ④ 악마가 지켜보는 곳 ⑤ 약속이 표현되는 곳

4 index fingers / cross 과거에는 행운을 비는 사람과 보조자가 하나로 합한 바람을 상징하기 위해 서로의 검지를 교차시켰다. 하지만 그 관습은 시간이 지나며 변했고 한 사람이 자신의 손가락을 교차시킴으로써 행운을 빌 수 있게 되었다.

Lesson 10

10B 1 height 2 spoil 3 purpose 4 spill 5 leap 6 underwater 7 drought 8 dim

10C 1 underwater 2 height 3 ethnic 4 spilled(spilt) 5 spoil 6 solution

10D 1 drowned 2 proposed 3 rainfall 4 starving

10E 1 ② 2 ④ 3 ② 4 ①

10F 전문 해석 지구는 지구 온난화의 결과로 점점 뜨거워지고 있다. 전문가들은 극지방의 만년설이 녹으면 물이 넘치고 결국 저지대와 섬에 있는 마을들이 물에 잠기게 될 것이라고 경고한다. 그러나 일부 과학자들은 세계 일조량의 감소라는 정반대의 것에 대해 걱정한다. 세계 일조량 감소는 공기를 오염시키고 지구의 표면에 도달하는 햇빛의 양을 줄이는 재와 매연과 같은 고체의 작은 입자들과 관련이 있다.
세계 일조량 감소는 지구 온난화의 해결책으로 보이지만 그것도 만만치 않게 지구에 해를 끼친다. 일조량 감소는 북반구를 식히는 효과가 있으며 대지와 바다의 온도를 떨어뜨리며 그리하여 강수량을 줄인다. 전문가들은 이 현상이 아프리카에 중대한 영향을 줄 수 있었다고 의견을 제시한다. 1980년대에 아프리카 대륙을 압도했으며 사람들을 굶어죽게 했던 가뭄이 세계 일조량 감소 때문이라고 전문가들은 믿는다.

1 ⑤ 세계적으로 일조량이 줄어드는 것은 지구 온난화의 해결책처럼 보이지만 사막화 등의 환경 문제를 야기할 수 있다는 내용의 글이므로 요지로는 ⑤가 가장 적절하다.

2 ③ 지구 온난화의 반대 개념은 지구 일조량의 감소이므로 ③ '정반대의'가 가장 적절하다.
① 긍정적인 전환 ② 재앙의 미리보기 ④ 온난화의 원인 ⑤ 예상치 못한 이득

3 ④ 전문가들은 세계 일조량의 감소가 아프리카에 가뭄을 유발했다고 믿고 있으므로 ④ '전문가들은 세계 일조량 감소가 아프리카를 위협할 수 있다고 경고한다.'가 글의 내용과 일치한다.
① 전문가들은 극지의 만년설이 녹고 있다는 것을 부인한다. ② 공기 중의 고체 분자들은 강수량을 증가 시킨다. ③ 세계 일조량 감소는 북반구를 더욱 덥게 하는 효과를 갖고 있다. ⑤ 세계 일조량의 감소는 홍수를 유발할 것으로 예상된다.

4 rainfall / droughts 지구 일조량 감소의 부정적인 효과는 무엇인가? → 그것은 북반구를 냉각시키고 강수량을 줄여서 가뭄을 유발한다.

Lesson 11

11B 1 passport 2 aptitude 3 logical 4 reject 5 permit 6 useless 7 intelligent 8 security

11C 1 intelligent 2 aptitude 3 useless 4 predict 5 sheet 6 logical

11D 1 security 2 turned out 3 passport 4 rule

11E 1 ② 2 ③ 3 ① 4 ④

11F 전문 해석 어떤 의미에서는, 원거리 통신의 디지털 혁명은 이미 시작되었다. 정보 기술 산업이 호황이다. 마이크로

프로세서의 효율이 18개월마다 두 배가 된다고 선언한 무어의 법칙은 유지되고 있다. 같은 맥락에서, (인터넷의) 사용 가능한 대역폭이 12개월마다 세 배가 된다는 길더의 법칙은 인터넷 사용 비용을 적절하게 한다. 인터넷 접속은 업무와 사생활 모두에서 매우 중요한 부분이 되었다. 게다가, 우리는 전자기기가 인터넷과 연결되면 기기의 가치가 증가한다는 것을 쉽게 예측할 수 있다. 초인종을 예로 들어 보자. 누군가 초인종을 눌렀고 집에 아무도 없으면 그것은 쓸모없는 기계가 된다. 하지만 초인종을 휴대전화와 연결하면 마을의 반대편에 있어도 답할 수 있다. 여러분은 비디오카메라를 통해 '벨을 누른 사람'을 인식하고 그와 이야기를 나눈다. 여러분은 그 후에 그를 집에 들어오게 할 것인가 말 것인가를 결정할 수 있다. 새로운 초인종은 여러분에게 더 높은 수준의 보안을 확보하도록 할 수 있을 것이다!

1 ① 디지털화 추세는 사람들로 하여금 기기를 인터넷에 연결하여 좀 더 편리한 방향으로 삶의 방식을 바꾸고 있다는 내용의 글이므로 이 글의 요지로는 ①이 가장 적절하다.

2 ③ 인터넷에 연결되면 전자 기기가 더 많은 일을 할 수 있다는 내용이므로 빈칸에는 ③ '전자 기기의 가치가 증가한다'가 가장 적절하다.
① 우리의 새로운 전자 기기를 자랑한다. ② 전자 기기의 가격이 떨어진다. ④ 우리는 전자 기기 사용법을 배워야 한다. ⑤ 전자 기기의 복잡함이 줄어든다.

3 ④ 주어진 문장의 him과 ringer를 알아야 문을 열어줄지 결정할 수 있으므로 주어진 문장은 문을 열어줄 것을 결정한다는 문장과 누군가 초인종을 누른다는 문장 사이에 들어가야 한다.

4 have easier access / at lower prices 무어의 법칙과 길더의 법칙이 암시하는 것은 무엇인가? → 사람들은 전자 기기와 인터넷 서비스를 더욱 저렴한 가격으로 편리하게 사용할 수 있다.

Lesson 12

12B 1 recipes 2 amusement 3 shadow 4 principal 5 legend 6 resemble 7 ideal 8 advantage

12C 1 robbed 2 determine 3 otherwise 4 endangered 5 celebration 6 hibernate 7 crawled

12D 1 ideal 2 consult 3 exposure 4 advantages

12E 1 ④ 2 ② 3 ① 4 ④

12F 전문 해석 펜실베니아의 Punxsutawney[pʌŋksətɔ́:ni]는 털복숭이 일기 예보관 중에서 가장 유명한 Punxsutawney Phil의 고향이다. 그들은 매년 2월 2일 굴에서 천천히 나와 겨울이 얼마나 더 지속될 것인가를 예측한다. 2월 초에 이 작은 마을은 흡사 대도시와 유사하다. 그리고 성촉절(聖燭節, Groundhog Day)로 불리는 2월 2일에는 그 지역 지도자들이 Phil과 상의하기 위해 Gobbler's Knob에 모이고 Phil은 자신의 동면 장소에서 기어 나와 자신의 그림자를 보거나 또는 보지 못한다. 전통에 따르면, Phil이 자신의 그림자를 보면 그것은 겨울이 앞으로 6주 동안 지속될 것임을 의미하고, 반면에 Phil이 자신의 그림자를 보지 못하면 봄이 머지 않았다고 한다.
누구도 이 전통이 언제 시작되었는지를 정확히 알지 못한다. 그것은 처음으로 18세기에 아마도 성촉절(聖燭節, Candlemas) 기념과 관련되어 언급되었는데, 성촉절은 그해 겨울의 첫 날과 봄의 첫 날 사이 중간의 날이다. 그리고 날짜가 똑같지는 않지만 성촉절의 날씨가 봄이 얼마나 빨리 올지를 결정한다는 믿음은 마멋(woodchuck)으로 번역되었는데, 마멋은 보통 2월 초에 겨울잠을 끝내는 동면 동물이었다. 하지만 요즘에는 Phil의 예보가 맞는지조차 중요하지 않다. 그것은 함께 모여 '공휴일'을 기념하고 작거나 평범할 뿐인 Punxsutawney 마을을 알리려는 구실에 지나지 않는다.

1 ③ 성촉절(聖燭節)이 어떻게 해서 생겨나게 되었는지에 관한 글이므로, 이 글의 제목으로는 '성촉절의 기원'이 가장 적절하다.

2 ⑤ 주어진 문장은 역접(however)의 연결사로 시작되며 Phil의 예보가 맞고 틀리고는 중요하지 않다는 내용이므로, 모두 모여 '공휴일'을 축하하기 위한 구실이라는 문장 앞에 오는 것이 문맥상 자연스럽다.

3 ④ Candlemas는 겨울의 첫 날과 봄의 첫 날 사이 중간에 있는 날이라 했으므로 보통 2월 초를 나타낸다.

4 six / begin(start) 전통에 따르면, Phil이 자신의 그림자를 보고 자신의 굴로 돌아간다면 이것은 겨울이 6주간 더 지속되는 것을 의미한다. Phil이 그림자를 보지 못한다면 봄은 곧 시작될 것이다.

Lesson 13

13B 1 bubble 2 refresh 3 liquid 4 lifelong 5 disabled 6 organ 7 acid 8 clone

13C 1 damaged 2 stomach 3 clone 4 dissolved 5 lifelong 6 organ 7 break down

13D 1 react 2 liquid 3 nutrients 4 backbone

13E 1 ① 2 ② 3 ④ 4 ③

13F 전문 해석 빵 한 조각을 입에 몇 분간 물고 있으면 잠시 후 단맛을 느낄 것이다. 침 속의 효소가 음식을 녹이기 시작하기 때문에 그것은 소화의 시작이다. 다음 단계는 음식을 삼키는 것이다. 위 속에서 산, 효소와 다른 액체들이 음식을 추가로 분해한다. 그 산 성분은 쇠못을 녹일 수 있을 정도로 강할 것이다. 다행히 위에는 그 화학물질들이 위를 상하게 하지 못하게 막는 특별한 내벽이 있다. 음식은 이제 액체 형태이고 5미터의 돌돌 말린 소장으로 밀어 넣어진다. 음식이 도착하면, 소장은 더 많은 소화액을 분비하는 것으로 반응하고 다음에는 결국 그것들을 소장으로부터 밀어낸다. 이제 몸은 음식으로부터 신체를 유지하는데 필요한 영양소를 흡수했다. 다음 목적지는 대장이다. 그곳에서, 남아 있는 수분은 뭐든지 음식으로부터 흡수되고 그것은 찌꺼기 덩어리로 내려간다. 몸으로부터 음식 안의 공기방울들이 새어나온다. 이제 여러분이 화장실에 갈 때이다!

1 ③ 위 글은 소화가 진행되는 과정을 설명하고 있으므로 글의 주제로는 '몸 안에서의 소화 과정'이 가장 적절하다.

2 ④ 주어진 문장의 That acid는 위산을 가리킨다. 위산을 먼저 소개한 다음 위산의 강도에 대해 부연설명을 하는 것이 자연스럽기 때문에 주어진 문장은 ④에 들어가는 것이 적절하다.

3 ④ 빵을 입에 두고 몇 분 후 단맛을 느끼는 것은 침 속의 효소 때문이라는 문장이 있으므로 ④가 적절하다.

4 digestive juices / nutrients 소장은 음식에 소화액을 더하고 음식을 대장으로 밀어내기 전에 신체를 유지하기 위해 필요한 영양소를 흡수한다.

Lesson 14

14B 1 evidence 2 complex 3 harmful 4 progress 5 relationships 6 reward 7 informal 8 unselfish

14C 1 charity 2 donation 3 specifically 4 relationship 5 similarities 6 heritage

14D 1 contact 2 committed 3 informal 4 significant

14E 1 ① 2 ③ 3 ② 4 ①

14F 전문 해석 Oregon 대학교의 Bill Harbaugh 교수와 그의 팀은 뇌와 경제적인 결정 사이의 관계를 명확하게 관찰했다. 겉으로 복잡하게 보이는 관계를 밝히려는 그들의 실험 중 하나에서, 연구자들은 사람들이 자선 단체에 기부하는 것이 신경 세포의 영향을 받는지를 알아보려고 해보았다. 19명의 여성들에게 컴퓨터 자선 게임을 위한 100달러가 지급되었다. 그들은 자선 단체에 기부를 할지 안 할지를 결정할 수 있었고 각각의 결정은 그들이 돈을 벌거나 잃을 수 있는 다른 상황으로 이어졌다. 게임이 끝나면 실험 대상자들은 자신의 계좌에 남아 있는 돈을 모두 가져갈 수 있었다.

실험 대상자들이 게임을 하는 동안 과학자들이 그들의 뇌를 정밀 촬영했다. 그들은 사람들이 얼마나 좋은 감정을 느끼는가를 통제하는 뇌의 '쾌락 중추'를 관찰했다. 대부분의 실험 대상자들이 자선 단체에 돈을 기부할 때 그들의 쾌락 중추가 뇌 정밀 촬영에서 밝아졌다. 몇몇은 자신의 기부금에 세금을 부여받았을 때에도 밝아졌다. 두 결과는 모두 뇌의 쾌락 중추가 사심이 없는 행동에 보상을 받는다는 것을 시사한다. 게다가, 사람들이 더 많이 기부하면 할수록, 그들의 쾌락 중추가 더 많이 밝아졌다. 몇몇 사람들의 쾌락 중추는 추가의 돈을 자신이 간직할 때보다 컴퓨터가 자선 단체에 기부할 때 밝아졌다. 과학자들은 이것이 순수한 이타주의에 관한 최초의 신경계적 증거라고 언급하며, 순수한 이타주의는 정말로 생물학적인 관련이 있을 수도 있다는 것을 의미 한다고 한다.

1 ③ 이 글은 이타주의가 뇌의 쾌락 중추와 관련이 있다는 내용이므로, 이 글의 주제로는 '이타주의와 생물학 사이의 관계'가 가장 적절하다.

2 ③ 남을 도우면 뇌의 쾌락 중추가 환해지면서 사람들이 많은 기쁨을 느낀다는 것이므로, 빈칸에 들어갈 말로는 biological(생물학적인)이 가장 적절하다.

3 ③ ⓒ는 the scientists를 가리키고 나머지는 모두 the subjects를 가리킨다.

4 feel good(happy) / give(donate) 순수한 이타주의란 사람들이 타인에게 사심 없이 무언가를 베풀었을 때 즐거움을 느끼는 것을 의미한다.

Lesson 15

15B 1 temporary 2 extend 3 earthquake 4 experiment 5 material 6 dispute 7 degree 8 landscape

15C 1 earthquake 2 experiment 3 dispute 4 landscape 5 harmony 6 forecast 7 route

15D 1 concentrate 2 consist 3 horizon / horizons 4 technology

15E 1 ② 2 ④ 3 ① 4 ④

15F 전문 해석 우리의 태양은 두 개의 항성과 이를 따르는 행성들로 이루어진 이중 항성 구조의 한 부분이라는 학설이 존재한다. 두 개의 태양이 있다면 지구의 풍경은 무척 다르고 하루에 두 번 일몰을 보게 될 것이다. 사실, 우리의 태양계는 다른 한 개의 태양계 주위를 돌고 있기 때문에 우리는 수평선에서 뜨는 한 개의 태양만을 볼 수 있다. 다른 태양계가 도는 궤도나 경로는 우리의 태양계에 묶여 있고 그들은 25,920년 마다 만난다. 그래서 우리는 두 번째 태양과의 다음 '만남'을 예측할 수 있다. 우리가 가진 기술은 우리의 태양에게 다른 한 짝이 있는지 여부를 입증할 수 있다. 일련의 실험을 통해 NASA는 또 다른 태양에 대한 증거를 모았지만 그것이 일으킬 논란 때문에 숨겨지지(→ 공표되지) 않았다. 다른 태양은 우리의 시각에서 보면 매우 멀고 작은 갈색별일 뿐이다. 어느 정도는 이치에 맞는다. 은하의 80퍼센트의 항성이 이중 항성이며 그들이 모두 완벽한 조화를 이루고 있다고 알려져 있다.

1 ② 이 글은 태양계에 항성이 두 개 있을 수 있다는 학설을 소개하고 있으므로 제목으로는 ② '정말 우리에게 두 개의 태양이 있을까?'가 가장 적절하다.

2 ⑤ 대중들에게 논란을 불러일으킬 것을 우려하여 NASA가 다른 항성의 존재에 대해 밝히지 않았다는 내용이므로 concealed 대신 released나 confirmed 등의 말을 쓰는 것이 적절하다.

3 ① 태양이 두 개 있다고 주장하는 학설에 대해 필자는 '동조하는' 입장이므로 ①이 적절하다.
② 회의적인 ③ 비판적인 ④ 무관심한 ⑤ 분석적인

4 disputes / create 왜 NASA는 두 개의 태양 학설에 대한 증거를 숨기는가? → 그들은 그것이 일으킬 논란을 두려워하고 있다.

Lesson 16

16B 1 suffer 2 be susceptible to 3 wildlife 4 invasion 5 yawn 6 mankind 7 awful 8 blame

16C 1 spread 2 threaten 3 invasion 4 wander 5 yawn 6 wildlife 7 cruel

16D 1 mammals 2 blame 3 death 4 increase

16E 1 ④ 2 ③ 3 ④ 4 ②

16F 전문 해석 마멋은 다람쥐 과에 속하며 고양이 정도의 크기이다. 그들의 눈은 크고 둥글며 입과 코는 작아서 귀엽고 순진해 보인다. 하지만 그들은 인류의 끔직한 적이 될 수 있다. 몽골의 초원 지역에서 발견되는 한 종의 마멋은 흔히 림프절 흑사병으로 알려져 있으며 예르시니아 흑사병으로 유발되는 폐의 전염병에 유전적으로 취약하다. 그 병은 인간을 위협하고 심각하게 기침을 하게 한다. 야생 상태일 때, 마멋은 근처의 생물들에게 기침을 하고 벼룩, 쥐, 인간을 감염시켜 그것을 주위에 치료한다 → 퍼뜨린다. 그 후, 박테리아가 다른 생명체에 옮겨진다. 감염된 마멋은 그 지역을 이리저리 돌아다니며 다른 생물들을 전염시킨다. "마멋의 침략"은 동아시아와 유럽을 휩쓴 모든 거대한 역병의 원인으로 비난받는다. 마멋과 인간들이 그 역병에 걸리면, 고열이 나고 림프선이 부으면서 검게 변한다. 몽골 사람들은 마멋의 고기를 좋아하지만 그들은 마멋의 겨드랑이에 "죽은 사냥꾼의 영혼이 있다."고 믿기에 그 부위를 먹지 않는다.

1 ⑤ 마멋이 옮기는 전염성 호흡기 질환의 위험성에 관한 글이므로 요지로는 ⑤가 가장 적절하다.

2 ③ 야생 상태에서 마멋이 옮기는 병은 기침을 통해 주위로 퍼져나가므로 treat 대신 spread를 쓰는 것이 글의 흐름상 적절하다.

3 ⑤ 몽골인들은 마멋의 겨드랑이 고기를 먹지 않는다고 했으므로 ⑤ '몽골인들은 마멋의 겨드랑이 고기를 먹기 좋아한다.' 는 글의 내용과 일치하지 않는다.
① 한 종의 마멋이 몽골의 초원 지역에 산다. ② 마멋이 림프절 흑사병에 걸리면 기침을 한다. ③ 마멋의 병은 인간을 위협할 수 있다. ④ 병든 마멋의 림프선은 부어오른다.

4 invasion / spread 동아시아에서 유럽까지 휩쓴 거대한 역병은 어떻게 설명될 수 있는가? → 마멋의 침략, 즉 마멋이 퍼뜨리는 림프절 흑사병이 그 재앙에 책임이 있다.

Lesson 17

17B 1 compare 2 keep track of 3 judge 4 accurate 5 divide 6 pitcher 7 athlete 8 complicated

17C 1 contribute 2 Athletes 3 divided 4 accurate 5 scout 6 compared 7 pitcher

17D 1 breeze 2 sore 3 appreciated 4 athlete

17E 1 ② 2 ③ 3 ① 4 ③

17F 전문 해석 통계는 아마 다른 어떤 운동에서보다 야구에 있어 매우 중요하다. 야구 경기는 매우 (A) 구조적인 흐름으로 진행되기 때문에 게임의 결과를 예측하는 것이 쉽다. 전문가들은 확률의 정확한 계산이 가능하다고 말한다. (B) 복잡하게 느껴지겠지만 일단 정보를 활용하는 법을 배우게 되면 통계를 파악하는 것은 매우 쉬운 일이다. 전통적으로 타자의 평균 타율(타석에 나선 수로 공을 친 수를 나눈 것)과 출루 평균(9회 동안 투수가 허용한 대략의 출루 수)이 중요하게 여겨진다.
이런 통계는 선수의 경기 성과를 더욱 잘 (C) 평가하기 위해 고안되어 있다. 팀 감독과 코치들은 통계에 근거해서 각각의 선수가 얼마나 팀에 공헌했는지 평가한다. 야구 스카우트 담당자들은 서로 다른 능력을 가진 선수들을 비교하기 위해 통계를 사용한다. 통계는 상대 팀을 이기기 위한 전략을 세우는 데 이용된다. 예를 들어, 감독은 경기를 하는 동안 타선에 누구를 기용할 것인가 또는 구원 투수로 누구를 부를 것인가 등에 대한 결정을 하는 데 있어 자주 통계를 사용한다.

1 ⑤ (A) 야구에서 통계가 중요한 이유를 설명하며 야구의 흐름이 예측 가능하다는 내용이므로 '구조적인' 이 적절하다. unexpected는 '의외의, 뜻밖의' 의 의미이다. (B) 처음에는 복잡해 보여도 활용법을 배우면 쉽다는 내용이므로 '복잡한' 이 적절하다. (C) 통계를 이용해 야구선수들의 성과를 평가하고 전략을 세울 수 있다는 내용이므로 '평가' 가 적절하다. compliment는 '칭찬' 의 의미이다.

2 ⑤ 감독들은 통계에 근거하여 구원투수를 결정한다고 했으므로 ⑤는 글의 내용과 일치하지 않는다.

3 ④ 글에서 밝힌 대로 타자의 평균 배팅 성적이 중요하게 여겨진다.
① 아웃을 시킨 평균 ② 구원 투수 등판 수 ③ 회당 평균 투구 수 ⑤ 투수의 총 투구 수

4 managers / coaches / scouts 야구 종목에서 누가 통계를 사용하는가? → 팀 감독, 코치, 스카우트 담당자들이 통계를 사용한다.

Lesson 18

18B 1 theory 2 honor 3 convert 4 spectator 5 sew 6 achievement 7 flour 8 identify

18C 1 decorate 2 amount 3 flour 4 theory 5 Rinse 6 Revolution

18D 1 mention 2 odd 3 honor 4 function

18E 1 ④ 2 ③ 3 ④ 4 ④

18F 전문 해석 우리가 하는 복장은 우리의 정체성을 보여준다. 예를 들어, 판매원들은 정장에 넥타이를 착용한다. 야구 선수들은 모자를 쓴다. 그럼 요리사들은 어떤가? 이론상 모든 종류의 모자를 사용할 수 있지만 그들은 대개 추한 머리그물이나 위쪽이 긴 이상한 하얀 모자를 쓴다. 정말 요리사의 모자 모양에 타당한 기능이 있는 것인가?
로마시대와 같은 고대에는 최고의 요리사들은 특별한 모자를 받음으로써 그들의 업적에 대한 인정을 받았다. 그들에게는 월계수가 장식된 모자가 가장 큰 영예였다.
17세기까지 프랑스에서는 요리사들은 지위에 따라 다양한 색의 모자를 상으로 받았다. 18세기 초반에는 탈레랑의 요리사가 그의 직원 전원에게 하얀 모자를 쓰라고 요구했다. 그는 그 모자가 밀가루나 버터 같은 재료들을 반죽하는 동안 요리사의 머리카락이 음식에 들어가지 않게 하려 고안되었다고 자신의 요리책에서 언급했다. 하지만 원래 이 모자는 납작했다. 높은 모자는 점차 인기를 얻게 되었는데, 항상 아주 뜨거운 환경에서 일하는 요리사들의 머리에 환기를 제공할 수 있었기 때문이었다. 요리사의 머리에서 발생한 많은 양의 열은 위로 올라간 다음 모자에서 빠져나가며 머리를 식혔다.

1 ④ 위로 높은 모양의 요리사 모자가 생기게 된 역사를 시대에 따라 서술하고 있으므로, 제목으로는 ④ '긴 요리사 모자의 역사'가 가장 적절하다.
① 모자: 정체성을 보여주는 것 ② 높은 모자: 자부심의 표현 ③ 요리사들에 의해 애호된 모자의 디자인 ⑤ 요리사 모자의 색상 변화

2 ③ 이어지는 문단에서 요리사 모자의 기능에 따른 변화를 설명하고 있으므로 빈칸에는 ③이 들어가는 것이 가장 적절하다.

3 ④ 탈레랑의 요리사가 직원들에게 흰 모자를 쓰도록 한 것은 맞지만 그 모자는 납작한 모양이라고 했으므로 ④ '탈레랑의 요리사는 직원들에게 긴 모자를 쓰도록 요구했다.'는 내용과 일치하지 않는다.
① 로마인들은 요리사들에게 월계수가 장식된 모자를 주었다. ② 프랑스에서 요리사들은 다양한 색의 모자를 썼다. ③ 탈레랑의 요리사는 흰 모자가 좋다고 믿었다. ⑤ 흰색의 긴 모자는 요리사들 사이에서 인기를 얻었다.

4 flat / cooled / heat 처음에는 요리사 모자들은 납작했지만 나중에 그것은 위쪽이 길어졌다. 위쪽이 긴 모자는 공기가 모자 안으로 들어왔다가 빠져나가게 함으로써 요리하는 동안 요리사의 머리에 생긴 열기를 식혔다.

Answer Key

Lesson 19

19B 1 worldwide 2 traffic 3 genes 4 population 5 zone 6 capable 7 species 8 possess

19C 1 organization 2 southern 3 protect 4 solid 5 continent 6 surround

19D 1 capable 2 motion 3 attack 4 population

19E 1 ③ 2 ④ 3 ① 4 ①

19F 전문 해석 새들은 걸을 수도, 날 수도 있다. 그러나 지구에는 날지 못하는 새보다 날 수 있는 새들이 더 많다. 한 종의 새가 날지 걸을지 선택하는 것은 서식 환경에 달려 있다. 나는 것은 걷는 것보다 더 많은 에너지를 필요로 한다. (A) 따라서 원래 서식지에서 포식자에 의한 공격의 두려움이 없는 새들은 결국 날지 못하게 되기 마련이다. 다른 대륙으로부터 멀리 떨어진 작은 대륙인 호주에는 날지 못하는 새들이 많이 있다. 그리고 태평양과 인도양의 섬에서 다수의 날지 못하는 새들이 보고되었다. 그곳에서는 자연이 걷기에 더 적합한 유전자를 '골랐다'. 대개 대지가 물로 둘러싸여 있고 천적의 수가 줄어드는 곳에서는 새들의 걷는 능력이 향상된다. 사실 '걷는다'는 것은 새들의 동작을 적절하게 묘사하는 용어가 아니다. 더 많은 수의 새들은 걷는다기보다는 총총 뛰어다닌다. 세계적으로 타조나 홍학처럼 걷거나 뛰어다니는 새들은 긴 다리를 갖고 있고 넓으며 사방이 뚫린 공간에서 산다. (B) 대조적으로, 나무 위에서 사는 대부분의 새들은 총총 뛰어다닌다. 이는 걷거나 나는 것 보다 이 가지에서 저 가지로 뛰어서 이동하는 것이 더 쉽기 때문이다.

1 ④ 새들에게는 나는 것보다 걷는 것이 에너지를 덜 소모하기 때문에 천적이 없는 곳에서는 날지 않게 된다는 내용의 글이므로 요지로는 ④가 가장 적절하다.

2 ③ (A) 앞선 문장은 걷는 것보다 나는 데에 에너지가 더 필요하다는 내용이고, 이어지는 문장은 포식자가 없으면 날지 않게 된다는 내용이므로 인과관계를 나타내는 Therefore를 쓰는 것이 적절하다. (B) 열린 공간에서 살며 걷거나 뛰어다니는 새들과 나무에서 총총 뛰어다니는 새들을 대조하고 있으므로 대조의 연결어인 In contrast를 쓰는 것이 적절하다.

3 ⑤ 주어진 문장은 걷는다는 표현이 새들의 동작을 묘사하기에는 적절치 않다는 내용이므로, 대부분의 다른 새들은 걸어다니는 것이 아니라 총총 뛰어다닌다고 하는 내용이 시작되기 전인 ⓔ에 들어가는 것이 적절하다.

4 Environment / fly / walk 무엇이 한 종의 새로 하여금 날거나 걷는 것을 선택하게 하는가? → 환경이 가장 중요한 역할을 한다. 자세히 말하자면, 포식자들이 거의 없으면 새들은 날지 않는 경향이 있다. 나무가 있으면 가지 주변을 총총 뛰어다니고 나무가 거의 없으면 땅 위에서 걷거나 뛰어다닌다.

Lesson 20

20B 1 immigrant 2 affairs 3 faint 4 establish 5 primary 6 benefit 7 courage 8 military

20C 1 government 2 illusion 3 courage 4 conductor 5 benefit 6 detective

20D 1 confuse 2 affair 3 impressed 4 agent

20E 1 ④ 2 ② 3 ④ 4 ①

20F 전문 해석 스파이는 국제 관계의 분야에서 자주 쓰인다. 예를 들어, 1756년에 루이 15세에 의해 고용된 프랑스의 요원인 Chevalier D'Eon은 자국의 이익을 위해 러시아의 여황제와 비밀 조약을 맺었다. 외국에서 온 남자는 그 여황제를 만날 기회를 갖을 수 없기 때문에 D'Eon은 여자로 변장해서 접견을 확보하고 조약을 성사시킬 용기가 있었다.

프랑스의 황제인 나폴레옹은 위대한 전술가이기도 했지만 그와는 별개로 오스트리아와 벌인 전쟁에서 입증한 것처럼 간첩 행위의 기술에서도 대가였다. 1804년에 그는 자신의 가장 노련한 스파이인 Karl Schulmeister를 비엔나로 파견했고 그곳에서 Schulmeister는 자신이 프랑스에서 추방되었다는 이야기를 했다. 그는 오스트리아의 군대 수장인 Marshall Mack과 친분을 쌓았다. 그는 Schulmeister가 가진 프랑스 군사 상황에 관한 지식에 너무나 감명 받아서 그를 오스트리아 정보 참모부장으로 임명했다. 그는 Schulmeister에 대해 의심의 징후가 없었다. 이 보직에 있으면서 Schulmeister는 나폴레옹의 군대에 대한 그릇된 환상을 심어주어서 Mack을 혼란시켰고, 결국 오스트리아 군대의 패배를 야기할 수 있었다.

1 ② 두 명의 유명한 스파이의 이야기를 다룬 내용이므로 제목으로는 ② '위대한 스파이들과 그들의 업적'이 가장 적절하다.
① 스파이 전쟁: 감춰졌지만 맹렬한 ③ 나폴레옹: 스파이 전쟁의 위대한 장인 ④ 작전 중에 스파이들이 직면하는 장애물 ⑤ 사용 가능한 정보에 의해 영향을 받는 정치

2 ③ Schulmeister가 의심을 받지 않았기 때문에 활동을 성공적으로 했다고 보는 것이 자연스럽다. 따라서 빈칸에 들어갈 말로는 ③ '~에 대한 의심의 징후가 없는'이 가장 적절하다.

3 ④ ④는 Marshall Mack을 가리킨다.

4 treaty / government official / false 유명한 스파이가 두 명 있다. 첫 번째 사람인 Chevalier D'Eon은 러시아에 가서 여황제와 조약을 맺었다. 두 번째 사람인 Karl Schulmeister는 오스트리아에 가서 정부 관리가 되어 프랑스의 이익을 위해 나폴레옹 군대에 대한 잘못된 정보를 주었다.

Lesson 21

21B 1 greedy 2 pretend 3 profit 4 wisdom 5 childhood 6 creative 7 struggle 8 encourage

21C 1 childhood 2 creative 3 attitudes 4 opinions 5 pretend 6 greedy

21D 1 scratched 2 overcome 3 shoot 4 compromise

21E 1 ① 2 ② 3 ② 4 ②

21F 전문 해석 Sylvester Stallone은 어린 시절을 힘들게 보냈다. 성인이 되어서도 그의 상황은 크게 나아지지 않았다. 안정적인 수입원이 없었고 전기세를 내는 데 보태기 위해 개를 25달러에 팔아야 했으며 그는 그러한 많은 어려움에 직면했다. 하지만 그는 자신에 대한 믿음을 잃지 않았고 어려움을 헤치고 나아갔다. 완전히 처음부터 시작하여 거의 20시간 만에 Rocky의 영화 대본을 쓴 것은 바로 개를 판 후 단 2주일이 지나서였다. 그는 그것을 많은 영화사에 보냈다. 결국, 1,500번의 거절을 당한 다음에야 Stallone은 United Artists로부터 12만 5천 달러에 승락을 받았는데 단 그가 주연을 맡지 않는 조건이었다. 그들은 그가 너무 욕심이 많다고 생각했다. 하지만 Stallone은 그가 주연을 맡지 않는다면 수락할 생각이 없었다. 결국 그들이 양보했다. 캐스팅 담당 감독이 그에게 전화를 했다.

그는 Stallone이 Rocky에서 주연을 맡도록 허락하지만 그에게 3만 5천 달러만 주고 수익의 1퍼센트를 주겠다고 했다. 그는 받아들였고 촬영이 시작되었다. Rocky는 제작에 백만 달러가 들었지만 2억 달러의 총수익을 거둬들였다! 전체의 Rocky 시리즈는 십억 달러 이상을 벌었다. 성공은 좌절 후에 온다. 중요한 것은 당신의 태도이다.

1 ⑤ Stallone에 대한 필자의 태도는 '칭찬하는' 것에 가까우므로 ⑤가 가장 적절하다.
① 회의적인 ② 질투하는 ③ 중립적인 ④ 만족스러운

2 ④ ④는 casting director를 가리키고, 나머지는 모두 Stallone을 가리킨다.

3 ② Stallone은 Rocky의 대본을 20시간만에 완성했다고 했으므로 ②는 글의 내용과 일치하지 않는다.

4 star in 왜 Stallone은 United Artists의 12만 5천 달러의 첫 번째 제안을 거절했는가? → 그는 그 영화의 주연을 맡고 싶었기 때문이다.

Lesson 22

22B 1 volunteer 2 foolish 3 exchange 4 preserve 5 adopt 6 electricity 7 artificial 8 communicate

22C 1 preserve 2 electricity 3 volunteers 4 skyscraper 5 rubber 6 exchange 7 ancestors

22D 1 string 2 commercial 3 coal 4 steam

22E 1 ④ 2 ③ 3 ③ 4 ②

22F 전문 해석 암호 기계는 전기로 작동되며 비밀 메시지를 교환하는 용도의 휴대 장비를 가리킨다. 그것은 메시지를 일련의 문자로 암호화하고 다른 상대편에서 그 암호를 해독한다. 컴퓨터의 조상이기도한 그것은 타자기의 키보드를 닮았다.

이것이 상용화되어 사용되었다는 기록은 없지만 2차 세계대전 때 독일군은 그것을 (A) 사용했다. 독일군은 어리석게도 연합군이 그 암호기의 암호를 풀 수 없을 것이라고 믿었다. 그렇지만 서로 의사소통 하는 것이 매우 (B) 어렵긴 했다. 매일 각각의 설정내용이 암호기와 해독기에 전송되어야 했다. 하루가 지나면 세팅은 삭제됐고 기록은 보관되지 않았다. 그러나 이 설정내용은 자주 연합군의 (C) 손에 들어가곤 했다. 게다가 암호기를 도난당했고 암호가 풀려 중요한 정보가 새어나갔다. 암호기 중 한 대가 폴란드에서 탈취되어서 영국으로 보내졌다. 암호를 푸는 데 자원한 폴란드 수학자들의 도움에 힘입어 영국의 전문가들은 그들이 입수한 많은 수의 나치 메시지의 암호를 푸는 데 성공했고 그것으로부터 귀중한 군사 정보를 얻었다.

1 ⑤ 암호 기계가 2차 세계대전에서 사용되었지만 사용법이 어려웠고, 가끔 적에게 탈취되어서 암호가 해독되기도 했다는 내용이므로 주제로는 ⑤가 가장 적절하다.

2 ③ (A) 독일군이 암호 기계를 채택했으므로 adopted가 적절하다. destroy는 '파괴하다'의 의미이다. (B) 암호 기계의 설정내용이 매일 삭제되어서 사용하기 힘들었다는 내용이므로 difficult가 적절하다. valued는 '소중한'의 의미이다. (C) 암호 기계가 적군에게 탈취되어서 암호가 풀렸다는 내용이 있으므로 captured가 적절하다.

3 ③ 매일 삭제되었던 것은 암호 기계가 문자를 조합한 구성이었으므로 ③이 가장 적절하다.
① 암호의 메시지 ② 작전의 암호 ④ 암호기와 해독기의 정체 ⑤ 암호를 주고 받는 지역

4 adopted / break / codes / intercept 암호 기계는 암호를 생성하고 2차 세계대전에서 독일군은 그것을 사용했다. 매일 바뀌는 설정내용은 기계를 사용하는 것을 더욱 어렵게 했다. 하지만 연합군은 그 암호를 풀어 비밀 메시지를 가로챌 수 있었다.

Lesson **23**

23B 1 responsible 2 sign up for 3 show up 4 dump 5 poverty 6 proof 7 pupil 8 passionate

23C 1 criticize 2 uncomfortable 3 negative 4 chairperson 5 proof 6 poverty 7 idle

23D 1 academic 2 discovered 3 cure 4 efficient

23E 1 ④ 2 ③ 3 ④ 4 ①

23F [전문 해석] Tony는 학업에 있어서는 별로 성공적이지 않았다. 오히려 그는 마을에서 가장 말을 안 듣는 말썽꾸러기였다. 나는 주말 리더십 훈련에서 Tony를 만났다. 학교의 모든 학생들은 그 훈련에 등록하도록 초청받았다.
(B) 훈련에서, 그들은 학교에서 일어났던 긍정적인 일과 부정적인 일들에 대해 말했다. Tony는 비판하지 않고 들어주었기 때문에 그의 모둠에 있던 아이들은 그의 말을 기꺼이 받아들였다. Tony는 자신이 모둠의 일원이라는 감정을 느꼈다. Tony와 다른 아이들은 노숙자 프로젝트 팀에 가입했다.
(A) 그는 가난, 굶주림, 절망에 대해 어느정도 알고 있었다. 팀의 아이들은 그의 열정적인 관심과 아이디어에 감명받았다. 그들은 Tony를 팀의 공동 의장으로 선출했다. 선생님들은 그것에 대해 불편해 했지만 아이들은 그들의 반응에 신경 쓰지 않았다. Tony는 식량 모으기 운동을 담당했고 학생회는 Tony의 지시를 따랐다.
(C) 2주 후, Tony와 그의 친구들은 2,854개의 통조림을 모집함으로써 새로운 학교 기록을 세웠다. Tony는 매일 학교에 나오기 시작했고 선생님들의 질문에 대답했다. Tony는 부러졌던 날개를 고치기만 하면 모든 새들이 날 수 있다는 것을 증명했다.

1 ② Tony는 문제아였지만 (B) 리더십 훈련에서 학생들과 친해졌고 (A) 학생들에 의해 프로젝트의 공동 책임자로 선출되었으며 (C) 프로젝트는 훌륭한 결과를 거두었고, Tony는 다시 매일 학교에 나오게 되었다는 글이므로 ②가 가장 적절하다.

2 ④ Tony와 친구들이 2,854개의 통조림을 모았다는 내용이 있으므로 ④는 글의 내용과 일치한다.

3 ③ ⓒ의 their는 교사들을 가리킨다.

4 passionate / criticize 아이들은 리더십 훈련에서 Tony에 대해 어떻게 느꼈는가? → 그들은 Tony의 열정적인 관심과 아이디어에 감명 받았다. 그들은 또한 그가 평가하거나 비판하지 않고 경청하며 이해하려 노력한다고 느꼈다.

Lesson 24

24B 1 bitter 2 eastern 3 when it comes to 4 bunch 5 attract 6 crash 7 mend 8 oar

24C 1 broadcast 2 bunch 3 dictation 4 played a part in 5 Unfortunately 6 regions 7 borders

24D 1 composed 2 conquered 3 attracted 4 broadcast

24E 1 ④ 2 ② 3 ③ 4 ①

24F 전문 해석 강은 항상 사람들이 살고 있거나 모이는 곳 사이의 경계가 되어 왔고 현재에도 계속 그러하다. 고대시대에 강은 자연적인 경계선이었다. 한 마을에 살고 있는 사람들은 강의 한 편에 작물을 심고, 강의 같은 편에 주거지를 짓고, 그리고 일반적으로 강의 다른 편의 땅을 필요로 하지 않았다. 특히 강이 넓을 때는 노를 저어 강을 건너는 것은 안타깝게도 너무 힘든 일이었다. 물론 여러분이 건너편의 사람들을 정복하고 싶을 때를 제외하고 말이다. 강은 과거에 많은 정복자들의 침략 속도를 늦춰왔다. '현대화된' 20세기에도 강은 국가를 침략으로부터 보호하고 호전적인 주변국으로부터의 공격 속도를 늦추는 데 주요한 역할을 해왔다.

강은 자연 경계선이 된다. 한 무리의 측량사를 데려다가 어렵게 경계선을 표시하는 것보다 Missouri 주의 대부분의 동쪽 경계선은 Mississippi 강이라고 말하는 것이 훨씬 더 수월하다. 미국의 지도를 확인해 보라. 경계선이 강을 포함하고 있는지 찾아보라. Nebraska의 동쪽 경계선 또한 Missouri 강이라는 것을 알게 될 것이다.

강은 또한 주와 도시를 위한 경계선이기도 하다. 여러분이 사는 곳이나 다른 지역의 지도에서 몇몇의 강을 발견할 수 있을 것이다. 그리고 그것은 미국만의 경우가 아니다. Huang He 강은 중국 Shensi 지방의 동쪽 경계선을 나타낸다. Danube 강은 루마니아와 불가리아 사이의 국경을 형성하는 데 도움이 되었다. 경계선에 관해서라면, 강보다 훨씬 더 자연스러운 경계선을 찾지 못할 것이다.

1 ① 이 글은 고대부터 현대까지 강이 나라와 도시들 사이의 경계선 역할을 해왔다는 내용이므로, 이 글의 제목으로는 '경계선으로서의 강'이 가장 적절하다.

2 ④ 전체적으로 나라와 도시의 경계선 역할을 하는 강의 의미에 대해 언급하고 있으므로, 빈칸에 들어갈 말로는 '훨씬 더 자연스러운 경계선을 찾지 못한다'가 가장 적절하다.

3 ② 고대 사람들은 강의 한쪽 편에만 작물을 심었다.

4 ⓐ the (wide) river ⓑ the map of the United States

Lesson 25

25B 1 crisis 2 optional 3 pollution 4 dominant 5 defend 6 civilizations 7 harsh 8 approach

25C 1 professional 2 widespread 3 development 4 standard 5 tremble 6 concept

25D 1 widespread 2 compete 3 crisis 4 dominant

25E 1 ① 2 ③ 3 ④ 4 ④

25F 전문 해석 화폐 발달에 정통한 전문가들에 따르면, 동전 형태의 화폐는 기원전 약 600년부터 존재해왔다. 당시 경제와 문명에서 지배적이었던 그리스 · 로마 문명이 동전을 돈으로 받아들이기 시작했으며 나머지 대부분의 국가들도 선례를 따랐다. 동전은 여전히 오늘날에도 사용되지만 보통은 지폐의 일부분으로 받아들여진다.

최초의 지폐는 13세기의 중국에서 발행되었다. 그 개념은 이후 400년이 지난 후에야 비로소 서양에서 일반화 되었다. 지폐 달러가 독립 전쟁 이후로 미국에 나타났고 서서히 국가 화폐의 기준이 되었다.

몇 가지 열거하여 수표, 우편환, 국채를 포함한 오늘날 화폐의 일반적인 형태의 대부분은 달러에 기반을 두고 있다. 미국의 (그리고 심지어 세계의) 대다수의 사람들은 그것을 교환의 수단으로 받아들인다. 역사적 측면에서 달러는 새로운 형태의 한 가지 화폐이지만 그것은 세계 대부분의 곳에서 통용된다.

더욱 새로운 하나의 화폐 형태는 전자 화폐이다. 오늘날 컴퓨터가 광범위하게 사용됨에 따라 상상할 수 없을 정도로 많은 거래가 전자결재로 이루어진다. 물리적인 형태의 화폐는 여전히 존재하고 문서 기록은 선택적이다. 달러와 센트는 비트와 바이트에 의해 나타내진다. 기준은 변하지 않았고, 교환의 방법만 변했다.

1 ③ 이 글은 화폐가 동전에서부터 지폐, 그리고 전자 화폐로 변화한 역사에 대한 것이므로, 이 글의 제목으로는 '역사를 거쳐 온 화폐'

2 ④ 물리적인 화폐는 그대로인데 전자 화폐의 출현으로 결제 방법이 달라진 것일 뿐이므로, 빈칸에 들어갈 말로는 '교환 방법'이 가장 적절하다.

3 ① follow suit는 '선례를 따르다'는 뜻으로 여기서는 그리스 · 로마 문명이 동전을 돈으로 받아들이자 다른 대부분의 국가들도 똑같이 했다는 의미를 나타낸다.

4 coin / paper money / electronic money 최초의 화폐 형태는 동전이었는데, 이는 요즘에도 사용된다. 지폐는 13세기 중국에서 최초로 사용되었다. 컴퓨터가 널리 보급되면서 전자 화폐의 사용이 일반적이게 되었다.

[숨마 주니어®]는

고교 상위권 선호도 1위 브랜드 숨마쿰라우데®가 만든
중학생들을 위한 혁신적인 **중등 브랜드**입니다!

숨마 주니어®

중학 영어 교과서 WORD MANUAL 시리즈

시리즈 단계	권별 학습	시리즈 전체 학습
WORD MANUAL ❶	중1 필수 어휘 450개 중1 확장 어휘 200개 독해 지문 30개	중학 필수 어휘 1,450개 + 중학 확장 어휘 750개 **총 어휘 2,200개** **독해 지문 80개**
WORD MANUAL ❷	중2 필수 어휘 500개 중2 확장 어휘 250개 독해 지문 25개	
WORD MANUAL ❸	중3 필수 어휘 500개 중3 확장 어휘 300개 독해 지문 25개	

본 교재만의 독특한 **4단계 학습 구성**으로
학생의 수준과 계획에 따라 다음의 2가지 방법 중 선택 학습이 가능합니다.

- 학습 Plan **1** : 어휘 집중 **학습형**
- 학습 Plan **2** : 어휘+독해 **학습형**

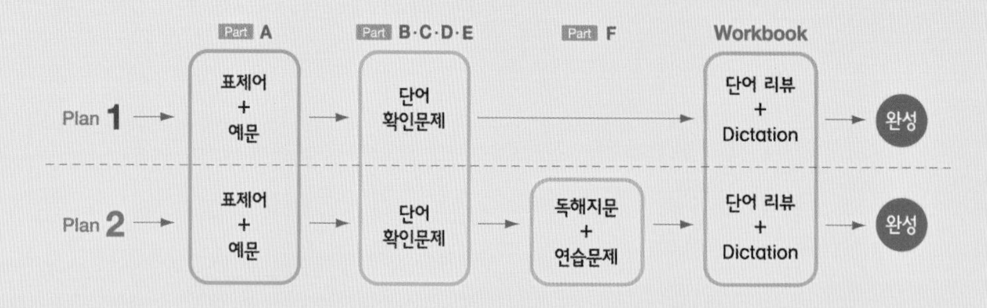

• 본 교재의 **mp3 파일**은 이룸이앤비 홈페이지(**www.erumenb.com**)에서 무료로 다운 받을 수 있습니다.

학습 교재의 새로운 신화! 이룸이앤비가 만듭니다!

기본은 **꾹꾹**, 실력은 **쑥쑥**

숨마 주니어®

S

SUMMA CUM LAUDE 「최우등 졸업」을 의미하는 라틴어

WORD MANUAL